College
Business
Mathematics

College Business Mathematics

Second Edition

Lloyd D. Brooks

Department of Management
Information Systems

Fogelman College of Business and Economics
Memphis State University

Memphis, Tennessee

SCIENCE RESEARCH ASSOCIATES, INC.
Chicago, Henley-on-Thames, Sydney, Toronto

An IBM Company

Acquisition Editor	Ann Meyer
Development Editor	Kevin Neely
Copy Editor	Kevin Neely
Cover Design	Paul Adams
Text Design	Maureen Langer & Paul Adams
Composition and Illustrations	The Clarinda Company

Library of Congress Cataloging-in-Publication Data

Brooks, Lloyd D., 1942-
  College business mathematics / Lloyd D. Brooks.—2nd. ed.
    p. cm.
  Rev. ed. of: Practical business mathematics. c1984.
  Includes index.
  ISBN 0-574-20085-1
  1. Business mathematics.   I. Brooks, Lloyd D., 1942-   Practical
business mathematics.   II. Title.
HF5691.B764   1987
513′.93—dc19   87-29038
                                                                      CIP

Originally published under the title *Practical Business Mathematics*.

Printed in the United States of America

10 9 8 7 6 5 4 3 2 1

CONTENTS

UNIT 6 Business Finance   277

ACKNOWLEDGMENTS

Many people provided assistance and motivation during the preparation of this text. Special thanks, however, go to a few notable people who took time to contribute to the development of the manuscript.

Reviewers of the first edition contributed many useful suggestions to ensure that the text provides a sound foundation for teaching practical business mathematics. These reviewers included Virginia Crawford, Robert Morris College (Pennsylvania); C.S. "Pete" Everett, Des Moines Area Community College (Iowa); Clo Hampton, West Valley College (California); Faye Ledbetter, Palm Beach Junior College (Florida); Janet Martin, Pensacola Junior College (Florida); Edward McCollough, Rogers State College (Oklahoma); Charles Peselnick, DeVry Institute (Ohio); and Billye Peterson, Oscar Rose Junior College (Oklahoma).

Reviewers of the second edition expended much effort to provide suggestions for refining the content and placement of material, as well as "tips" for making the presentations and illustrations more interesting and understandable for students. For their effort, professional attitude, and suggestions, I express sincere gratitude to the following reviewers: Helen Albides, American Business Institute (Massachusetts); Peter Astalos, Rutledge College (North Carolina); Dorothy Doran, Yavapai College (Arizona); Kathy Hughston, Bradford School of Business (Texas); Dennis Mathern, Bowling Green University (Ohio); and Doris Sadovy, San Jose City College (California).

Appreciation is also expressed to Tracye Gee for her work with the *Resource Manual and Test Bank* and the *Solutions Manual.* Deep appreciation is also expressed to Susan Brooks for proofreading the manuscript and for her encouragement throughout the project and to Linda Purcell for proofreading the book in its production stages. Kevin Neely, the project's development editor at Science Research Associates, also deserves "a big word of thanks" for his many excellent suggestions and his devotion to the project.

Lloyd Brooks
Memphis, 1988

TO THE STUDENT

Business mathematics affects career and personal activities on an almost daily basis. A knowledge of business mathematics will help you whether your future leads you to a career in a bank, government office, department store, legal or medical office, accounting office, or any other area in which computational skills are essential for day-to-day business operations.

Electronic calculators are now an accepted tool. All problems and examples in this text are presented in a format that can be adapted to solution with an electronic calculator. Spreadsheet software is now used with microcomputers to solve many types of computational problems. You will be shown throughout the text how spreadsheets and calculators can be used, but you do not need these tools to solve any of the problems or assignments in this text. No prior knowledge of these tools is assumed or required.

The text is arranged into 9 units and 33 chapters that divide the instruction into easy-to-use modules. Each chapter begins with introductory material and is followed by explanations, examples, and illustrations. Many examples present a problem and solution that you can readily relate to assignments in the text and problems that you will encounter later on your job. Each chapter concludes with one or more assignments, and each unit concludes with a self-test to allow you to test your understanding of the material in the unit or to let you know which areas you may need to study further. Each unit also includes spreadsheet application problems. These problems can be readily completed, however, with or without the use of microcomputers and spreadsheet software.

Working with *College Business Mathematics* will show you how decimals, percents, and other values can be used to solve problems relating to marketing, banking, finance, accounting, and other areas. You will practice and develop skills in solving problems typically found on civil service and employment tests. You will also develop an understanding of math procedures that will help you to handle your tax returns and bank statements, deal successfully with consumer credit problems, and cope with financial situations in business and home environments.

This text has been carefully designed to make learning as enjoyable and easy as possible. The business math skills that you build will help you to successfully complete other courses in areas such as finance and accounting that require strong math skills. As the world becomes increasingly automated, good business math skills are more important than ever before.

Lloyd Brooks
Memphis, 1988.

TO THE INSTRUCTOR

Introduction

The second edition of *College Business Mathematics* is designed to provide the foundation your students need to complete related courses and to handle jobs in the business world. It offers a wide range of practical topics with clear and concise explanations, easy-to-follow examples, and numerous exercises. All examples are formatted to allow efficient solution on an electronic calculator, if desired.

Program Components

A separate *Solutions Manual* provides the instructor with answers and worked-out solutions for text-workbook assignments. A *Resource Manual and Test Bank* is also provided that contains transparency masters for classroom use and a variety of exercises and/or test problems. In addition to providing additional exercises for each chapter, the test bank includes alternate tests for each unit and answers to all exercises and test problems. An optional computerized test bank containing objective problems for each chapter is also available to adopters of the text.

The text-workbook is the component that students will use, and it has been designed to meet both their learning needs and your teaching goals. Its pages are perforated to enable students to hand in any completed exercises you may wish to review or grade.

Text-Workbook Design

Organization. The text-workbook consists of 9 units divided into 33 chapters. Each chapter is independent of the others to give you the flexibility to structure your course according to your students' particular needs. The ability levels of your students will determine how much time you spend on the early chapters and how fast you are able to progress.

Fundamentals Review. Unit 1 helps students to develop speed and accuracy with the basic operations of addition, subtraction, multiplication, and division. Even students taking advanced mathematics courses often exhibit weaknesses in performing these basic operations accurately. Unit 2 presents a thorough review of decimals.

Calculator Use. Students will find it beneficial to use electronic calculators to complete problems beginning with Unit 3. All examples in the text-workbook are shown in a format that illustrates step-by-step use of electronic calculators. For your convenience, the *Solutions Manual* shows solutions in the order that steps will be followed for solving problems with electronic calculators.

Topic Coverage. Math fundamentals are covered in the first two units. The five chapters in Unit 3 cover "Percentage in Business" and show how percentage is applied to pricing merchandise, borrowing money, computing taxes, and determining consumer credit. Unit 4 covers "Marketing Mathematics" and includes computation of cash and trade discounts, markup and markdown, and commission. Unit 5 deals with math computations that relate to accounting and financial control. Unit 6 examines the value of money and the costs associated with its use (interest, insurance, and annuities).

Unit 7 shows how statistical data can be analyzed and grouped in summary or graphic form and also introduces computations related to stocks and bonds. Unit 8 presents a series of problems in an electronic spreadsheet format. However, as with *all* problems in this text shown in a spreadsheet format, a computer is not necessary to complete these assignments. Unit 9 displays problems that are typical of those found on employment tests.

Spreadsheet Design. Problems in a spreadsheet format are included at the end of each unit in Units 2 through 7 and in Unit 8. Students learn how computers can be used to solve problems, but manual computation or electronic calculators can be used to complete the exercises. A computer is not needed.

Individualized versus Group Instruction

The organization of the material and the clear explanations and examples will enable some students to progress through the text-workbook at an individualized pace. An instruction in the text-workbook indicates when sufficient material has been covered to permit completion of a specific assignment or the unit self-test. This structure permits students to learn material in short segments with reinforcement.

The self-directed approach is also facilitated by the self-test that concludes each unit. These tests permit students to evaluate their mastery of the material presented in one unit prior to taking a test and/or continuing to the next unit. Answers to the self-tests are included in the back of the text-workbook to allow students to check their answers and review relevant sections of the text as needed to improve their understanding and skills.

You can, of course, use group instruction methods and explain chapter content and examples to the entire class at the same time. Students will then complete assignments and take the unit tests as you direct and in the timeframes you specify.

Many instructors prefer to use a combination of individualized and group instruction. In this case, you may want to review some of the highlights of a particular unit before allowing students to complete assignments in the unit at an individualized pace.

Evaluation

Some instructors prefer to grade chapter assignments and unit tests, whereas others will choose to grade only the unit tests and will use the chapter assignments as learning aids. You can grade the chapter assignments in the text-workbook, the unit and chapter tests from the *Resource Manual and Test Bank*, tests from the computerized test bank, or a combination of both the assignments and the tests.

An "Achievement Chart" is provided in the back of the text-workbook to allow students to record their scores for each chapter assignment and unit self-test as they complete them.

Grading can be more difficult in business mathematics than in many other courses. Should a grade in an easier chapter, for example, count the same as a grade in a more difficult chapter? Most instructors give the grade for each chapter the same weight based on the premise that the easier chapters and the more difficult ones will "balance out" over the course of instruction.

You may want to assign weights to types of problems. For example, you might assign a value of "1" to each answer in problems that are not word problems and assign a value of "2" to each answer for word problems. You would then divide the number of points awarded by the number of points possible for the assignment or test to compute a score for that assignment or test.

Changes in the Second Edition

This second edition of *College Business Mathematics* includes several new features. Some of these are listed below.

The format of examples has been changed to facilitate students' comprehension. Most examples present a problem situation followed by a step-by-step solution.

The chapter on "Using an Electronic Calculator" has been moved closer to the front of the text to give you the option of having students use this tool after the basic math operations have been covered.

Each unit includes business applications in a spreadsheet format. However, students can complete these assignments using manual methods, a calculator, or a microcomputer. Students learn spreadsheet logic regardless of the method used to complete the assignments.

A complete unit on analyzing data in a spreadsheet format has also been added. Here students learn in a non-threatening way how to analyze, read, and use electronic spreadsheets. Once again, a microcomputer or calculator is not necessary.

The order of topic presentation has been changed to enable instructors to review arithmetic fundamentals but also present realistic problems from the beginning of the course.

New problems have been added, and others have been revised. Where needed, content has been revised to make it more logical and easier to learn. For example, chapters involving percentage computations have been standardized to include amount/rate/base terminology. All material has been updated to reflect current prices, amounts, and rates. The second edition also presents more problems in a word format.

Chapters on income taxes and depreciation have been revised to reflect new tax laws.

A separate *Solutions Manual* is provided to instructors who adopt the text. This manual contains detailed calculations and answers to problems in the chapter assignments. A check sheet of answers to odd-numbered student assignment word problems is included in the *Solutions Manual*. If desired, instructors may duplicate this sheet and distribute copies to students.

A *Resource Manual and Test Bank* is also provided to instructors who adopt the text. This manual contains a complete testing program, including tests for each chapter and alternate unit tests. An optional computerized testing program is also available that contains objective tests for each chapter. The *Resource Manual and Test Bank* also contains more than 100 transparency masters for visually displaying graphs, tables, and examples to the entire class.

A Final Note

This text provides the foundation that your students need to master the content of other courses in their program of study (accounting, statistics, finance, data processing, etc.). Throughout the text, discussion of sound business practices and attitudes are integrated with the presentation of math problems. The "whys" of math operations are emphasized, and examples and exercises illustrate the how-to approach of *College Business Mathematics*. This combination of skills and concepts, presented in a logical format, will make business mathematics easy to learn. The components provide you with a business mathematics program that is efficient and effective to implement.

Lloyd Brooks
Memphis, 1988

Basic Mathematic Operations

Unit 1 provides practice with the basic operations of mathematics with applications designed to develop speed and accuracy.

Some skills you can achieve in this unit include the following:

- Determining place value and reading numbers.
- Performing horizontal addition of numerical values.
- Performing addition, subtraction, multiplication, and division computations.
- Using shortcut methods to perform basic computations.
- Verifying the accuracy of basic computations.
- Estimating the accuracy of basic computations.
- Utilizing business applications relating to basic computations.

UNIT 1

ACCURATE ADDITION

The growth of microcomputers has made the processing of numerical data even more important than in the past. This equipment can process millions of values in a few seconds. Ironically, however, the electronic equipment in use today makes the study of business mathematics more essential than ever. To use the equipment effectively, you must first understand business mathematical procedures.

Place Value

From prehistoric times to the present, people have used symbols to represent quantities. The Romans used seven letters to express numerical values, whereas the Egyptians used symbols. Most modern countries use the decimal number system, which is based on the ten digits 0, 1, 2, 3, 4, 5, 6, 7, 8, and 9.

Electronic calculators and computers use the decimal system to process numerical values. The value of each digit depends on its place in relation to the decimal point. Each number place has a value ten times greater than the number place to its right. For example, 40 is ten times greater than 4, and 400 is 10 times greater than 40.

Number place determines a number's actual value. Example 1.1 shows the values of various positions to the left and right of the decimal point.

EXAMPLE   **Place value chart**

1.1

Hundred Thousands	Ten Thousands	Thousands	Hundreds	Tens	Units	Decimal Point	Tenths	Hundredths	Thousandths
						.			

Reading Values

Numbers are read according to their position in the place value chart. Example 1.2 illustrates how numbers are read:

CHAPTER 1

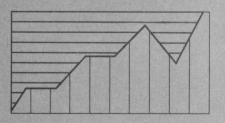

EXAMPLE   **Reading numbers**

1.2

7	read *seven*
214	read *two hundred fourteen*
12,716	read *twelve thousand, seven hundred sixteen*
7,204,000	read *seven million, two hundred four thousand*
4.2	read *four and two tenths*
18.35	read *eighteen and thirty-five hundredths*
0.421	read *four hundred twenty-one thousandths*
$12.45	read *twelve dollars and forty-five cents*
18%	read *eighteen percent*

Reading numbers is especially important when communicating by telephone. For example, a customer requesting an account balance will be misinformed if an amount is read incorrectly.

Increasing Speed by Grouping

Speed is important when making mathematical computations by hand. One way to add numbers quickly is to identify groupings of two or more numbers that total 10, because addition in groups of 10 is relatively fast. See Example 1.3.

EXAMPLE   **Addition in groups of 10**

1.3

$$
\begin{array}{ccc}
\left.\begin{array}{c}6\\4\end{array}\right\}10 & \left.\begin{array}{c}1\\2\end{array}\right\}10 & \left.\begin{array}{c}7\\2\end{array}\right\}10 \\
\left.\begin{array}{c}3\\7\end{array}\right\}10 & \left.\begin{array}{c}7\\8\end{array}\right. & 10\left\{\begin{array}{c}3\\8\end{array}\right. \\
\underline{8} & \left.\begin{array}{c}8\\\underline{2}\end{array}\right\}10 & \underline{1} \\
28 & 20 & 21
\end{array}
$$

Practice makes grouping values easier and increases speed in manual addition. When a calculator or computer is used, the numbers should be entered in order without grouping because the values are recorded into memory as they are entered from the keyboard.

In Example 1.4, group the numbers from top to bottom as you add. To check the accuracy of your answer, add the numbers again by grouping the values from bottom to top. If you obtain the same answer twice, you can be reasonably certain that the answer is correct. Even when using a calculator, performing the addition twice is always recommended.

Checking the accuracy of addition   EXAMPLE

1.4

788	763
272	124
835	343
125	768
988	132
3,008	2,130

Increasing Accuracy by Estimating

A second way to increase accuracy is to estimate the answer first and then compare the estimated answer with the computed answer to see if they are similar. To estimate, round the numbers to a specific digit such as the hundreds place or the tenths place.

In *rounding* to the hundreds place, for example, first convert all digits to the right of the hundreds place to zeros. Then, if the digit in the tens place is 5 or more, increase the digit in the hundreds place by 1. Otherwise, the digit in the hundreds place is unchanged. Example 1.5 illustrates typical rounding of numbers.

Rounding values   EXAMPLE

1.5

46	rounded to tens	50
342	rounded to hundreds	300
562	rounded to hundreds	600
3,728	rounded to thousands	4,000
8.65	rounded to tenths	8.7
29.42	rounded to tenths	29.4
9.236	rounded to hundredths	9.24
8.923	rounded to hundredths	8.92
5.34%	rounded to tenths	5.3%
$4.55	rounded to dollars	$5.00

After rounding, zeros to the far right of the decimal point are usually dropped. For example, 8.65 rounds to 8.7.

Perform the exercise in Example 1.6 to determine if your answer equals the answer given. First, compute the exact answer. Then compute the estimated answer to see if they are close.

EXAMPLE   **Estimating answers: Whole numbers**

1.6

Exact	Rounded to hundreds
345.28	300
450.38	500
2,562.36	2,600
650.00	700
4,008.02	4,100

Example 1.6 shows that the estimated answer is close to the exact answer. If the estimated answer is much different from the computed exact answer, the numbers should be added again.

Rounding can also be used to estimate the answer when adding decimal values, as shown in Example 1.7.

EXAMPLE   **Estimating answers: Decimals**

1.7

Exact	Rounded to tenths
4.35	4.4
10.57	10.6
5.26	5.3
20.18	20.3

The estimated answer is reasonably close to the exact answer. This comparison is another way to ensure that computations are accurate.

Adding Figures Horizontally

In hand calculations, horizontal addition is more difficult because the numbers are not aligned vertically for ease of reading. As in vertical addition, add the digits in the ones place first, then the digits in the tens place, and so on. With a calculator, of course, horizontal addition is as easy as vertical addition. Example 1.8 demonstrates horizontal addition.

EXAMPLE   **Horizontal addition**

1.8

$$145 + 25 + 68 = \_ \_ \underline{8} \quad \text{(carry 1 to tens place)}$$

$$145 + 25 + 68 = \_ \underline{3} \underline{8} \quad \text{(carry 1 to hundreds place)}$$

$$145 + 25 + 68 = \underline{2} \underline{3} \underline{8}$$

The accuracy of horizontal addition can be checked by adding the values horizontally and vertically as shown in Example 1.9. The sum of the vertical totals and the sum of the horizontal totals should be the same if all individual sums have been added correctly.

Checking horizontal addition   EXAMPLE

1.9

$$42 + 36 + 45 = 123$$
$$32 + 18 + 19 = 69$$
$$\underline{35} + \underline{16} + \underline{32} = \underline{83}$$
$$109 + 70 + 96 = \mathbf{275}$$

● **Complete Assignment 1.1** ●

● **Complete Assignment 1.2** ●

ASSIGNMENT 1.1   ADDITION

1. Add the following numbers. Group by tens when possible.

(a) 859	**(c)** 983	**(e)** 899	**(g)** 937	**(i)** 419	**(k)** 282	**(m)** 587	
941	817	381	862	364	673	368	
228	272	528	121	237	652	783	

(b) 894	**(d)** 972	**(f)** 895	**(h)** 426	**(j)** 764	**(l)** 143	**(n)** 547	
786	728	385	319	589	679	428	
323	282	928	208	405	187	913	

2. Add the following numbers. Check the accuracy of your addition.

(a) $128.37	**(c)** $126.84	**(e)** $727.18	**(g)** $62.85	**(i)** $35.89
26.45	832.67	107.40	47.63	43.67
389.71	289.85	87.98	52.52	18.34
$	$	$	$	$

(b) $38.72	**(d)** $168.01	**(f)** $ 30.57	**(h)** $306.75	**(j)** $176.88
142.19	78.15	105.41	42.18	14.62
321.86	5.89	52.18	5.67	934.22
$	$	$	$	$

3. Add the following numbers. Check the accuracy of your addition.

(a) $248.62	**(c)** $481.65	**(e)** $387.43	**(g)** $ 245.78	**(i)** $ 837.49
381.28	328.25	285.09	246.74	18,768.48
429.74	526.72	683.11	467.28	87,987.53
384.36	815.18	748.67	9,217.86	43,816.76
$	$	$	$	$

(b) $368.45	**(d)** $144.62	**(f)** $1,326.43	**(h)** $ 693.23	**(j)** $87,286.19
52.18	68.76	248.67	35.48	89,286.37
327.53	15.63	425.68	768.16	68,394.83
426.17	757.49	7,328.47	9,783.67	73,837.51
$	$	$	$	$

4. Round each of the following values to hundreds. Compute the exact and estimated answers for each problem.

	Exact	Rounded		Exact	Rounded		Exact	Rounded
(a)	146		**(c)**	850		**(e)**	762	
	258			745			2,569	
	1,267	_____		874	_____		4,287	_____
	____	____		____	____		____	____
(b)	258		**(d)**	2,562		**(f)**	896	
	490			6,729			509	
	589	_____		3,896	_____		845	_____
	____	____		____	____		____	____

5. Round each of the following values to tenths. Compute the exact and estimated answers for each problem.

	Exact	Rounded		Exact	Rounded		Exact	Rounded
(a)	2.456		**(c)**	3.51		**(e)**	4.239	
	3.609			12.58			5.89	
	3.781	_____		6.55	_____		4.247	_____
	____	____		____	____		____	____
(b)	0.578		**(d)**	12.4		**(f)**	3.591	
	3.528			0.583			6.249	
	9.446	_____		5.68	_____		2.009	_____
	____	____		____	____		____	____

6. Frank McKenzie estimates that one manufacturer's microcomputer will cost $2,489 and a second manufacturer's will cost $1,986. Round each price to hundreds and compute the estimated cost of purchasing both.

7. Concord Lighting Company sells three lamps for the following prices: $79.87, $59.23, and $24.15. Round each price to tens and compute the estimated total cost of the three lamps.

8. The Kilgore Pet Shop sells three dogs for the following prices: $189.45, $134.50, and $89.50. Round each price to tens and compute the estimated total cost of the three dogs.

9. The Cycle Store had the following total sales for the past three days: Monday, $2,422.55; Tuesday, $1,254.18; and Wednesday, $2,450.25. Round each daily sales total to hundreds and compute the estimated total sales for the three days.

10

ASSIGNMENT 1.2 Addition

1. Add the following values vertically and horizontally. The grand totals of the vertical and horizontal totals should agree.

(a) 4 + 13 + 3 + 7 = _____

(b) 27 + 33 + 87 + 13 = _____

(c) 18 + 22 + 46 + 34 = _____

(d) 78 + 12 + 43 + 87 = _____

(e) 43 + 57 + 97 + 89 = _____

(f) 41 + 75 + 38 + 59 = _____

(g) 52 + 48 + 96 + 87 = _____

(h) 86 + 74 + 39 + 38 = _____

(i) 37 + 41 + 16 + 23 = _____

(j) _____ + **(k)** _____ + **(l)** _____ + **(m)** _____ = **(n)** _____

2. The following chart lists the number of units produced by 6 employees in a manufacturing plant. Compute the number of units produced each day, the number of units produced by each employee, and the total number of units produced.

Employee Number	Units Produced Each Day					Totals
	Monday	Tuesday	Wednesday	Thursday	Friday	
101	184	216	198	180	191	_____
102	176	204	213	197	184	_____
103	204	188	216	182	232	_____
104	162	175	183	175	184	_____
105	189	182	178	194	177	_____
106	173	190	192	166	196	_____
Totals	_____	_____	_____	_____	_____	_____

3. The following chart lists sales made by each salesperson for each day of the week. Indicate the total sales for each salesperson, total sales for each day, and total sales for all salespersons during the week.

Day	Salesperson						Totals
	Abel	Collins	Hayes	Kendel	Munson	Rowe	
Monday	$623.14	$537.48	$462.37	$389.72	$518.37	$487.36	$ _____
Tuesday	587.56	489.72	523.87	417.69	507.20	518.27	$ _____
Wednesday	586.41	473.68	529.43	428.47	534.28	398.41	$ _____
Thursday	602.43	525.18	763.31	581.45	369.71	406.41	$ _____
Friday	368.45	415.32	602.10	513.47	423.87	523.62	$ _____
Totals	$ _____	$ _____	$ _____	$ _____	$ _____	$ _____	$ _____

4. Find the sum for each of the following problems. Then copy the addends as neatly as possible and find the sum a second time. Analyze the neatness of your figures and compare the results to ensure that the sums are the same for both solutions of each problem.

		Copy			Copy			Copy
(a)	53		**(c)**	40		**(e)**	$34.81	
	45			97			73.28	
	37			88			16.90	
	82			20			96.96	
	26			32				
	_____	_____		_____	_____		$ _____	_____

(b)	86		**(d)**	$13.82		**(f)**	$26.89	
	75			4.67			74.83	
	12			3.89			18.32	
	48			98.25			92.78	
	97							
	_____	_____		$ _____	_____		$ _____	_____

12

SUBTRACTION, MULTIPLICATION, AND DIVISION

Many people apply mathematics every day. Their uses of mathematics range from computing the cost of their lunch to computing the monthly payment on a home mortgage. Even complex formulas for making business decisions require accuracy in addition, subtraction, multiplication, and division. Addition was discussed in Chapter 1. This chapter covers subtraction, multiplication, and division.

Subtraction

Finding the difference between two values is often necessary in business and personal applications. As shown in Example 2.1, the number subtracted is called the *subtrahend*, the number subtracted from is called the *minuend*, and the resulting answer is called the *difference* or *remainder*. See Example 2.1.

EXAMPLE   **Components of subtraction**

2.1

$$
\begin{array}{ll}
\$4,\!274.45 & \text{Minuend} \\
-\,1,\!121.28 & \text{Subtrahend} \\
\hline
\$3,\!153.17 & \text{Difference (Remainder)}
\end{array}
$$

Proof in Subtraction

Subtraction is the opposite of addition. Therefore, you can check or prove the accuracy of subtraction by adding the difference to the subtrahend to see if the resulting sum equals the minuend. You can check the subtraction in Example 2.1 by adding $1,121.28 + 3,153.17 = $4,274.45.

Horizontal Subtraction

Accounting records, journals, invoices, and charge account statements are often written in a horizontal format, as in $24 - 13 = 11$. This horizontal arrangement makes it more difficult to align decimal points, as in $2.189 - 1.2 = .989$, but the method used for horizontal subtraction is the same as for vertical subtraction.

CHAPTER 2

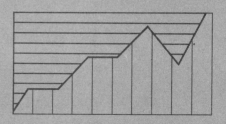

Estimating Answers in Subtraction

Estimating answers is also useful in subtraction. The procedure for rounding is like the one used for addition discussed in Chapter 1. The subtrahend and minuend should be rounded to the same place, for example, tenth or hundredth. This technique is illustrated in Example 2.2.

EXAMPLE **Estimating answers in subtraction**

2.2

	Actual	Estimated
	4,269	4,200
	− 1,138	− 1,100
	3,131	3,100

Notice that the estimated answer is reasonably close to the actual answer. This is another safeguard to obtain the correct answer. Estimating becomes even more important when using a calculator because merely striking a wrong key can result in an error. Estimating fairly simple computations can be done mentally.

● **Complete Assignment 2.1** ●

Multiplication

Multiplication is used to compute taxes, interest on loans, discounts on sales, insurance rates, and other business applications. The number that is multiplied is called the *multiplicand,* the number by which one multiplies is called the *multiplier,* and the resulting answer is called the *product.* As shown in Example 2.3, in the computation 8 × 23 = 184, the multiplicand is 23, the multiplier is 8, and the product is 184.

EXAMPLE **Multiplication**

2.3

23	238	235	Multiplicand
× 8	× 135	× 11	Multiplier
184	1 190	235	Partial products
	7 14	2 35	
	23 8	2,585	Product
	32,130		

Notice that the multiplicand and the multiplier are written so that their figures are aligned at the right. In the second problem, the multiplicand is first multiplied by the digit of the multiplier farthest to the right (238 × 5). The multiplicand is then multiplied by the second digit from the right in the multiplier (238 × 3). This process is continued until the multiplicand has been multiplied by each digit in the multiplier.

Also notice that the result of each individual multiplication is aligned under the digit in the multiplier, as shown in Example 2.3. These results are called *partial products*. The sum of the partial products equals the product.

Estimating Answers in Multiplication

In multiplication, even a small error in one step can result in a large error in the product. To estimate the answer to a multiplication problem, round the multiplicand and the multiplier to the same place (tens, hundreds, or thousands, etc.) and then multiply. The problem in Example 2.4 has been rounded to the nearest ten.

Estimating answers in multiplication   EXAMPLE

2.4

Exact: $55.34 \times 44 = 2,434.96$
Estimated: $60 \times 40 = 2,400$

Comparing the exact and estimated answers will show whether any gross errors have been made. In this chapter, the number of decimal places to the right of the decimal point will be two. More advanced problems that involve placing the decimal point are presented in Chapter 8.

Checking the Accuracy of Multiplication

To check the accuracy of multiplication, divide the product by either the multiplicand or the multiplier. If accurate, the answer to that division should equal the third number in the calculation as shown in Example 2.5.

Checking the accuracy of multiplication   EXAMPLE

2.5

Problem: $25 \times 5 = 125$
Check: $125 \div 5 = 25$
or $125 \div 25 = 5$

• Complete Assignment 2.2 •

Division

Division is used in many mathematical computations, such as computing the average daily sales of a department store. Division is the process of determining how many times one number can be divided into another number. Four terms apply to the numbers involved in basic division. The number to be divided is the *dividend*, the number the dividend is divided by is the *divisor*, and the answer is the *quotient*. If the divisor does not divide into the dividend evenly, the part that is left is the *remainder*. Example 2.6 illustrates different formats that can be used for division problems. In Example 2.6, 18 is the dividend, 3 is the divisor, and 6 is the quotient; there is no remainder.

EXAMPLE   **Division**

2.6

$$18 \div 3 = 6$$

$$18/3 = 6$$

$$\begin{array}{r} 6 \\ 3\overline{)18} \end{array}$$

In division, always remember to keep the numbers properly aligned. Example 2.7 shows a division problem with a remainder.

EXAMPLE   **Alignment in division**

2.7

$$
\begin{array}{r}
756 + \text{remainder of 5} \\
20\overline{)15125} \\
\underline{140} \\
112 \\
\underline{100} \\
125 \\
\underline{120} \\
5 \quad \text{(remainder)}
\end{array}
$$

Estimating Answers in Division

To estimate the answer to a division problem, round off both the divisor and the dividend to the same place as shown in Example 2.8.

Estimating answers in division   EXAMPLE

2.8

Actual: 4218 divided by 69 equals 61 with a remainder of 9
Estimated: 4200 divided by 70 equals 60

Checking the Accuracy of Division

To verify the accuracy of division, multiply the quotient by the divisor and then add any remainder. The result should equal the dividend. Example 2.9 illustrates checking the accuracy of division.

Checking the accuracy of division   EXAMPLE

2.9

Problem: 675/25   = 27
   Check: 25 $\times$ 27 = 675

Problem: 191/2 = 95 with a remainder of 1
   Check: (95 $\times$ 2) + 1 = 191

Division Applications

Although division is not used as often in business as addition, subtraction, and multiplication, it is frequently used in statistical computations to compute means, profit-and-loss ratios, and standard deviations.

To find the mean or average of a group of numbers, first find the sum of that group of numbers and then divide by the number of numbers in the group. For example, assume that Rita McGuire had scores of 75, 85, 92, and 88 on 4 tests. Example 2.10 illustrates how to find her mean (average) score on the 4 tests.

Finding the average of 4 test scores   EXAMPLE

2.10

Sum: 75 + 85 + 92 + 88 = 340
Average: 340/4 = 85

Thus Rita McGuire's average score for the 4 tests was 85.

● **Complete Assignment 2.3** ●

● **Complete Assignment 2.4** ●

ASSIGNMENT 2.1 Subtraction

1. Find the difference and check answers for each of the following problems:

(a) 68	(b) 207	(c) 88	(d) 87	(e) 8,520	(f) 76,712	(g) 1,008,235
29	89	53	48	3,245	53,891	609,487

_____ _____ _____ _____ _____ _____ _____

_____ _____ _____ _____ _____ _____ _____

2. Find the difference for each of the following problems:

(a) $15 - 7 =$ _____   (d) $87 - 49 =$ _____   (g) $383 - 178 =$ _____

(b) $82 - 15 =$ _____   (e) $123 - 18 =$ _____   (h) $357 - 289 =$ _____

(c) $57 - 29 =$ _____   (f) $187 - 138 =$ _____   (i) $1,762 - 835 =$ _____

3. Compute the markup (the difference between the cost price and the selling price) for each of the following problems. Then compute totals for each column.

	First Period				Second Period		
Item	Selling Price	Cost Price	Markup	Item	Selling Price	Cost Price	Markup
A	$ 6.73	$ 5.49	_____	AA	$ 13.52	$ 11.76	_____
B	8.26	6.84	_____	BB	19.89	13.52	_____
C	7.35	4.79	_____	CC	17.81	15.49	_____
D	6.40	5.38	_____	DD	38.89	32.92	_____
E	8.49	5.75	_____	EE	162.71	153.89	_____
F	9.28	7.67	_____	FF	165.98	139.52	_____
TOTALS	$ _____	$ _____	$ _____		$ _____	$ _____	$ _____

20

4. Estimate the sums of each of the following problems:

Actual	Estimated	Actual	Estimated	Actual	Estimated
(a) 56	60	**(b)** 31	30	**(c)** 528	500
78	_____	22	_____	763	_____
42	_____	46	_____	581	_____
54	_____	53	_____	730	_____
_____	_____	_____	_____	279	_____
				_____	_____

5. A desk can be purchased at Midtown Furniture Center for $898.23 or at Denver Furniture Company for $913.35. How much can be saved by buying the desk at Midtown Furniture Center?

$ _____

6. One basic application of addition and subtraction is maintaining a checkbook balance. Deposits are added, whereas checks written and service charges are deducted from the balance. Compute the balance after each transaction in the check register shown below.

CHECK NO	DATE	CHECK ISSUED TO	BAL. BR'T. F'R'D.	V	6,389	72
341	1/3/__	TO Lucky Seven Beauty Shop FOR personal services	AMOUNT OF CHECK OR DEPOSIT BALANCE		17	21
342	1/3/__	TO Lotus Restaurant FOR lunch for client - Collins	AMOUNT OF CHECK OR DEPOSIT BALANCE		37	25
343	1/4/__	TO Lance and Associates FOR consulting services	AMOUNT OF CHECK OR DEPOSIT BALANCE		300	00
—	1/4/__	TO Deposit - #43 FOR weekly receipts #53	AMOUNT OF CHECK OR DEPOSIT BALANCE		2,640	75
344	1/4/__	TO Lorenz Photography FOR office photography	AMOUNT OF CHECK OR DEPOSIT BALANCE		175	80
345	1/4/__	TO Luellen Building Supplies FOR building materials	AMOUNT OF CHECK OR DEPOSIT BALANCE		463	17
346	1/5/__	TO City Nursing Home FOR donation	AMOUNT OF CHECK OR DEPOSIT BALANCE		100	00
347	1/5/__	TO Kaye Furniture Store FOR office furniture	AMOUNT OF CHECK OR DEPOSIT BALANCE		898	72
—	1/5/__	TO Service charge FOR statement #12	AMOUNT OF CHECK OR DEPOSIT BALANCE		10	22
348	1/6/__	TO Easy Care Lawn Center FOR lawn services	AMOUNT OF CHECK OR DEPOSIT BALANCE		82	95
349	1/6/__	TO Norris Office Supply FOR office supplies	AMOUNT OF CHECK OR DEPOSIT BALANCE		114	23
350	1/7/__	TO Hunt, Hunt, & James FOR attorney fees	AMOUNT OF CHECK OR DEPOSIT BALANCE		420	00
351	1/7/__	TO Moran Insurance Agency FOR policy #31306	AMOUNT OF CHECK OR DEPOSIT BALANCE		179	24

Ending balance $ _____

ASSIGNMENT 2.2 Multiplication

1. Compute the actual and estimated products of each of the following problems:

	Actual	Estimated		Actual	Estimated		Actual	Estimated
(a)	93 ×27	_____	**(c)**	27 ×18	_____	**(e)**	198 × 92	_____
(b)	86 ×13	_____	**(d)**	121 × 54	_____	**(f)**	316 ×302	_____

2. Multiply the unit price by the quantity to determine the total price for each item on the following invoice:

Quantity	Item Stock Number	Unit Price	Total
89	101-B	$14.00	$ _____
73	102-X	38.00	$ _____
27	819-A	17.25	$ _____
35	723-Z	24.16	$ _____
27	814-P	32.50	$ _____
32	916-F	16.82	$ _____
			$ _____

3. A secretary has an average typing speed of 53 words per minute. How many words can the secretary type in 17 minutes?

_____

4. Bill Jones makes $8.85 per hour. How much will he earn for working 23 hours?

$ _____

5. A certain machine can produce 37 items per minute. How many items will be produced in (a) 42 minutes? (a) 3 hours?

(a) _____

(b) _____

6. A car is driven 13,128 miles during the first year. How many miles will the car be driven in 7 years if it is driven the same number of miles each year?

_____

7. A man drives a car at an average speed of 55 miles per hour. How many miles will he travel in 9 hours?

_____

8. A carton contains 24 cans of tomato juice. How many cans will 38 cartons contain?

_____

9. A secretary can take shorthand dictation at 120 words per minute. How many words can the secretary take in 37 minutes?

_____

22

ASSIGNMENT 2.3   Division

1. Find the quotient for each of the following problems:

(a) $4\overline{)196}$ (e) $3\overline{)561}$ (i) $132\overline{)6,996}$ (m) $102\overline{)38,862}$

(b) $5\overline{)175}$ (f) $9\overline{)2,502}$ (j) $128\overline{)73,728}$ (n) $231\overline{)27,951}$

(c) $3\overline{)192}$ (g) $7\overline{)3,948}$ (k) $218\overline{)14,606}$

(d) $8\overline{)248}$ (h) $8\overline{)37,456}$ (l) $231\overline{)92,862}$

2. Compute the unit cost for each of the following items:

Item	Total Cost	No. of Units	Unit Cost
A	$ 28.75	23	$ _____
B	33.04	14	$ _____
C	31.50	18	$ _____
D	26.35	31	$ _____
E	412.32	16	$ _____

3. Compute the actual and estimated quotients for each of the following problems:

Actual	Estimated	Actual	Estimated

(a) 22)‾638‾

(e) 42)‾2,478‾

(b) 38)‾1,976‾

(f) 898)‾35,920‾

(c) 294)‾14,994‾

(g) 29)‾928‾

(d) 306)‾11,934‾

(h) 198)‾8,316‾

ASSIGNMENT 2.4 **Division**

1. Compute the quotient for each of the following problems. Check the accuracy of your division by multiplying the quotient by the divisor, and then adding any remainder.

(a) $37\overline{)1,665}$

(d) $16\overline{)370}$

(g) $121\overline{)4,235}$

(b) $30\overline{)600}$

(e) $38\overline{)1,599}$

(h) $206\overline{)31,518}$

(c) $18\overline{)1,118}$

(f) $26\overline{)1,204}$

(i) $316\overline{)64,780}$

2. Sarah Dower received the following scores in accounting class: 88, 79, 94, 80, 84. What is her average score?

_____

3. Jerry Caldwell drives his car 1,404 miles and uses 39 gallons of gasoline. On the average, how many miles can he drive per gallon?

_____

4. Don Roberts earns gross pay of $1,408 for 22 working days. What is his average daily pay?

$ _____

5. Dorothy Ling drove 468 miles in 9 hours. What was her average miles per hour?

_____

6. Carol Poulos's annual salary is $19,476. What is her monthly salary?

$ _____

7. Jim Baker drove the following miles during a 5-day period: 420, 430, 418, 413, and 434. How many average miles per day did he drive?

_____

8. Sales at Barney's Fitness Center for 3 months were as follows: $21,680.20, $22,819.62, and $23,736.68. Find the average monthly sales for the 3-month period.

$ _____

9. Four candidates received the following numbers of votes: 22,100, 28,450, 24,600, and 25,862. What was the average number of votes received by the 4 candidates?

_____

MERCHANDISE RECORDS

Merchandise is products that businesses purchase for resale to consumers or other businesses. The size and type of a business determine the way that it maintains merchandise and sales records. For example, an automobile agency that sells relatively few large items each day will maintain a record for each automobile sold, but a department store that sells hundreds of small items each day will need more detailed records. All businesses need to maintain records to keep track of what merchandise has been sold. A separate record may be kept for each item (such as an automobile), or a summary record may be kept on total sales (such as total sales of fruit in a supermarket).

Sales Records

Many retail stores issue sales slips to provide a record of the sale. This slip normally indicates the quantity, description, price, sales taxes, and amount due for items sold. A handwritten sales slip is shown in Example 3.1.

EXAMPLE   Sales slip

3.1

SALES SLIP

- Chin Office Supply
- 4828 Tift Avenue
- Hyattsville, MO 20782

Customer's Order No. *1123* Phone No. *761-2317* Date *3/8* 19 __

Sold To *John Smith*

Address *1823 Carbondale Lane - City*

SOLD BY	CASH	C. O. D.	CHARGE	ON ACCT.	MDSE. RETD.	PAID OUT
LD	✓					

QUAN.	DESCRIPTION	PRICE	AMOUNT	
3	5 1/4" Diskettes	1.50	4	50
1	Keyboard Cover	6.95	6	95
2	Calculator (P16)	21.50	43	00
5	Pens (T16-4)	3.95	19	75
			74	20
		TAX	4	88
		TOTAL	79	08

ALL claims and returned goods MUST be accompanied by this bill.

018001   Rec'd by *JJ*

Many stores continue to use handwritten sales slips, but some stores now use computerized cash register slips. The sales clerk can simply enter the product number, and the computer then records the description and price of the item sold on the cash register tape. The computer can also monitor the number of products in stock and notify the store to reorder products when needed. Example 3.2 illustrates a computerized sales slip.

• Complete Assignment 3.1 •

EXAMPLE   Computerized sales slip

3.2

```
12/06/86  15:44  3778 8292 020            27

G MEMBER 49323959 S BROOKS

    4 @ 3.09
    15071  RIBBON 600              12.36  T
    3388   GUCCI 1.0 OZ             7.99  T
    10290  SPICE DROPS              2.19  T
    13581  BOOT SOX                 3.69  T
    13581  BOOT SOX                 3.69  T

           5% UPCHARGE              1.50
           TAX DUE                  2.43
           BALANCE DUE             33.85

           CASH                    40.00
           CHANGE DUE               6.15
```

Stores must maintain a record of merchandise purchased and sold in order to know when to reorder merchandise and to determine which items are selling fast and which are selling slowly. This record is called an *inventory* and may be kept in computer memory or on handwritten cards. The record must indicate sales, purchases, and balances for each item. Example 3.3 is a typical inventory record.

RENYO WATCH	PRODUCT NO. RW726–89			
	COST PRICE: $ 69.45			
	SALE PRICE: $139.99			
Date	**Transaction**	**Increase**	**Decrease**	**Balance**
03/01	Beg. Balance			18
03/07	Sale		3	15
03/08	Sale		2	13
03/21	Purchase	8		21
03/26	Sale		4	17

Notice that each purchase of merchandise by the store increases the inventory or number of items available for resale to customers. Similarly, each sale to a customer is deducted from the store's inventory, and fewer items are then available for resale.

Shipping Merchandise

Many stores operate catalog departments that ship products to the customer. A *sales invoice* shipped with the merchandise states the product description, price, quantity, and other information about the order. This invoice must be much more complete than a sales slip because it also serves as a bill. Manufacturers and wholesalers that regularly ship merchandise to retailers usually use sales invoices. Example 3.4 illustrates a typical sales invoice.

		INVOICE NO.
INVOICE		25702

SOLD TO		SHIP TO	
Barcelona & Cofer, Attorneys		Same	
290 53d Street			
Brooklyn, NY 11232			

CUSTOMER ORDER NO.		SALESMAN	TERMS	SHIPPED VIA	F.O.B	DATE
6729		Smith	C. O. D.	Truck		3/17/—

QUANTITY ORDERED	QUANTITY SHIPPED	DESCRIPTION	UNIT PRICE		AMOUNT	
12	12	Single-Strike Ribbon (43872 REM)	9	10	109	20
5 doz.	5	Pocket Secretary Refills (3462 TAZ)	6	25	31	25
7	7	Stationery Cabinet (8BC-BW-1 LIT)	40	95	286	65
———	---	***Total			427	10

● **Complete Assignment 3.2.** ●

ASSIGNMENT 3.1 Sales Slips

1. The following items were sold on account to Robert Newport, 925 Carpenter Crossing, Folcroft, PA 19032. Complete the sales slip, including both the price and amount columns. Use the current date.

   3 pairs shoes @   42.75
   4 shirts   @   13.95
   2 ties   @   8.50
   6 pairs socks @   4.99
   Sales Tax   10.37

2. The following items were sold cash on delivery to Roberta Rawls, 716 North Wells Street, Chicago, IL 60610. Complete the sales slip using the current date.

   7 cases diskettes   @   8.75
   5 printer ribbons   @   8.25
   2 computer cables   @   29.95
   3 books   @   19.95
   1 type cleaner   @   8.50
   Sales tax   10.11

SALES SLIP

Customer's Order No.	Phone No.	Date_____ 19 ___	

Sold To_____

Address_____

SOLD BY	CASH	C. O. D.	CHARGE	ON ACCT.	MDSE. RETD.	PAID OUT	

QUAN.	DESCRIPTION	PRICE	AMOUNT
		TAX	
		TOTAL	

ALL claims and returned goods MUST be accompanied by this bill.

018003   Rec'd by

Sales Slip Problem 1.

SALES SLIP

Customer's Order No.	Phone No.	Date_____ 19 ___	

Sold To_____

Address_____

SOLD BY	CASH	C. O. D.	CHARGE	ON ACCT.	MDSE. RETD.	PAID OUT	

QUAN.	DESCRIPTION	PRICE	AMOUNT
		TAX	
		TOTAL	

ALL claims and returned goods MUST be accompanied by this bill.

018002   Rec'd by

Sales Slip Problem 2.

31

3. Compute exact and estimated amounts for each of the following items:

Item No.	Quantity	Price	Exact Amount	Estimated Amount
1	23	$ 1.35	_____	_____
2	45	2.49	_____	_____
3	12	0.85	_____	_____
4	17	12.45	_____	_____
5	15	8.47	_____	_____

4. Compute and estimate the amounts for each of the following items:

Product	Price	Quantity	Exact Amount	Estimated Amount
Golf Balls	$ 0.45	48	_____	_____
Binoculars	39.95	6	_____	_____
Jackets	79.95	3	_____	_____
Candles	1.25	50	_____	_____
Watches	39.95	2	_____	_____

5. The Slumber Rest Co. sells bedspreads for $41.37 each. What amount would an invoice for 12 bedspreads show?

$ _____

6. Newson Appliances sells washing machines for $399.95 each. What amount would an invoice for 3 machines show?

$ _____

7. Newson Appliances sells table lamps for $59.99 each. What amount would an invoice for 5 lamps show?

$ _____

8. The Best Discount Store sells electronic calculators for $29.95 each. What amount would an invoice for 36 calculators show?

$ _____

32

ASSIGNMENT 3.2   Sales Invoices

1. Compute the amounts in each line and the total for the following invoice. Assume that no sales tax is charged.

INVOICE

INVOICE NO.
25701

SOLD TO
International Importers

744 Western Avenue

Boston, MA 02135

SHIP TO
Same

CUSTOMER ORDER NO.	SALESMAN	TERMS	SHIPPED VIA	F.O.B.	DATE
30741	Upton	C. O. D.	Truck		8/28/--

QUANTITY ORDERED	QUANTITY SHIPPED	DESCRIPTION	UNIT PRICE		AMOUNT	
12	12	Memo Holders (1373-1 ELD)	6	59		
15	15	Diskette Cleaning Kit (11250 DEE)	9	59		
8	8	Rotary Card File (SR48C-DE)	34	95		
6	6	Ledger Sheets (K2E FR)	16	05		
13	13	Computer Labels--4 x 1 7/16 (2044 RVE)	13	25		
15	15	Staple Gun (80007 HFH)	16	59		
37	37	Weekly Appointment Books (340-53-5 COL)	3	75		
125	125	Looseleaf Desk Calendar (P34-00 JJ)	7	95		
---	---	***Total				

ORIGINAL

THANK YOU

2. Martina Meade sold 40 items at $12.35 each. Sarah Rasch sold 38 items at $12.55 each. Who made the larger sale?

3. Tim Brandon sold 12 items at $14.95 each. Brenda Miller sold 14 items at $14.75 each. Who made the larger sale?

4. The Town and Country Furniture Center normally sells a ceramic table lamp for $69.99. During a special sale, the lamps are offered for $59.95 each if three or more are purchased. What is the cost of three lamps?

$ _____

5. The Buy-Rite Food Store can purchase dinner rolls for $9.59 per case. What is the cost of 17 cases?

$ _____

6. The Computer Center normally sells a dot matrix printer for $289.59. During a sales promotion, the price of each printer is reduced by $30.00. If 5 printers are sold, what is the (a) regular and (b) reduced total sales amount for the five printers?

(a) $ _____

(b) $ _____

7. For each mile driven, City Car Rental charges $0.27. Michelle Hanson rented a car for an 837-mile trip. What amount was she charged?

$ _____

8. The Arco Sports Center sells one brand of basketball for $23.95 each. What is the cost of 7 basketballs?

$ _____

9. The Brandon Discount Center sells calculators for $24.95 each. What is the cost of 4 calculators?

$ _____

34

RECONCILING A BANK STATEMENT

Bank depositors place money into an account that permits withdrawal of funds from the account by writing checks against the balance. This type of account is called a *checking account*. Periodically, the bank sends a statement that reflects deposits, withdrawals, charges, and other transactions affecting the account. The depositor also keeps a record of these transactions in a checkbook. *Reconciliation of the bank balance* involves comparing the transactions recorded in the bank statement with those recorded in the checkbook. Adjustments are made or errors are corrected to make the balances equal. This chapter presents information about banking records and shows you how to reconcile your checkbook record with the bank's record of your account. A typical bank statement is shown in Example 4.1.

EXAMPLE   A bank statement

4.1

Customer Statement

FIRST TENNESSEE BANK 1st

JOHN Q. PUBLIC
201 SOUTH MAIN STREET
ANYWHERE, TENNESSEE   38118

ACCOUNT NUMBER	LAST STATEMENT DATE	CURRENT DATE
00-1234567	3/10/--	4/08/--

CHECKING ACCOUNT SUMMARY:

	BALANCE OF YOUR FUNDS
PREVIOUS BALANCE	$ 468.50
2 DEPOSITS TOTALING	$ 905.26
17 WITHDRAWALS TOTALING	$ 1198.34
NEW BALANCE ON STATEMENT DATE	$ 177.42

CHECKING ACCOUNT TRANSACTION:

DATE:	AMOUNT:	TRANSACTION:
3/14	452.63	DEPOSIT THRU AUTOMATIC PAYROLL PLAN
3/20	20.00	AUTOMATIC SAVINGS TRANSFER
3/21	50.00	WITHDRAWAL - FIRST BANKING TELLER
4/01	10.00	WITHDRAWAL - FIRST BANKING TELLER
4/08	452.63	DEPOSIT THRU AUTOMATIC PAYROLL PLAN

DATE:	CHECK NO:	AMOUNT:	DATE:	CHECK NO:	AMOUNT:
3/25	944	25.99	4/04	994	200.00
3/14	985**	156.89	4/07	996**	25.00
3/14	986	225.00	4/08	997	90.69
3/16	987	289.35			
3/17	988	55.87			
3/16	989	12.36			
3/21	990	12.69			
3/18	991	15.00			
4/04	992	5.00			
4/06	993	2.50			

** PREVIOUS CHECK NUMBER(S) MISSING   * SEE REVERSE SIDE FOR IMPORTANT INFORMATION

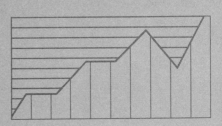

Making a Deposit

To write checks to pay bills and to obtain cash, bank customers must have funds in their checking accounts. Bank customers deposit and withdraw funds periodically during the month as money is available or needed. A typical deposit ticket and check are shown in Examples 4.2 and 4.3.

EXAMPLE   **Deposit ticket**

4.2

EXAMPLE   **Check**

4.3

Maintaining a Record of Checks and Deposits

Bank customers maintain check registers or check stub records to show deposit and withdrawal transactions and a running balance. Charges made by the bank, such as service charges, check purchases, and return check charges, or additions such as interest earned on the account, should also be shown on the check register or check stub record. A typical check register is shown in Example 4.4.

Check register   EXAMPLE

4.4

CHECK NO	DATE	CHECK ISSUED TO	BAL. BR'T. F'R'D.	V		
		TO	AMOUNT OF CHECK OR DEPOSIT			
		FOR	BALANCE			
		TO	AMOUNT OF CHECK OR DEPOSIT			
		FOR	BALANCE			
		TO	AMOUNT OF CHECK OR DEPOSIT			
		FOR	BALANCE			
		TO	AMOUNT OF CHECK OR DEPOSIT			
		FOR	BALANCE			
		TO	AMOUNT OF CHECK OR DEPOSIT			
		FOR	BALANCE			
		TO	AMOUNT OF CHECK OR DEPOSIT			
		FOR	BALANCE			

Banks offer a variety of checking account plans. Some charge a fee if the balance falls below a specified level, whereas others may charge a fee (such as 20 cents) for each check written during the month. Some banks do not charge a fee, and some banks may pay interest on all or a portion of the account balance. These items will be shown on the bank statement and should be used to adjust the check stub balance while reconciling the bank balance.

Reconciling the Bank Statement

The balance shown on the bank statement is reconciled (made to agree) with the check stub balance by adjusting each balance or by correcting errors. Reconciliation simply involves making adjustments to one balance for transactions that have already been reflected in the other balance. For example, a recent deposit may not be reflected on the bank statement but may have been added to the check stub balance on the day of the deposit. This adjustment will require the late deposit to be added to the bank balance. Except for correcting errors, this process is repeated for each item that is reflected in one balance but not in the other. Of course, the late deposit will eventually be added to the bank balance and reflected on a future statement. Typical items that may need to be adjusted are discussed below.

Subtractions from the Bank Statement Balance

Outstanding checks are checks that have been written and recorded by the depositor but have not yet been paid by the bank and are thus not shown on the bank statement.

Withdrawals from an automatic teller machine were made too late to be reflected on the bank statement but were deducted from the check stub. An automatic funds transfer to another account will also fall into this category.

Additions to the Bank Statement Balance

Deposits in transit are deposits that were made too late for inclusion on the statement. These must also be accounted for in reconciling the bank statement.

Subtractions from the Check Stub Balance

Bank service fees based on the number of checks written, account balance, or overdrafts must be deducted. These charges will be shown on the statement.

The *bank charge* for printing new checks must also be deducted.

Rejected or returned checks are checks that cannot be paid to your account because the party who gave the check to you stopped payment on the check or does not have sufficient funds to cover the amount of the check. Such checks must also be accounted for in reconciling the statement.

Additions to the Check Stub Balance

The amount of a *note collected* by the bank that was credited to your account must be added.

Electronic funds transferred from another account (such as a payroll check) into the checking account must be added.

Interest earned on the account balance during the period must be added.

Remember that the bank statement and check stub amounts should be carefully studied to determine entries on one record that should be reflected on the other record as either subtractions or additions to the balance. After this is completed, the new balances of the two records should be the same. In other words, the bank balance and check stub balance must be in agreement so that the reconciliation is complete.

Assume that the bank statement shows a balance of $379.50 and a service charge of $3.50. A review shows outstanding checks (No. 113 for $15 and No. 115 for $10) amounting to $25 and a deposit in transit for $20. The check stub balance is $378.00. The reconciliation of the bank balance for this situation is shown in Example 4.5.

Reconciliation of bank balance   EXAMPLE

Bank Balance		$379.50	Check stub balance		$378.00
Deduct:			Deduct:		
Check No. 113	$15.00		Service charge		3.50
Check No. 115	$10.00	25.00			
		$354.50			$374.50
Add:			Add:		
Deposit in transit		20.00			0.00
			Adjusted check stub		
Adjusted bank balance		$374.50	balance		$374.50

After reconciliation, you are ready to begin a new period with a "clean slate" knowing that your check stub balance correctly reflects your checking account balance. Notice that the adjusted bank balance and the adjusted check stub balance must be equal. A form for bank reconciliation such as the one depicted in Example 4.6 is sometimes provided by the bank to help customers to make their check stub balance equal to the bank statement balance.

Bank statement reconciliation form   EXAMPLE

RECONCILIATION OF BANK STATEMENT			
Bank statement balance	$_____	Check stub balance	$_____
Add late deposits	_____	Add interest	_____
Total	$_____	Total	$_____
Deduct outstanding check	_____	Deduct service charge	_____
Adjusted bank balance	$_____	Adjusted stub balance	$_____

● **Complete Assignment 4.1** ●

● **Complete Assignment 4.2** ●

ASSIGNMENT 4.1 Bank Statement Reconciliation

1. Checks and deposits made during the month are listed below with a summary of the bank statement for Alicia Caesar. Find the check stub balance after each entry and reconcile the bank statement.

Check Stub			Bank Statement	
Beginning balance	$945.45		Beginning balance	$945.45
Deposit	100.50		Checks: #101 $30.00	
			#105 50.25	
Balance	**(a)** $ _____		#103 125.40	
Check #101	30.00		#104 67.35	
Balance	**(b)** $ _____		Deposits: $100.50	
Check #102	75.50		Service charge: 7.50	
Balance	**(c)** $ _____		Ending Balance	$765.45
Check #103	125.40			
Balance	**(d)** $ _____			
Check #104	67.35			
Balance	**(e)** $ _____			
Deposit	300.50			
Balance	**(f)** $ _____			
Check #105	50.25			
Balance	**(g)** $ _____			

(Problems 2 and 3 on reverse page)

2. Use the following information to reconcile the bank statement for June O'Brien:

Bank balance: $3,675.82
Check stub balance: $2,358.62

Checks outstanding: No. 1801 for $540.20
                       No. 1803 for $75.20
                       No. 1804 for $80.30

Bank service charge: $3.50

Note collected by bank and credited to account: $750.00

Deposit in transit: $50.00

A check, No. 1795, for $75.00 was omitted from the check stub but was included on her bank statement.

Bank Balance	Check Stub Balance
Deduct:	Deduct:
Add:	Add:
Adjusted Balance:	Adjusted Balance:

3. Use the following information to reconcile the bank statement for Michelle Oliver:

Bank balance: $760.50
Check stub balance: $729.42

Checks outstanding: No. 314 for $50.80
                       No. 315 for $75.25
                       No. 316 for $60.48

Interest credited to account on bank statement: $8.50

Service charge: $5.00

Check deposited and returned by bank: $50.45

Deposit in transit: $100.00

Charges for printing checks: $8.50

Bank Balance	Check Stub Balance
Deduct:	Deduct:
Add:	Add:
Adjusted Balance:	Adjusted Balance:

42

ASSIGNMENT 4.2 Bank Statement Reconciliation

1. A list of checking account transactions is given below. Write a, b, c, or d in the blank to show whether the transaction requires an adjustment that (a) subtracts from the bank balance, (b) subtracts from the check stub balance, (c) adds to the bank balance, or (d) adds to the check stub balance in order to reconcile the bank statement.

    (a) A check that was deposited after the date of the bank statement. ⎯⎯⎯⎯⎯

    (b) A note that was collected by the bank and credited to the account. ⎯⎯⎯⎯⎯

    (c) An electronic funds transfer of the payroll check that was credited to the account. ⎯⎯⎯⎯⎯

    (d) An outstanding check that was written by the customer but was written too late to be reflected on the bank statement. ⎯⎯⎯⎯⎯

    (e) A bank service charge made because the balance fell below $500 during the month. ⎯⎯⎯⎯⎯

    (f) A check that was deposited into the account but was returned because the person who wrote the check did not have sufficient funds to cover it. ⎯⎯⎯⎯⎯

    (g) Interest earned on the average daily balance in the account. ⎯⎯⎯⎯⎯

    (h) A charge made by the bank for printing a new supply of checks. ⎯⎯⎯⎯⎯

    (i) A check for $8.97 that was incorrectly entered in the check stub as $8.79. ⎯⎯⎯⎯⎯

2. Study the check register transactions shown below. Enter the correct balance after each transaction.

CHECK NO.	DATE	CHECK ISSUED TO			✓	4,869	50
579	4/6/--	TO *Naysmith Clock Shoppe*	AMOUNT OF CHECK OR DEPOSIT			1,309	89
		FOR *grandfather clock*	BALANCE				
580	4/6/--	TO *Elliotts' Supermarket*	AMOUNT OF CHECK OR DEPOSIT			108	16
		FOR *groceries*	BALANCE				
—	4/7/--	TO *Deposit #92*	AMOUNT OF CHECK OR DEPOSIT			583	93
		FOR *weekly payroll*	BALANCE				
581	4/7/--	TO *Hathaway Glassware*	AMOUNT OF CHECK OR DEPOSIT			207	10
		FOR *china*	BALANCE				
582	4/8/--	TO *Midland Telephone*	AMOUNT OF CHECK OR DEPOSIT			59	39
		FOR *phone bill*	BALANCE				
—	4/8/--	TO *Service charge*	AMOUNT OF CHECK OR DEPOSIT			15	00
		FOR *returned check*	BALANCE				

Ending balance $ ⎯⎯⎯⎯⎯⎯⎯⎯⎯⎯

3. Doyle Whitherspoon received a bank statement that shows an ending balance of $1,814.37. His check stub balance shows a balance of $1,796.92. A review of his records indicates that the adjustments shown below are needed. Reconcile the bank statement on the form provided. Use the last day of last month as the date.

Interest added to the account	$ 7.45
Outstanding check: No. 1103 for	$30.00
Deposit in transit	$15.00
Bank service charge	$ 5.00

<table>
<tr><td colspan="4" align="center">Doyle Whitherspoon</td></tr>
<tr><td colspan="4" align="center">RECONCILIATION OF BANK STATEMENT</td></tr>
<tr><td>Bank statement balance</td><td>$_____</td><td>Check stub balance</td><td>$_____</td></tr>
<tr><td>Plus late deposits</td><td>_____</td><td>Plus interest</td><td>_____</td></tr>
<tr><td>Total</td><td>$_____</td><td>Total</td><td>$_____</td></tr>
<tr><td>Less outstanding check</td><td>_____</td><td>Less service charge</td><td>_____</td></tr>
<tr><td>Adjusted bank balance</td><td>$_____</td><td>Adjusted stub balance</td><td>$_____</td></tr>
</table>

4. Dennis Bower received a bank statement that shows an electronic funds transfer of $1,728.15. If this is the only adjustment needed for his check stub balance of $2,609.24, what is the amount of his adjusted check stub balance?

$_____

5. Clara Robertson forgot to record check No. 908 for $38.76 in her check register. If this is the only adjustment needed for her check stub balance of $748.25, what is the amount of her adjusted check stub balance?

$_____

44

INFORMATION PROCESSING

The way that words and data are processed to provide useful information to business is continually changing. Students preparing for business careers must keep up with these changes to qualify for many jobs. The growing use of microcomputers in the work place affects many of the ways that business data is analyzed to make business decisions. Even though the microcomputer performs many computations formerly performed manually or with electronic calculators, persons in business need a thorough knowledge of business mathematics to use the microcomputer effectively.

Electronic Spreadsheet

The electronic spreadsheet, word processing, and database management have made it practical for many businesses to use microcomputers. The spreadsheet is a grid of rows and columns. Microprocessors perform calculations on numeric and alphabetic data entered on the spreadsheet. Formulas can then be entered to perform automatic calculations. Thus the spreadsheet combines many of the same functions as the word processor and the calculator. A sample spreadsheet is shown in Example 5.1.

EXAMPLE   **Sample spreadsheet**

5.1

```
            A              B          C
 1                   SAMPLE REPORT
 2         ------------------------------------
 3          Employee     Monthly    Annual
 4            Name        Salary     Salary
 5         ------------------------------------
 6       Collins, Wanda    1,450     17,400
 7       Goode,  Sarah     1,838     22,056
 8       Mendez,  Raul     1,378     16,536
 9       Poole,  Lee       1,675     20,100
10         ------------------------------------
11          Total          6,341     76,092
12         ------------------------------------
```

The numbers down the left side of the spreadsheet refer to *rows* across the spreadsheet, and the letters across the top refer to *columns* down the spreadsheet. Data can be entered across the rows and under the columns. The location where data is entered is called the *cell address.* For example, data entered in Row 8 under Column C is in cell address C8. When indicating cell addresses, the column designation is always given first, such as D4, G7, A10, and so forth.

CHAPTER 5

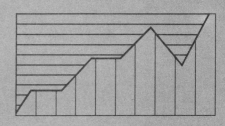

Study Example 5.2 to see how the cell addresses are assigned. Remember that the cell address gives the column letter first, followed by the row number.

EXAMPLE 5.2   Spreadsheet layout

```
          A           B           C           D
1      Cell A1     Cell B1     Cell C1
2
3      Cell A3                             Cell D3
4                  Cell B4
5                  Cell B5     Cell C5
6      Cell A6                             Cell D6
7      Cell A7     Cell B7     Cell C7
```

Spreadsheet Entries

Entries on the spreadsheet may be *labels* (text information such as someone's name or address), *values* (such as someone's salary or rate of pay), or *formulas* (such as one to find gross pay from hourly rates). The spreadsheet in Example 5.3 gives pay rate, hours worked, and gross pay amounts for four employees. Although these spreadsheet computations can be made using a calculator, with a microprocessor they automatically become part of the table.

EXAMPLE 5.3   Spreadsheet computations

```
            A           B           C           D
1                    **PAY RATES**
2       ==========================================
3       Employee      Pay       Hours         Wage
4       Name          Rate      Worked       Amount
5       ==========================================
6       Cofer         7.60         38        288.80
7       Dole          7.85         40        314.00
8       Fuller        6.95         40        278.00
9       Hanks         7.45         36        268.20
10      ==========================================
11      Total      ********       154      1,149.00
12      ==========================================
```

The spreadsheet problems and examples in this text can be solved by using a microcomputer spreadsheet software program, an electronic calculator, or manual methods. The method that you will use will depend on the preference of your instructor and the equipment available. Whatever method you use, you will learn how spreadsheet formats can be used to solve business mathematics problems.

● **Complete Assignment 5.1.** ●

● **Complete Assignment 5.2.** ●

● **Complete Assignment 5.3.** ●

● **Complete Assignment 5.4.** ●

ASSIGNMENT 5.1   Wage Computation Spreadsheet

The spreadsheet shown below is used to compute wages. The gross pay for each employee is computed by multiplying the hours worked by the pay rate. For example, the wage amount for A. Adams is computed by multiplying $5.75 per hour by 35 hours (201.14). This answer should be shown in Cell D6. Compute this and the gross pay for the other employees and enter their gross pays in Column D. Finally, compute the sum of all the employees' gross pays and enter that amount in Cell D18. As mentioned previously, all spreadsheet exercises in this textbook can be computed by using microcomputer spreadsheet software, an electronic calculator, or manual methods. Compute the amounts by hand or machine and enter in the corresponding cell addresses.

```
              A              B           C           D        E
  1                     **WAGE  COMPUTATION**
  2        ==========================================
  3                    Hours        Pay        Wage
  4        Employee    Worked       Rate       Amount
  5        ==========================================
  6        A. Adams      35         5.75
  7        T. Busey      24         5.75
  8        C. Guiez      34         6.20
  9        B. Ham        40         7.20
 1Ø        D. Houck      40         6.25
 11        J. Mann       36         6.35
 12        S. Mulllins   38         6.40
 13        E. Otto       28         5.95
 14        R. Poole      40         6.3Ø
 15        W. Rule       40         6.45
 16        A. Young      35         7.1Ø
 17        ==========================================
 18        Total Wages  *****************
 19        ==========================================
 2Ø
```

Use the data in the completed spreadsheet above to answer the following questions:

1. What was the gross pay for C. Guiez? $ _____

2. What was the gross pay for J. Mann? $ _____

3. What was the gross pay for R. Poole? $ _____

4. What was the gross pay for A. Young? $ _____

5. What was the number of hours worked by D. Houck?   _____

6. What was the number of hours worked by W. Rule?   _____

7. How many employees worked less than 40 hours?

_____

8. How many employees worked exactly 40 hours?

_____

9. How many employees earned more than $6.00 per hour?

_____

10. What was the total gross pay of all employees?

_____

ASSIGNMENT 5.2 Balance Computation Spreadsheet

The spreadsheet shown below is used to determine the ending balance for several bank accounts. Deduct each of the four payments from the beginning balance of each account to compute its ending balance. Record these balances in Column G. Compute the totals for Column B to Column G and record them in Row 19.

	A	B	C	D	E	F	G
1			**BALANCE COMPUTATIONS**				
2	===
3	Account	Beginning	First	Second	Third	Fourth	Ending
4	No.	Balance	Payment	Payment	Payment	Payment	Balance
5	===
6	AC12	1,254.44	89.75	98.34	102.38	78.54	
7	BW23	789.37	78.34	113.45	78.48	98.75	
8	CD75	1,221.39	83.45	187.34	73.56	102.34	
9	CD84	1,782.34	87.45	298.34	309.70	115.83	
10	DF44	1,538.92	119.34	127.54	211.77	406.38	
11	DF72	1,354.56	289.67	389.76	432.49	182.38	
12	DF99	1,829.46	254.67	347.10	300.75	309.48	
13	HE44	1,728.38	243.22	78.43	320.23	310.48	
14	JJ23	1,034.56	213.67	275.23	432.45	83.48	
15	KK34	734.58	198.67	89.43	306.71	37.56	
16	KK65	1,532.48	234.43	376.21	78.56	149.76	
17	MM65	789.56	38.65	47.98	78.48	38.66	
18	===
19	Totals						
20	===

Use the data in the completed spreadsheet above to answer the following questions:

1. What was the ending balance for Account No. AC12? $ _____

2. What was the ending balance for Account No. DF72? $ _____

3. What was the ending balance for Account No. KK65? $ _____

4. Which account number had the largest ending balance?   _____

5. Which account number had the smallest ending balance?   _____

6. How many ending balances were greater than $600.00?   _____

7. How many ending balances were smaller than $100.00?   _____

8. What was the total of the ending balance column? $ _____

9. Which of the four payments had the smallest total amount?   _____

10. What was the difference between the totals of the beginning and ending balance columns? $ _____

51

ASSIGNMENT 5.3 Units Sold Spreadsheet

The spreadsheet shown below can be used to determine the weekly total units sold by each employee and the total units sold on each day of the week. Add the units sold during each day to compute the weekly total for each employee. Record these amounts in Column G. Show the totals for each column in Row 19.

	A	B	C	D	E	F	G
1	Rice Variety Store			**UNITS SOLD**			
2	==						
3		No. on	No. on	No. on	No. on	No. on	Weekly
4	Employee	Monday	Tuesday	Wednesday	Thursday	Friday	Total
5	==						
6	Abson	27	32	32	32	21	
7	Burns	38	33	34	34	22	
8	Coozen	37	53	36	43	24	
9	Diez	28	56	43	55	26	
10	Fogelman	48	32	42	32	29	
11	Getz	34	34	41	33	23	
12	Halls	19	32	34	37	31	
13	Jensen	24	34	24	29	34	
14	Keels	28	43	23	26	29	
15	Lenz	32	22	26	32	37	
16	Martin	38	34	28	28	33	
17	Noonan	33	14	33	22	32	
18	==						
19	Totals						
20	==						

Use the data in the completed spreadsheet above to answer the following questions:

1. How many units did Getz sell on Wednesday?   _____

2. Which employee sold the most units on Tuesday?   _____

3. Which employee sold the fewest units on Friday?   _____

4. How many units did Fogelman sell during the week?   _____

5. How many units did Martin sell during the week?   _____

6. On which day of the week were the most units sold?   _____

7. On which day of the week did Halls sell the most units?   _____

8. How many total units were sold on Monday?   _____

9. How many total units were sold on Friday?   _____

10. How many total units were sold during the week?   _____

ASSIGNMENT 5.4 Monthly Absentee Report Spreadsheet

The spreadsheet shown below can be used to summarize employees' attendance records. Divide the number of days absent by the number of employees to find the average number of days absent per employee for each store. Record these averages in Column E. Divide the number of days present by the number of employees to compute the average number of days present per employee and record these averages in Column F. Record the totals of Columns E and F in Row 19.

	A	B	C	D	E	F
					Days	Days
					Absent	Present
					Per	Per
	Store	Days	Days	No. of	Employee	Employee
1	Howard Mfg. Co.		**MONTHLY ABSENTEE REPORT**			
2	==					
3					Days	Days
4					Absent	Present
5	Store	Days	Days	No. of	Per	Per
6	Code	Absent	Present	Employees	Employee	Employee
7	==					
8	Abbey	48	452	25		
9	Burley	42	658	35		
10	Cooper	61	459	26		
11	Drake	76	524	30		
12	Everett	40	400	22		
13	Hauck	46	674	36		
14	Kelsey	48	792	42		
15	Menslow	53	347	20		
16	Nelson	46	454	25		
17	Opal	38	522	28		
18	==					
19	Summary	498	5282	289		
20	==					

Use the data in the completed spreadsheet above to answer the following questions:

1. What was the average number of days absent per employee for the Everett store?   _____

2. What was the average number of days present per employee for the Burley store?   _____

3. Which store had the largest average number of days absent per employee?   _____

4. Which store had the smallest average number of days absent per employee?   _____

5. For how many stores was the average number of days absent per employee greater than 1.72?   _____

6. Which store employed the greatest number of employees?   _____

7. What was the total number of days absent for all stores combined? _____

8. How many employees were employed by all stores combined? _____

9. What was the average number of days absent per employee for all stores combined? _____

10. What was the average number of days present per employee for all stores combined? _____

• **Complete Unit 1 Self-Test** •

56

UNIT 1 SELF-TEST Basic Mathematic Operations

1. Joe Chang made the following purchases: $128.45, $236.77, $17.89, and $173.23. What was the total amount of his purchases?

    $ _____

2. The Melrose Heating Company sells 3 heaters for the following prices: $24.56, $37.28, and $48.75. Round each price to tens and compute the estimated total cost of the three heaters.

    $ _____

3. Store A had total sales of $43,387.53. Store B had total sales of $52,173.12. By how much did Store B's sales exceed Store A's sales?

    $ _____

4. Joe Vocca had a beginning balance of $789.45 in his checking account. He made a $239.45 deposit. He wrote checks for the following amounts: $23.78, $89.34, and $75.04. What was his ending balance?

    $ _____

5. The Connie Forde Auto Center sold 207 automobiles with an average price of $3,818. Round all figures to hundreds and compute the estimated total sales amount.

    $ _____

6. Carl Dickerson drives his car at an average speed of 55 miles per hour. How many miles will he drive in 7 hours?

    _____

7. Brenda Everett earned $289.40 for five days of work. What was her average earnings per day?

    $ _____

8. A secretary needs to type a report containing 837 words. If the secretary can type 65 words per minute, how many minutes will be required to type the report? (Round to one decimal place.)

_____

9. The following items were sold to a customer. Compute the amount per item and the total cost.

Item	Quantity	Price	Amount
A	13	8.98	_____
B	9	14.95	_____
C	7	8.59	_____
D	9	19.98	_____
Total Cost			_____

10. Jim Brock's check stub balance was $789.14. His bank statement balance was $786.89. A review of his banking records showed a $5.00 bank charge that had not been recorded in the check stub. There were two outstanding checks ($20.50 and $17.25) and a late deposit ($35.00) that were not recorded on the bank statement. What was the reconciled balance of his account?

_____

11. Clara Fuller forgot to record Check No. 723 for $137.89 in her check stub. If this is the only adjustment that needs to be made to her check stub balance of $625.30, what is her adjusted check stub balance?

_____

12. Roy Jones received a bank statement that included an electronic funds transfer of $1,353.78. If this is the only adjustment that needs to be made to his check stub balance of $3,721.53, what is his adjusted check stub balance?

_____

58

Decimals

To be computed by computers and electronic calculators, numbers must be in decimal form. Most business math problems include computations that require the use of decimal values. Accuracy in computation and placement of the decimal point is essential because one undetected error can cause a mistake of thousands of dollars.

Some skills you can achieve in this unit include the following:

- **Using a place value chart and reading decimal values.**
- **Converting fractions to mixed numbers.**
- **Converting fractions to decimal values.**
- **Adding, subtracting, multiplying, and dividing decimal values.**
- **Aligning decimal points and rounding decimal values to an appropriate number of places to the right of the decimal.**
- **Placing the decimal point at the appropriate position when multiplying or dividing decimal values.**
- **Using the electronic calculator to make computations related to decimal values.**

UNIT 2

DECIMALS: AN OVERVIEW

As computers and electronic calculators become increasingly common and necessary business tools, most figures are stated in decimal form because computations performed with this equipment must be in decimal form. This chapter provides background knowledge needed to perform the fundamental processes of addition, subtraction, multiplication, and division using decimal values.

Decimal Values

Many values in business and everyday use are stated in decimal form. Examples include product prices, interest rates, discounts, speedometer readings, and measurements. The *decimal places* to the right of a decimal point (period) represent one or more tenths, hundredths, thousandths, and so forth of a single number such as 0.1 or 0.15. A mixed decimal is a decimal number that combines a whole number and a decimal fraction, such as 5.1 or 5.65.

Place value with fractions, as with whole numbers, is important. The chart in Example 6.1 is similar to the one used in Chapter 1 to show place value for whole numbers. Notice that the first place to the right of the decimal point is the tenths place, and each position to the right is a power of 10 (hundredths, thousandths, ten thousandths, and so forth). The value of each number place decreases as it appears further to the right of the decimal point. For example, 0.8 is greater than 0.08, and 0.2 is greater than 0.02 because of place value. In Example 6.1, a 2 is in the hundreds place and a 3 is in the tens place.

EXAMPLE   Place value chart

6.1

Millions	Hundred Thousands	Ten Thousands	Thousands	Hundreds	Tens	Units	Decimal Point	Tenths	Hundredths	Thousandths	Ten Thousandths	Hundred Thousandths	Millionths
4	9	7	8	2	3	2	•	0	1	9	6	2	1
10^6	10^5	10^4	10^3	10^2	10^1	10^0		0.1	0.01	0.001	0.0001	0.00001	0.000001

←Increases in Value   0 Decreases in Value →

CHAPTER 6

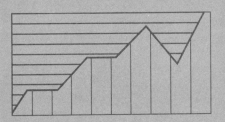

Example 6.2 shows how decimals are read. The fractional equivalents of the decimals are also indicated.

EXAMPLE 6.2 Reading decimals

Decimal Value	Place Value	Pronounced	Fractional Value
0.5	Tenths	Five Tenths	5/10
0.06	Hundredths	Six Hundredths	6/100
0.072	Thousandths	Seventy-Two Thousandths	72/1,000
0.0002	Ten-Thousandths	Two Ten-Thousandths	2/10,000
0.00003	Hundred-Thousandths	Three Hundred-Thousandths	3/100,000
0.000008	Millionths	Eight Millionths	8/1,000,000
3.15	Hundredths	Three and Fifteen Hundredths	3 15/100
114.7	Tenths	One Hundred Fourteen and Seven Tenths	114 7/10
5.08	Hundredths	Five and Eight Hundredths	5 8/100

Some people prefer to pronounce the decimal point. For example, 2.67 is read "two point sixty-seven," and 0.07 is read "zero point zero seven."

Equivalent Decimals and Fractions

Fractions can be converted to decimal equivalents and decimals can be converted to fractional equivalents. Example 6.3 shows how to convert the decimal .34 to a fraction.

EXAMPLE 6.3 Converting the decimal .34 to a fraction

Step 1. Read the decimal.

Read .34 as thirty-four hundredths.

Step 2. Write the decimal as a fraction by placing its digits in the numerator. The denominator is 1 followed by as many zeros as the number of places to the right of the decimal point.

34/100

Step 3. Reduce the fraction to its lowest terms.

34/100 = 17/50

Therefore, .34 equals 34/100 or 17/50.

Mixed decimals can be changed to mixed numbers using the same procedure. Example 6.4 shows how to change 10.250 to its mixed number equivalent.

Converting the decimal 10.250 to a fraction   EXAMPLE

6.4

Step 1.   Ten and two hundred fifty thousandths

Step 2.   10 250/1,000

Step 3.   10 250/1,000 = 10 1/4

Notice that the whole number in the mixed decimal remains the same when converted to a mixed number.

A fraction can be changed to a decimal by simply dividing the numerator by the denominator of the fraction. For example, 1/4 becomes 0.25 as shown in Example 6.5. Zeros are added to the right of the decimal until the division ends or until it appears that the denominator cannot be divided into the numerator evenly. In that case, the remainder is placed as a numerator over the divisor, and this fraction is placed to the right of the quotient. Both of these situations are shown in Example 6.5.

Converting a fraction to a decimal   EXAMPLE

6.5

$$1/4 = 0.25 \qquad 4\overline{)1.0} \atop \begin{array}{r} 0.25 \\ \underline{8} \\ 20 \\ \underline{20} \end{array}$$

$$1/3 = 0.333\ 1/3 \qquad 3\overline{)1.000} \atop \begin{array}{r} 0.333\ 1/3 \\ \underline{9} \\ 10 \\ \underline{9} \\ 10 \\ \underline{9} \\ 1 \end{array}$$

• **Complete Assignment 6.1** •

ASSIGNMENT 6.1 Decimals

1. Evaluate each of the following pairs of decimal values and indicate which of the two numbers in each pair is larger.

(a) .2 or .3 _____   (d) .725 or .81 _____

(b) .25 or .125 _____   (e) 4.8 or 4.08 _____

(c) .367 or .286 _____   (f) 3.11 or 3.2 _____

2. Indicate the place value of the digit on the extreme right in each of the following numbers:

(a) 0.2 _____   (d) 0.000001 _____

(b) 0.25 _____   (e) 3.289 _____

(c) 0.3451 _____   (f) 4.8 _____

3. Write out in words how the following decimal values are read or pronounced:

(a) 0.3 _____

(b) .08 _____

(c) 0.85 _____

(d) 0.003 _____

(e) 0.0017 _____

(f) 0.00001 _____

(g) 3.2 _____

(h) 4.25 _____

4. Convert the following fractions to decimals or decimals to fractions:

	Decimal	Fraction		Decimal	Fraction
(a)	0.25	_____	**(f)**	0.375	_____
(b)	2.5	_____	**(g)**	0.875	_____
(c)	_____	3/10	**(h)**	0.025	_____
(d)	_____	1/8	**(i)**	_____	2/3
(e)	_____	3/4	**(j)**	_____	3/8

66

DECIMALS: ADDITION AND SUBTRACTION

Many applications require the addition and/or subtraction of decimals, such as deducting payments on account, computing statement balances, determining a customer's account balance, and computing payrolls. In this chapter, you will practice adding and subtracting decimal values and solving appropriate problems.

Addition of Decimals

Adding decimal values is similar to adding whole numbers except that when adding by hand the alignment of the decimal point must be considered. If you are using a calculator, however, it will automatically align the decimal point. In other words, the decimal point must be aligned for each value, as shown in Example 7.1 when adding 1.23, 1.456, 16.71, and 293.1. Notice that zeros can be added onto the extreme right of the decimal point to help you add decimal values without affecting the value. For example, 1.23 equals 1.230 or 1.2300. Some people prefer to add sufficient zeros so that the values, or addends, align evenly on the right side as shown in Example 7.1.

EXAMPLE **Alignment of decimals**

7.1

$$
\begin{array}{r}
1.23 \\
1.456 \\
16.71 \\
+293.1 \\
\hline
312.496 \text{ sum}
\end{array}
\Big\} \text{addends} \quad \text{or} \quad
\begin{array}{r}
1.230 \\
1.456 \\
16.710 \\
+293.100 \\
\hline
312.496
\end{array}
$$

Decimal values can be added in the same manner as whole numbers if the decimal point in the answer is placed in the same vertical line as the other decimal points. Most computers and electronic calculators will align the decimal point automatically if the decimal point is keyboarded (entered) in the proper place along with each decimal place. While using the equipment, decimal values can be arranged in either horizontal or vertical column order. However, manual addition (or subtraction) of decimal values is easier to perform if the values are arranged in vertical order with the decimal points properly aligned. If an electronic calculator or computer is used, most problems in this and other chapters should first be solved manually and then with equipment in order to gain practice unless your instructor directs otherwise.

CHAPTER 7

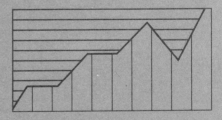

Rounding Numbers

Any number can be rounded to the desired number of places. As a general rule, addition or subtraction of dollar values should be carried to three places to the right of the decimal point and rounded to two places to the right of the decimal point. Note that rounding to two decimal places is normally done only after the final answer has been obtained.

A general rule for problems in this text and for making business calculations that involve multiplication or division is to round off numbers to four decimal places and then round off the answer to two decimal places. See Examples 7.2 and 7.3.

EXAMPLE

7.2

Rule for rounding off numbers

Step 1.   Decide the decimal digit to which the value will be rounded, such as the fourth decimal place. (It is a good idea to underline that digit.)

Step 2.   If the next digit to the right is 5 or greater, add 1 to the digit in the position to be rounded. If the next digit to the right is 4 or less, leave the digit in the position to be rounded unchanged.

Step 3.   Add the values after rounding. Then round the answer to the desired decimal place using Steps 1 and 2 above.

EXAMPLE

7.3

**Rounding of decimal values
(four places with the answer to two places)**

Step 1.   14.325<u>8</u>7
6.425<u>8</u>51
3.289<u>4</u>2
5.267<u>8</u>48

Step 2.   14.3259
6.4259
3.2894
+ 5.2678
29.30<u>9</u>0

Step 3.   29.3090 = 29.31

If the original values had *not* been rounded, the actual sum would have been 29.308989. In this instance, the actual sum rounded to two decimal places would have been 29.31, which is the same as the sum obtained by rounding off. There may be a few instances in which the final sums will be inaccurate due to rounding of addends, but if the above rules for addition and subtraction problems are followed, the rounding usually balances out.

● Complete Assignment 7.1. ●

Subtraction of Decimals

The rule for aligning the decimal point in addition of decimals also applies to the subtraction of decimals. However, adding zeros to the right of the decimal point is required in subtraction so that both values have the same number of places to the right of the decimal point. This is illustrated in the following examples in which 8.112 is subtracted from 11.238, 1.243 is subtracted from 8.380, and 3.20 is subtracted from 7.25.

$$
\begin{array}{r} 11.238 \\ -\ 8.112 \\ \hline 3.126 \end{array}
\qquad
\begin{array}{r} 8.380 \\ -1.243 \\ \hline 7.137 \end{array}
\qquad
\begin{array}{r} 7.25 \\ -3.20 \\ \hline 4.05 \end{array}
$$

In the middle example, notice that the value 1 can be "borrowed" from the left digit to add 10 to the value. For example, 1 was borrowed from the value 8 (making the 8 a 7) to add 10 to the value 0. Then, 3 was subtracted from 10 to produce the value 7 in the answer.

After sufficient zeros have been added to right-justify (make even on the right side) the two values and the decimal point has been properly aligned, subtraction is performed in the same manner as subtraction with whole numbers. Because correct placement of the decimal point in the answer is so important, estimation and verification of answers are essential when making computations with decimals.

● Complete Assignment 7.2 ●

ASSIGNMENT 7.1 Decimals: Addition

1. Before adding the amounts for each problem, rewrite each value vertically with the decimal points properly aligned. (Do not round off.)

(a) 27.2, 31.41, 32.192

_____

(b) 148.3, 16.075, 63.7052

_____

(c) 214.3789, 109.0003, 63.1

_____

(d) 807.2, 19.00901, 16.143

_____

(e) 167.1, 819.202, 16.8009

_____

(f) 15.81765, 189.7624, 1.81

_____

(g) 90.009, 45.25, 76.1124

_____

(h) 814.04, 782.009, 484.4, 21.8

_____

(i) 975.87, 0.50906, 3.6145, 3.12

_____

(j) 87.007, 70.0081, 134.83, 8.8

_____

(k) 0.608, 913.21, 4.0098

_____

(l) 164.29, 14.009, 62.137, 18.423

_____

2. A person bought the following items at the grocery store: bread, $1.07; produce, $6.27; cheese, $4.19; and meat, $8.83. Determine the total amount due for the merchandise.

$ _____

3. A family spent the following amounts on various items in the family budget: rent, $480.00; food, $395.87; clothing, $162.37; miscellaneous, $405.95; and savings, $275.14. Determine the family's total monthly income.

$ _____

4. Round the following numbers as indicated:

(a) 384 to the nearest ten _____

(b) 426 to the nearest ten _____

(c) 3,062 to the nearest hundred _____

(d) 452 to the nearest hundred _____

(e) 87,653 to the nearest thousand _____

(f) 87.521 to one decimal place _____

(g) 1,214.253 to one decimal place _____

(h) 16.895 to two decimal places _____

(i) 142.314 to two decimal places _____

(j) 16.21894 to two decimal places _____

(k) 162.21936 to three decimal places _____

(l) 14.89567 to four decimal places _____

(m) 6.89501 to three decimal places _____

(n) 152.155 to two decimal places _____

(o) 52.0504 to one decimal place _____

(p) 23,762.8951 to two decimal places _____

72

ASSIGNMENT 7.2 Decimals: Subtraction

1. Rewrite each of the following values with the decimal points correctly aligned, then subtract. (Do not round.)

(a) $12.32 - 4.1 =$

_____

(b) $28.6 - 9.42 =$

_____

(c) $516.382 - 28.197 =$

_____

(d) $472.4 - 36.817 =$

_____

(e) $73.001 - 28.73 =$

_____

(f) $0.216 - 0.1725 =$

_____

(g) $0.8783 - 0.527 =$

_____

(h) $1.0 - 0.264 =$

_____

(i) $25.006 - 13.7268 =$

_____

(j) $7.6 - 0.01254 =$

_____

(k) $86{,}412.8 - 0.0739 =$

_____

(l) $1.009 - 0.6873 =$

_____

2. Juan Rodriquez had a beginning checking account balance of $1,623.81. He then wrote checks for the following amounts: $14.67, $37.14, $289.34, $56.78, and $4.23. What was his ending balance after deducting these checks?

$ _____

3. G. H. Polawski had gross income of $423.13 for the week. The following amounts were deducted: income taxes, $98.86; retirement fund, $113.87; other state and federal taxes, $48.08. What was the amount of her paycheck (called the *net pay*) after all deductions were subtracted?

$ _____

4. An account statement for medical services for Albert Schaefer for the past month is shown below. Complete the statement by adding charges to the balance and subtracting payments made to the account.

Day	Charge	Payment	Balance
		STATEMENT: ALBERT SCHAEFER	
		3989 POPLAR AVENUE	
		MEMPHIS, TENNESSEE 38111	
1			$143.14
3	24.23		$ _____
7	62.37		$ _____
9		39.82	$ _____
15	27.89		$ _____
19		26.39	$ _____
21		14.26	$ _____
25		17.82	$ _____

5. Constance Rosetti had $647.13 at the beginning of the day. After counting her money at the end of the day, she had $378.26. How much did she spend during the day?

$ _____

6. Avron Goldsmith drove his car for one month. At the beginning of the month, his odometer read 26714.6 miles. At the end of the month, his odometer read 27638.3. How many miles did he drive during the month?

_____

7. Marla Smithson purchased a new car for $13,898.18 last year. This year, a new car with similar equipment costs $15,149.01. How much did the price of the car increase this year?

$ _____

8. The promoter of a rock concert sold 13,750 tickets for $16.65 each for a total income of $228,937.50. Total expenses were $189,989.14. How much profit did the promoter make?

$ _____

74

DECIMALS: MULTIPLICATION AND DIVISION

8

Business applications in areas such as accounting, finance, statistics, real estate, and data processing require a thorough knowledge of multiplication and division of decimal values because many business computations deal with decimal values. This chapter provides skill and knowledge needed to solve problems that involve decimal values.

Multiplication of Decimals

Multiplication of decimal values is performed in much the same way as multiplication of whole numbers. A difference is that in multiplication of decimal values the decimal point must be placed at the proper position in the answer. The rule for determining where the decimal point should be placed in the product is to count from right to left the number of decimal places in the multiplier and multiplicand combined. This is illustrated in Example 8.1 below, where 4.231 is multiplied by 4.5.

EXAMPLE **Rule for placing the decimal point in the product**

8.1

Step 1. Multiply the decimal values as whole numbers.

$$
\begin{array}{r}
4.231 \text{ multiplicand} \\
\times \quad 4.5 \text{ multiplier} \\
\hline
21155 \\
16924 \quad \\
\hline
190395 \text{ product}
\end{array}
$$

Step 2. Count the number of decimal places in the multiplicand and multiplier combined.

4.231 (3 places) + 4.5 (1 place) = 4 decimal places

Step 3. Place the decimal point at the number of places (counting from right to left) in the product that corresponds to the sum obtained in Step 2.

19.0395

Whole numbers have an assumed decimal point at the right of the ones place. In Example 8.2, one of the factors is a whole number.

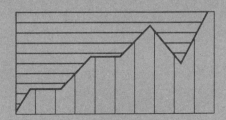

75

EXAMPLE
8.2

Multiplying 4.216 by 23

```
        4.216 (3 decimal places)
     ×     23 (0 decimal places)
        12648
         8432
        96.968 (3 + 0 = 3 decimal places)
```

Example 8.3 shows how to count decimal places when small decimals are multiplied.

EXAMPLE
8.3

Multiplying .003 by .0004

```
       .003 (3 decimal places)
     × .0004 (4 decimal places)
      .0000012 (3 + 4 = 7 decimal places)
```

The rule in Example 8.3 also applies when several decimal values are multiplied. As shown in Example 8.4, the number of places to the right of the decimal point in the product equals the sum of decimal places in all factors.

EXAMPLE
8.4

Multiplying 2.52 by 1.2 by 2.5

```
        2.52 (2 decimal places)
     ×   1.2 (1 decimal place)
         504
         252
        3024
     ×   2.5 (1 decimal place)
       15120
        6048
       7.5600 (4 decimal places)
```

Note: This product can also be shown as 7.56 to omit the zeros without changing the value of the product.

Most electronic calculators will automatically place the decimal point correctly in the product. Example 8.5 shows how the previous problem would be displayed on an electronic calculator.

Multiplication with an electronic calculator   EXAMPLE

8.5

$$2.52 \times 1.2 = \underline{3.024} \times 2.5 = \underline{7.56}$$

Rounding Numbers

There is no universally accepted rule for deciding how far to carry out a decimal product or quotient. The preceding chapter indicated that computations involving dollars and cents should be carried to five decimal places and rounded to four decimal places and the final answer rounded to two decimal places. That is a good rule for multiplication and division computations as well.

For decimals other than money amounts, a general rule is to carry out the product to the total number of decimal places contained in the two largest factors. For example, the problem $2.34 \times 3.583 \times 2.3$ will have a product rounded to five decimal places, but the problem 2.3×1.4 will be rounded to two decimal places. Answers to these problems will be 19.28371 and 3.22 respectively.

A general rule for division is to carry out the decimal place in the quotient to four places or to the number of decimal places in the divisor and the dividend combined, whichever is greater. For example, the problem $0.13 \div 0.7$ will be rounded to three decimal places, and the quotient will be 0.186.

The rules in this chapter and the preceding chapter for rounding numbers should be used for rounding all problems in this text unless directions indicate otherwise.

● **Complete Assignment 8.1** ●

Division of Decimals

Division of decimal values is similar to the division of whole numbers except that correct placement of the decimal in the divisor, dividend, and quotient is essential. Placement of the decimal point is outlined in Example 8.6.

Correct placement of the decimal point in division   EXAMPLE

8.6

Problem: $1.5\overline{)3.525}$

Solution: Step 1.   If the divisor is not a whole number, move the decimal point to the right of the divisor and move it the same number of places in the dividend.

$15\overline{)35.25}$

Step 2.   Place a decimal point in the quotient directly above the decimal point in the dividend and perform the division.

$$
\begin{array}{r}
2.35 \\
15\overline{)35.25} \\
\underline{30} \\
52 \\
\underline{45} \\
75 \\
\underline{75} \\
\end{array}
$$

Remember that the decimal point in the quotient must be directly above the decimal point in the dividend. Also remember that the decimal point must be moved the same number of places in the dividend as in the divisor (unless the divisor is a whole number). See Example 8.7.

EXAMPLE   Placement of decimal point in division

8.7

(a) .35 ÷ 7 = .05

$$
\begin{array}{r}
.05 \\
7\overline{)\,.35} \\
\underline{35} \\
\end{array}
$$

(b) 75 ÷ .5 = 150.

$$
\begin{array}{r}
150.0 \\
5\overline{)750.} \\
\underline{5} \\
25 \\
\underline{25} \\
00 \\
\underline{00} \\
\end{array}
$$

(c) 11.25 ÷ 5 = 2.25

$$
\begin{array}{r}
2.25 \\
5\overline{)11.25} \\
\underline{10} \\
12 \\
\underline{10} \\
25 \\
\underline{25} \\
\end{array}
$$

(d) 10 ÷ .3 = 33.33 1/3

$$
\begin{array}{r}
33.33\ 1/3 \\
3\overline{)100.00} \\
\underline{9} \\
10 \\
\underline{9} \\
10 \\
\underline{9} \\
10 \\
\underline{9} \\
1 \\
\end{array}
$$

In Example 8.7d, notice that the dividend cannot be divided evenly by the divisor. This is an *infinite number* because the quotient will continue to contain a remainder. In this case, the decimal should be rounded off or shown with the quotient expressed as a decimal combined with a fraction. The final remainder is shown as the numerator and the divisor as the denominator of the fraction. Depending on how many places the quotient was carried, the quotient could have been 33.3 1/3, 33.33 1/3, 33.333 1/3, 33.3333 1/3, and so forth. Zeros can be added to the right of the decimal in the dividend, as needed, to carry the quotient the desired number of places. When calculators are used, the answer must be rounded because the display will not show fractions.

An electronic calculator will automatically place the decimal at the appropriate place in the quotient. The quotient that a calculator would display is underlined in the example below.

$$75 \div .5 = \underline{150}.$$

Most problems and examples in the text are formatted to be solved using electronic calculators. Unless otherwise directed by your instructor, problems should be solved manually to develop the thought process even if electronic calculators are also used. If calculators are available, problems can be solved both manually and with equipment to provide practice and check accuracy.

● **Complete Assignment 8.2** ●

ASSIGNMENT 8.1   Decimals: Multiplication

1. Multiply each of the following problems. Rewrite each problem in vertical columns before completing the multiplication.

(a) $2.4 \times 4.2 =$

(b) $3.54 \times 2.4 =$

(c) $14.231 \times 3 =$

(d) $\$14.26 \times 1.50 =$

(e) $\$128.60 \times 1.25 =$

(f) $0.6052 \times 5 =$

(g) $0.0026 \times 4 =$

(h) $0.0072 \times 7 =$

(i) $0.0091 \times 16 =$

(j) $0.0906 \times 1.5 =$

(k) $316 \times 0.25 =$

(l) $\$40.00 \times 0.75 =$

(m) $0.5 \times 0.25 =$

(n) $0.26 \times 0.48 =$

(o) $272 \times 0.201 =$

(p) $162 \times 0.003 =$

(q) $297 \times 0.0025 =$

(r) $318 \times 0.000037 =$

(s) $0.002 \times 0.004 =$

(t) $0.08 \times .0012 =$

2. Multiply each of the following problems. Round off each product to the proper number of places using the general rules presented in the text.

(a) 3.41 × 6.231 × 1.52 = _____

(d) 4.516 × 2.1 × 3.5 = _____

(b) 3.54 × 2.5 × 3.2 = _____

(e) 12.578 × 0.05 × 0.025 = _____

(c) 4.27 × 3.417 × 3.25 = _____

(f) 128.42 × 0.54 × 0.25 = _____

3. Claudia Akins made 257 silk flowers during the week. She is paid 85¢ for each one. What will her total earnings be?

$ _____

4. Will Bernstein worked 40 hours during the week and was paid $9.78 per hour. What was his gross pay?

$ _____

5. Marcell Perez typed 428 pages of manuscript material for a client. He charged $4.65 per page. How much did he earn for typing the manuscript?

$ _____

82

ASSIGNMENT 8.2   Decimals: Division

1. Divide each of the following problems. Rewrite each problem with the decimal point properly placed. Where rounding is needed, round problems to the proper place. Round problems involving money to two places.

(a) $54.25 \div 35 =$ 155

_____

(b) $14.875 \div 3.5 =$ 425

_____

(c) $10.44 \div 7.2 =$

_____

(d) $49.3125 \div .25 =$

_____

(e) $85 \div 2.5 =$

_____

(f) $96 \div 3.2 =$

_____

(g) $68 \div 5.2 =$

_____

(h) $79 \div 4.6 =$

_____

(i) $82 \div 0.5 =$

_____

(j) $75 \div 1.04 =$

_____

(k) $36.24 \div 8 =$

_____

(l) $96.48 \div 75 =$

_____

(m) $63.28 \div 8 =$

_____

(n) $0.69 \div 0.75 =$

_____

(o) $0.144 \div 0.03 =$

_____

2. Bowery Enterprises had a net profit of $12,627.75 for the year. The profit was divided equally among 3 partners. How much did each partner receive?

$ _____

3. Joe Cobb had to travel 1,786.6 miles in four days. On the average, how many miles did he travel each day?

_____

83

4. Jewell Gross drove 16,471 miles and used 1470.6 liters of gasoline. How many miles per liter did she travel?

_____

5. Bob Randolph assembled 3,800 pieces in 4.75 days. If he assembled an equal number of pieces each day, how many did he assemble each day?

_____

6. Rochelle Lawson, a television performer, signed an annual contract for $360,565.25. For each of the 365 days in the year, how much will her daily earnings be?

$_____

7. A professional baseball player in Japan hit 361 home runs in 9.5 years. On the average, how many home runs did he hit each year?

_____

8. Boxwood, Inc. employed 720 employees during the year. They missed a total of 5,940 days due to illness. On the average, how many days did each employee miss due to illness?

_____

9. Roger Whittaker earned $371.64 for working 38 hours. How much did he earn per hour?

$_____

84

UNIT 2 SPREADSHEET APPLICATION 1: Word Processing Charges

The spreadsheet shown below is used to determine word processing charges. Customers are charged a rate per line that depends on the type of document. The amount charged is computed by multiplying the number of lines produced by the cost per line. Show these amounts in Column F. Show the sum of the amounts charged in Cell F19.

```
        A            B              C           D      E      F      G       H
1   Clark Steno Service              *WORD PROCESSING CHARGES** ******
2   ========================================================|********
3       Job        Type of         Lines         Cost        |Amount  ********
4       Number     Document         Produced     Per Line     |Charged ********
5   ==============================================|==========|********
6   P23        Memo               120         0.10          |          Call
7   P24        Letter             175         0.09          |       761-2047
8   P25        Memo               128         0.10          |         for
9   P26        Table               95         0.14          |       Prompt
10  P27        Letter             185         0.09          |       Service
11  P28        Letter             173         0.09          |       ^^^^^^^^^
12  P29        Memo               145         0.10          |       Please
13  P30        Table              115         0.14          |       pay
14  P31        Manuscript         745         0.12          |       within
15  P32        Letter             165         0.09          |       15 days.
16  P33        Memo               125         0.10          |       ^^^^^^^^^
17  P34        Memo               132         0.10          |       Thanks
18  ==============================================|==========|for your
19  Amount Due    xxxxxxxxxxxxxxxxxxxxxxxxxxxxxx |          |business.
20  ==============================================|==========|********
```

Complete the spreadsheet and answer the following questions:

1. How many lines were produced for Job P26? _____

2. How many lines were produced for Job P34? _____

3. How many jobs were included on the report? _____

4. What type of document was completed for Job P28? _____

5. What amount was charged for Job P27? _____

6. What amount was charged for Job P31? _____

7. What amount was charged for Job P33? _____

8. For what type of document is the highest cost per line charged? _____

9. For which job was the highest amount charged? _____

10. What was the total amount billed for all the jobs? _____

UNIT 2 SPREADSHEET APPLICATION 2: Mileage Analysis

The spreadsheet shown below is used to determine the miles per gallon (called the *mileage* or *MPG*) and fuel cost for a fleet of automobiles. Divide the miles driven by the gallons of fuel used to compute the number of miles per gallon (round to one decimal place). Multiply the fuel used by the fuel cost per gallon to compute the fuel cost (round to two decimal places). Show the miles per gallon in Column E. Show the fuel cost in Column G. Show the sum of each column in Row 19.

```
            A          B         C      D      E      F      G     H      I
 1   City Fleet Service               **MPG ANALYSIS**          ***************
 2   ================================================================  **************
 3   Vehicle      Miles      Fuel  | Miles per |  Fuel  ***************
 4   ID           Driven     Used  |   Gallon  |  Cost  **************
 5   ================================|===========|=========  **************
 6   A41D8        876.8      48.3   |           |           ^^^^^^^^^^^^^^^^^
 7   B44B7        759.7      45.7   |           |           Fuel cost
 8   D4513        762.5      42.6   |           |           per gallon
 9   G44N36       763.3      40.1   |           |                 $0.869
10   H23H51       812.9      43.6   |           |           ^^^^^^^^^^^^^^^^^
11   JJ345A       805.2      45.7   |           |           ***************
12   M142M3       653.4      38.7   |           |           **************
13   P33P35       746.8      42.3   |           |           **************
14   P45N2        800.5      42.7   |           |           **************
15   U7610        783.7      40.2   |           |           **************
16   V44F5        752.4      39.5   |           |           ***************
17   Y6522        812.1      42.7   |           |           **************
18   ==============================|===========|=========  **************
19   Totals                        |XXXXXXXXXXX|           **************
20   ================================================================  **************
```

Complete the spreadsheet and answer the following questions:

1. What was the MPG for Vehicle D4513?   _____

2. What was the MPG for Vehicle P45N2?   _____

3. What was the fuel cost per gallon?   _____

4. What was the fuel cost for Vehicle H23H51?   _____

5. What was the fuel cost for Vehicle U7610?   _____

6. Which vehicle had the lowest MPG?   _____

7. Which vehicle had the highest fuel cost?   _____

8. How many vehicles had MPGs greater than 18.0?   _____

9. What was the amount of total fuel used by the fleet?   _____

10. What was the cost of total fuel used?   _____

• **Complete Unit 2 Self-Test** •

UNIT 2 SELF-TEST Decimals

1. Write the following fractional values out in words to show how they are read or pronounced.

   (a) 0.5   _____

   (b) 0.08   _____

   (c) 0.013   _____

   (d) 0.0018   _____

   (e) 0.00007   _____

   (f) 4.02   _____

   (g) 5.0071   _____

   (h) 17.123   _____

2. Convert the following fractions to decimals or decimals to fractions as indicated. (Reduce fractions to lowest terms.)

	Decimal	Fraction			Decimal	Fraction
(a)	0.3	_____	(e)		_____	7/10
(b)	0.25	_____	(f)		_____	4/5
(c)	2.75	_____	(g)		_____	1/2
(d)	5.8	_____	(h)		_____	5/8

3. Add the following decimal amounts with the decimal points correctly aligned. (Do not round off.)

   (a) 17.2 + 6.3   = _____   (d) 6.17 + 0.07 + 3.0098 = _____

   (b) 25.15 + 16.08   = _____   (e) 1.81 + 807.2 + 16.018 = _____

   (c) 13.001 + 25.08 + 6.27 = _____ (f) 8.121 + 2.13 + 301.01 = _____

4. Round the following numbers to the places indicated.

   (a)   567 to the nearest ten   _____

   (b)   3,492 to the nearest
thousand   _____

   (c)   555 to the nearest ten   _____

   (d)   65.549 to one decimal place   _____

   (e)   2.518 to two decimal places   _____

   (f)   10.752 to one decimal place   _____

   (g)   8.2384 to three decimal
places   _____

5. Complete the following subtractions. (Do not round off.)

   (a) $13.57 - 4.23$ = _____   **(d)** $38.251 - 15.3162$ = _____

   (b) $84.027 - 5.009$ = _____   **(e)** $618.25 - 52.819$ = _____

   (c) $37.008 - 17.215$ = _____   **(f)** $315.537 - 106.658$ = _____

6. Bonnie Oswalt owed $189.15 on her doctor's bill. She paid $13.89. How much remains to be paid?

   $ _____

7. Complete each of the following multiplications.

   (a) 3.5×1.2 = _____   **(d)** 152.3×3.125 = _____

   (b) 62.87×0.5 = _____   **(e)** 618×0.005 = _____

   (c) 20.88×5.25 _____   **(f)** 0.02×0.17 = _____

8. Complete each of the following divisions. Round each answer to the proper place.

   (a) $75.45 \div 15$ = _____   **(f)** $79 \div 4.6$ = _____

   (b) $52.56 \div 0.8$ = _____   **(g)** $181.86 \div 3.5$ = _____

   (c) $64.48 \div 1.6$ = _____   **(h)** $204.736 \div 5.6$ = _____

   (d) $32.20 \div 9.2$ = _____   **(i)** $16.28 \div 0.005$ = _____

   (e) $0.128 \div 0.75$ = _____   **(j)** $9.96 \div 0.75$ = _____

90

Percentage in Business

We compute percentages almost every day in our professional and personal lives. Pricing merchandise, determining payroll amounts, borrowing money, and computing taxes are a few of the applications of percentages.

Some skills you can achieve in this unit include the following:

- **Using percentages to make computations.**
- **Computing base, rate, and percentage.**
- **Learning the most commonly used aliquot parts while using $1 and $100 as the base.**
- **Converting mixed numbers and decimal values to aliquot parts.**
- **Computing finance charges based on previous balance and average daily balance.**
- **Using the Rule of 78 to compute cancelled finance charges.**

UNIT 3

USING AN ELECTRONIC CALCULATOR

Because electronic calculators have become relatively inexpensive in recent years, most students and businesspersons have access to this tool for making computations. A thorough knowledge of the fundamental principles of business mathematics is still necessary, but electronic calculators make computations easier and more accurate than manual methods of computation. This chapter illustrates some of the basic computations that can be easily made with an electronic calculator. Note that problems and illustrations in other chapters are in a format adaptable to solution with an electronic calculator.

Types of Calculation

Any calculation that can be performed manually can be performed using an electronic calculator or vice versa. Calculators should have at least an 8-digit or 10-digit display to be useful for solving business problems. In addition, more expensive calculators can print as well as display the entries and results visually. A calculator adequate for most purposes can be purchased for under $20. More sophisticated calculators and printing calculators are more expensive. Some calculators can be purchased for less than $5; more expensive models may cost several hundred dollars.

Scientific calculators perform a wide variety of calculations, such as trigonometric tangent, sine, and cosine functions. However, business calculators are simpler to operate with practical applications for solving business and consumer problems. These include addition, subtraction, multiplication, and division as well as special applications such as chain multiplication and division, multiplication and division by a constant, raising to powers, extraction of square root, percentage calculation, add-on and discount calculations, and various mixed calculations. Some of the more common business calculations are illustrated in this chapter.

Calculator Terminology

Although business calculators perform similar functions, some models have special keys and functions that are not found on others. Some of the labels on keys may also have slightly different designations. Most companies provide an operator's instruction booklet that describes the functions and provides sample problems. Examples in this chapter are typical and should help you to adapt quickly to the particular model that is available for your use. A typical keyboard is shown in Example 9.1.

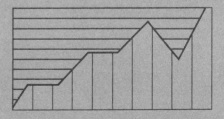

EXAMPLE   Typical calculator keyboard

9.1

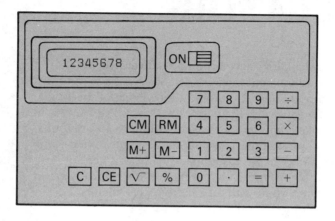

A calculator with a *floating decimal point* automatically places the decimal point to the maximum number of places available on the calculator's display. For calculators with a *fixed decimal point* feature, the decimal can be placed two places to the left to permit easy entry of values containing dollars and cents.

Some calculators have an *AC adapter* that permits the calculator to be used with batteries or regular current. Some models also permit the calculator to operate on energy from a light source.

The *power switch* turns the power on and off. In some models, the power will turn off automatically if the calculator is not used for a specified period of time (such as two minutes) to save the battery if the calculator is left on accidentally.

The *division, multiplication, subtraction, addition,* and *equal* keys ($\div$, $\times$, $-$, $+$, and $=$) have the same function as in arithmetic.

The *M+* or *M−* keys are used to obtain results, store those results in the calculator's memory, and add or subtract the displayed values to or from the stored results.

The *RM* key is used to recall the contents of the memory.

The *C* key is used to clear all registers except the memory.

The *CM* key is used to clear the contents of the memory.

The *%* key is used to perform percentage, add-on, and discount calculations.

The $\sqrt{}$ key is used to find the square root of the value displayed.

The *CE* key clears a value that has been keyboarded incorrectly from the display without clearing all registers.

Overflow means that the capacity of the display has been exceeded. A light, arrow, or special character indicates that an overflow condition exists. For example, a solution that contains 11 digits when the display only permits the display of 10 digits will cause an overflow condition.

A *decimal point* (.) is placed to the right of the whole number portion of a value, such as 14. or 13.23. Some models automatically place the comma in values of one thousand or more, such as 2,000.

Fundamental Calculations

Remember that various brands of calculators may be slightly different in operation. Some models offer special features that others do not. However, the following examples represent fundamental calculations that can be performed on most calculators. If the calculation does not work on your machine, read your operator's instruction booklet to determine why the calculation is not performed as indicated below. The calculator used to provide these solutions is in the floating-point mode.

**Fundamental calculations
using an electronic calculator**   EXAMPLE

9.2

---

1. Addition Calculation: $141 + 132 + 1,500 = 1,773$

   Keyboard Entry: [C] 141 [+] 132 [+] 1500 [=]

   Visual Display: 0.   141.   141.   132.   273.   1500.   1773.

2. Subtraction Calculation: $48.2 - 16.1 = 32.1$

   Keyboard Entry: [C] 48.2 [−] 16.1 [=]

   Visual Display: 0.   48.2   48.2   16.1   32.1

3. Multiplication Calculation: $5.8 \times 1.2 = 6.96$

   Keyboard Entry: [C]   5.8 [×] 1.2 [=]

   Visual Display: 0.   5.8   5.8   1.2   6.96

4. Division Calculation: $18 \div 7 = 2.571428571$

   Keyboard Entry: [C] 18 [÷] 7   [=]

   Visual Display: 0.   18.   18.   7.   2.571428571

   Note: This calculation was carried to 9 decimal places plus 1 place for the whole number, the maximum for a 10-digit display.

5. Multiplication Chain: $3 \times 4 \times 2 = 24$

   Keyboard Entry: [C] 3 [×] 4 [×] 2 [=]

   Visual Display: 0.   3.   3.   4.   12.   2.   24.

6. Division Chain: $18 \div 3 \div 2 = 3$

   Keyboard Entry: [C] 18 [÷] 3 [÷] 2 [=]

   Visual Display: 0.   18.   18.   3.   6.   2.   3.

7. Multiplication-Division
   Combination: $3 \times 50 \div 2 = 75$

   Keyboard Entry: [C] 3 [×] 50 [÷] 2 [=]

   Visual Display: 0.   3.   3.   50.   150.   2.   75.

(Continued on following page.)

8. Multiplication by a
   Constant: $4 \times 25 = 100$, $4 \times 50 = 200$, $4 \times 30 = 120$

   Note: For calculators with a *constant* feature.

   Keyboard Entry: [C] 4 [×] 25 [=] 50 [=] 30 [=]

   Visual Display: 0.   4.   4. 25. 100. 50. 200. 30. 120.

   OR

   Note: For calculators with a *memory register* but not a constant feature.

   Keyboard Entry: [C] 4 [M+] [×] 25 [=] [RM] [×] 50 [=] [RM]

   Visual Display: 0.   4.   4.^{M} 4.^{M} 25.^{M} 100.^{M} 4.^{M} 4.^{M} 50.^{M} 200.^{M} 4.^{M}

   Keyboard Entry: [×] 30 [=]

   Visual Display: 4.^{M} 30.^{M} 120.^{M}

   Note: On some machines, the M's will not appear on the visual display.

9. Division by a Constant: $48 \div 6 = 8$, $72 \div 6 = 12$, $36 \div 6 = 6$

   Note: For calculators with a *constant* feature.

   Keyboard Entry: [C] 48 [÷] 6 [=] 72 [=] 36 [=]

   Visual Display: 0. 48. 48.   6.   8. 72. 12. 36.   6.

   OR

   Note: For calculators with a *memory register* but not a constant feature.

   Keyboard Entry: [C] 6 [M+] [÷] 6 [=] 48 [÷] [RM] [=] 72 [÷] [RM]

   Visual Display: 0.   6.   6.   6.   6.   1. 48. 48.   6.   8. 72. 72.   6.

   Keyboard Entry: [=] 36 [÷] [RM] [=]

   Visual Display: 12. 36. 36.   6.   6.

   Note: Display shown here without M's, which appear on some machines.

10. Product of Two Sums: $(2 + 4) \times (3 + 2) = 30$

    USING MEMORY

    Keyboard Entry: [C] [CM] 2 [+] 4 [=] [M+] 3 [+] 2 [×] [RM] [=]

    Visual Display: 0.   0.   2.   2.   4.   6.   6.   3.   3.   2.   5.   6.   30.

11. Product of Sum and
    Difference: $(5 + 3) \times (7 - 2) = 40$

    USING MEMORY

    Keyboard Entry: [C] [CM] 5 [+] 3 [=] [M+] 7 [−] 2 [×] [RM] [=]

    Visual Display: 0.   0.   5.   5.   3.   8.   8.   7.   7.   2.   5.   8.   40.

● **Complete Assignment 9.1** ●

**Fundamental applications
using an electronic calculator   EXAMPLE**

9.3

1. Computing Percent: $160 \times 25\% = 40$

   Keyboard Entry: [C] 160 [×] 25 [%]

   Visual Display: 0. 160. 160. 25. <u>40.</u>

2. Computing a Mixed
   Calculation Percentage: $(25 + 45) \times 20\% = 14$

   Keyboard Entry: [C] 25 [+] 45 [=] [×] 20 [%]

   Visual Display: 0. 25. 25. 45. 70. 70. 20. <u>14.</u>

3. Invoicing Application:

   USING MEMORY

Quantity	Unit Price	Amount	Keyboard Entries	Final Display
20	$ 8.50	$ 170.00	[C] [CM] 20 [×] 8.50 [=] [M+]	170.
35	15.25	533.75	35 [×] 15.25 [=] [M+]	533.75
30	10.50	315.00	30 [×] 10.50 [=] [M+]	315.
Total Amount		$1,018.75	[RM]	1018.75
Discount 15%		152.81	[×] 15 [%]	152.8125
Net Amount		$ 865.94	[M−] [RM]	865.9375
Plus Packing Charge		3.50	[CM] [+] 3.50	
Total Due		$ 869.44	[=]	869.4375

4. Checkbook Balance Application:

   Opening balance   = $687.30

   Deposits   = $126.30 and $340.22

   Checks   = $10.13, $14.68, $213.40, and $89.30

   Computed balance = $826.31

   Keyboard Entry: [C] 687.30 [+] 126.30 [+] 340.22 [−] 10.13

   Visual Display: 0. 687.30 687.30 126.30 813.6 340.22 1153.82 10.13

   Keyboard Entry: [−] 14.68 [−] 213.40 [−] 89.30 [=]

   Visual Display: 1143.69. 14.68 1129.01 213.40 915.61 89.30 <u>826.31</u>

5. Computing Interest Application: $900 at 8% for 65 days = $13.00

   Keyboard Entry: [C] 900 [×] 0.08 [×] 65 [×] 360 [=]

   Visual Display: 0. 900. 900. 0.08 72. 65. 4680. 360. <u>13.</u>

   OR

   Keyboard Entry: [C] 900 [×] 8 [%] [×] 65 [=] [÷] 360 [=]

   Visual Display: 0. 900. 900. 8. 72. 72. 65. 4680. 4680. 360. <u>13.</u>

   (Continued on following page.)

OR

USING MEMORY

Keyboard Entry: [C] [CM] 900 [×] 0.08 [=] [M+] 65 [÷] 360

Visual Display: 0.   0.   900.   900.   0.08   72.   72.   65.   65.   360

Keyboard Entry: [×]   [RM]   [=]

Visual Display: 0.180555   72.   12.999996

Note: Final answer is slightly off due to rounding.

6. Square Root: $\sqrt{1316.9641} = 36.29$

Keyboard Entry: [C]   1316.9641   [√]

Visual Display: 0.   1316.9641   36.29

7. Square Root: $\sqrt{8 \times 8 + 80} = 12$

Keyboard Entry: [C] 8 [×] 8 [+] 80 [=] [√]

Visual Display: 0.   8.   8.   8.   64.   80.   144.   12.

● **Complete Assignment 9.2** ●

ASSIGNMENT 9.1 Basic Computations Using the Electronic Calculator

1. Addition

(a) $14 + 16 + 13 = $ _____

(b) $3.2 + 7.25 + 1.09 = $ _____

(c) $1.2 + 3.18 + 14.71 = $ _____

(d) $18 + 0.008 + 1.35 = $ _____

(e) $9.78 + 7.0028 + 15.002 = $ _____

(f) $1,264.31 + 9,362.48 = $ _____

2. Subtraction

(a) $4.2 - 3.1 = $ _____

(b) $16.38 - 3.4 = $ _____

(c) $7.89 - 0.0028 = $ _____

(d) $74.2 - 31.6 - 12.2 = $ _____

(e) $36.8 - 21.2 - 3.89 = $ _____

(f) $128.2 - 28 - 13.01 = $ _____

3. Multiplication

(a) $2 \times 3 \times 5 = $ _____

(b) $2.3 \times 4.5 = $ _____

(c) $3.89 \times 14.2 = $ _____

(d) $0.18 \times 7.1 = $ _____

(e) $14 \times 3 \times 3.5 = $ _____

(f) $36 \times 72 \times 0.005 = $ _____

4 Division

(a) $18 \div 3 \div 2 = $ _____

(b) $45 \div 30 \div 3 = $ _____

(c) $450.30 \div 1.5 = $ _____

(d) $0.0018 \div 0.006 = $ _____

(e) $731.25 \div 45 = $ _____

(f) $4,033.92 \div 88 = $ _____

5. Mixed addition and subtraction

(a) $18 + 18 - 3 - 2 = $ _____

(b) $38 - 14 + 23 - 8 = $ _____

(c) $72 - 50 + 18 - 9 = $ _____

(d) $9.2 + 1.3 - 7.6 = $ _____

(e) $13.2 - 0.002 + 3.01 = $ _____

(f) $18.16 + 17.14 - 8.09 = $ _____

6. Mixed multiplication and division

(a) $9 \times 3 \div 2 = $ _____

(b) $16 \div 2 \times 89.2 = $ _____

(c) $14.28 \times 7.35 \div 0.02 = $ _____

(d) $7.8 \div 0.05 \times 1.25 = $ _____

(e) $3.1 \times 14.25 \times 11.78 \div 50 = $ _____

(f) $4.50 \div 1.5 \times 11.689 = $ _____

7. Multiplication by a constant

(a) $18 \times 6 =$ _____

$38 \times 6 =$ _____

$45 \times 6 =$ _____

(b) $62.30 \times 24 =$ _____

$76.18 \times 24 =$ _____

$80.20 \times 24 =$ _____

(c) $7.28 \times 13 =$ _____

$6.214 \times 13 =$ _____

$18.92 \times 13 =$ _____

(d) $14.2 \times 13.1 =$ _____

18.8×13.1 _____

$62.5 \times 13.1 =$ _____

8. Division by a constant

(a) $320 \div 16 =$ _____

$480 \div 16 =$ _____

$64 \div 16 =$ _____

(b) $4,340 \div 35 =$ _____

$5,670 \div 35 =$ _____

$4,970 \div 35 =$ _____

(c) $6,048 \div 25.2 =$ _____

$4,662 \div 25.2 =$ _____

$5,266.8 \div 25.2 =$ _____

(d) $149.5 \div 3.25 =$ _____

$1,319.5 \div 3.25 =$ _____

$354.25 \div 3.25 =$ _____

9. Product of two sums

(a) $(6 + 10) \times (3 + 2) =$ _____

(b) $(7 + 8) \times (13 + 2) =$ _____

(c) $(6 + 24) \times (18 + 7) =$ _____

(d) $(3.2 + 2.5) \times (3.1 + 7.9) =$ _____

(e) $(5.31 + 2.1) \times (3.1 + 6.9) =$ _____

(f) $(16.9 + 11.2) \times (3.8 + 1.7) =$ _____

10. Product of sum and difference

(a) $(6 + 7) \times (19 - 2) =$ _____

(b) $(5 + 3) \times (9 - 2) =$ _____

(c) $(4 + 6) \times (10.8 - 8.2) =$ _____

(d) $(15 + 3) \times (89 - 13) =$ _____

(e) $(132 + 89) \times (72 - 14) =$ _____

(f) $(76 + 132) \times (7.2 - 2.1) =$ _____

11. Square root

(a) $\sqrt{25} =$ _____

(b) $\sqrt{1,225} =$ _____

(c) $\sqrt{222.6064} =$ _____

(d) $\sqrt{9 \times 7 + 106} =$ _____

(e) $\sqrt{30 \times 500 + 206 - 77} =$ _____

(f) $\sqrt{2.5 \times 98.5 + 18.9 + 359.85} =$ _____

100

ASSIGNMENT 9.2 Business Applications Using the Electronic Calculator

1. Sylvia Novak had a beginning balance of $714.28 in her checking account. During the month, she made deposits of $114.87 and $213.64 and wrote checks for $14.28, $27.13, $123.89, $72.14, and $39.82. What was her balance at the end of the month?

   $ _____

2. George Kell had a beginning balance of $823.48 in his checking account. During the month, he wrote checks for $3.87, $13.08, $23.72, $14.97, $189.29, and $323.45 and made deposits of $616.06 and $19.83. What was his balance at the end of the month?

   $ _____

3. The Kennington Wholesale Supply Company sold the following items: 20 items @ $7.42, 14 items @ $9.27, and 8 items @ $8.58. A discount of 25% was provided on the total amount of the invoice. What was the (a) total amount, (b) discount amount, and (c) net amount?

   (a) $ _____

   (b) $ _____

   (c) $ _____

4. Joel House of Fashion sold the following items: 27 items @ $4.28, 31 items @ $16.32, 21 items @ $7.52, and 6 items @ $8.48. A discount of 35% was provided on the total amount of the invoice. What was the (a) total amount, (b) discount amount, and (c) net amount?

   (a) $ _____

   (b) $ _____

   (c) $ _____

5. Jamison Contractors purchased 237 stakes for $0.37 each, plus $5.26 sales tax. What was the total amount to be paid?

   $ _____

6. Space Flight candy bars sell for $0.45 each or $4.89 for a box of 12 bars. What will be the cost of 1200 bars (a) purchased individually and (b) purchased in boxes of 12?

   (a) $ _____

   (b) $ _____

7. George Barnes' sales for the day amounted to $362.60. If his commission was 15% of sales, how much commission did he earn?

   $ _____

8. Dianne Caron, a real estate agent, sold a house for $106,118 last week. If her company charges a 7% commission fee, how much commission will be charged for selling the house?

$ _____

9. Dave's Auto Company sells automobiles for a discount of 18% off the list price. If the list price was $12,360.00, what was the (a) discount and (b) selling price of the automobile?

(a) $ _____

(b) $ _____

10. John Drennon drove from Memphis to Johnson City, a distance of 462.8 miles. If his automobile gets 23.2 miles per gallon and gasoline costs $1.38 per gallon, what was the cost of the gasoline for the trip?

$ _____

11. The Coan Department Store has 89 sales clerks. Total sales for the day were $42,591.84. What was the average sales per salesperson?

$ _____

12. Phyllis Ray borrowed $1,280 at the First National Bank. She signed a 90-day, 8-3/4% (simple interest) note. What amounts of (a) interest and (b) total payment were due on the maturity date?

(a) $ _____

(b) $ _____

13. Richard's Manufacturing Company pays all employees $9.85 per hour. During the week, each employee worked the following number of hours: Abel, 38; Collier, 40; Dayton, 39; Fulmer, 37; Goodson, 35; Jenson, 40; Palson, 32; and Reynolds, 38. What was the total gross pay for all employees for the week?

$ _____

14. Juliet's Shoe Store pays employees a 15.8% sales commission. The clerks' weekly sales were as follows: Ball, $1,870; Hightower, $1,920; Kooney, $1,755; LaVerne, $1,905; and Woodcock, $2,005. What was the total commission earned by the sales force?

$ _____

15. One gallon equals 3.785 liters. Four cars were driven on a test drive for 420 miles. Compute the number of liters each car used during the test drive and the total liters used.

Car	Gallons	Liters
A	20.1 gallons	_____
B	18.8 gallons	_____
C	17.2 gallons	_____
D	16.5 gallons	_____
TOTAL		_____

102

PERCENTAGE AMOUNTS IN BUSINESS

Percentages are commonly used in both business and personal activities. A discount on an airline ticket purchase, interest on a home mortgage, sales taxes, and discounts on clothing purchases are only a few examples of applications that require percentage computations.

Conversions

The terms *percent* and *percentage* are often confused. Percent is the *rate* and has a percent sign after the number, such as 14%. Percentage is the *number represented by the percent*. For example, a professional basketball team won 80%, or 40, of the 50 games it played during the season. In this example, 80% is the percent and 40 is the percentage. Because percentage refers to an amount, the term *amount* will be used in chapter discussions and illustrations in place of the term *percentage*.

Rate is another way of expressing numbers as a *fractional part of 100*. A rate, such as 80%, means 80 parts out of 100 possible parts. This rate may also be written as 80/100. When converting a rate to a fraction, the numerator of the fraction is the specific rate, and the denominator is always 100. The fraction is normally reduced to its lowest terms. In this example, 80/100 reduces to 4/5.

A rate can be converted to a fraction as shown above. Other conversions include converting decimals to rates, rates to decimals, and fractions to rates.

Example 10.1 illustrates the relationship between 80%, 20%, and 100%. The entire circle represents 100%. The games won represent

---

EXAMPLE   **Percentage pie chart**

10.1

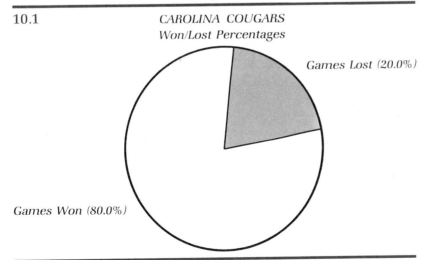

CAROLINA COUGARS
Won/Lost Percentages

Games Lost (20.0%)

Games Won (80.0%)

80 parts out of 100, or 80%. The games lost represent 20 parts out of 100, or 20%. The entire circle represents the total games played, or 100%. This chart was completed using graphic software and a microcomputer.

Converting Decimals to Percents

As shown in Example 10.2, a decimal is converted to a percent by (1) moving the decimal point two places to the right and (2) adding a percent sign at the end of the value.

EXAMPLE

10.2

Problem: Convert the following decimal values to rates expressed as a percent: .75, .253, .5, 3, 2.25, and .007.

Solution:
| .75 = 75% | .5 = 50% | 2.25 = 225% |
| .253 = 25.3% | 3. = 300% | .007 = .7% |

Notice that each conversion required the decimal point to be moved two places to the right. Some conversions require caution. For example, .007 converts to .7%, which is read seven-tenths percent, which is less than one percent. Notice that when .5 was converted to 50%, a zero was added in order to move the decimal point two places to the right.

Converting Percents to Decimals

Computations are often expressed as percents. For example, the cost of a dress may be reduced 25%, or an airline may offer a special fare that is 20% less than the regular fare. In order to make a computation, the percent should first be converted to a decimal. This conversion is the reverse of the one illustrated above.

To convert a percent to a decimal, you (1) drop the percent symbol and (2) move the decimal point two places to the *left*. If the percent includes a fraction, the fraction should be converted to a decimal. Example 10.3 demonstrates conversion of percents to decimal values.

EXAMPLE

10.3

Problem: Convert the following percents to decimal values: 24%, 15.8%, 125%, 75.3%, .8%, and 7 3/4%.

Solution:
| 24% = .24 | 125% = 1.25 | .8% = .08 |
| 15.8% = .158 | 75.3% = .753 | 7 3/4% = .0775 |

Converting Fractions to Percents

A fraction can be converted to a rate expressed as a percent by (1) dividing the numerator by the denominator, (2) moving the decimal point two places to the right, and (3) adding the percent sign, as shown in Example 10.4.

EXAMPLE

10.4

Problem: Convert the following fractions to percents: 3/4, 1/2, and 1/25.

Solution: 3/4 = .75 = 75%
1/2 = .5 = 50%
1/25 = .04 = 4%

Business Applications of Percentage

All percentage problems use the following basic formula: Amount = Base times the *R*ate or, abbreviated, A = B × R *or* B × R = P (if using a calculator). In this formula, *A* is amount, *B* is base, and *R* is rate. The relationship of these three components is shown in Example 10.5.

Percentage formula   **EXAMPLE**

10.5

$B \times R = A$

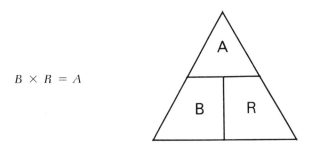

    The horizontal line represents a fraction bar. If you know the amount and the base and you want to find the rate, cover the R section. This gives the formula for the rate:

(Continued on following page.)

$$\frac{A}{B} = R$$

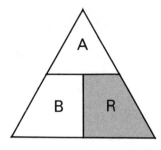

If you know the amount and the rate and you want to find the base, cover the B section to get the formula for the base:

$$\frac{A}{R} = B$$

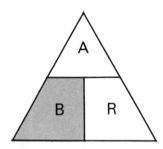

The vertical line in the triangle represents a multiplication sign. If you are trying to find the amount, cover the A section to get the formula for the amount:

$$B \times R = A$$

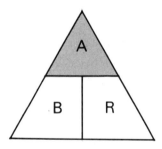

Notice that the percent is converted to a decimal value prior to making the calculation, as shown in Example 10.6.

EXAMPLE

10.6

Problem: The Seaside Fruit Stand estimates that 25% of the fruit will sell during the day. If the fruit is valued at $1,500, what amount of the fruit will sell today?

Solution: Base × Rate = Amount
$1,500 × .25 = $375

The amount may be larger than the base because the rate can be larger than 100%. However, the same basic computation is required. See Example 10.7.

EXAMPLE
10.7

Problem: Betty Weaver, a salesperson, had a $2,500 sales goal for the week. Her sales were 110 percent of her goal. How much were her sales?

Solution: Base × Rate = Amount
$2,500 × 1.10 = $2,750

The rate may also be expressed in fractions instead of percents, as shown in Example 10.8.

EXAMPLE
10.8

Problem: The Ace Furniture Store had 80 recliners in the warehouse. During a rainstorm, 1/4 of the recliners were damaged. How many were damaged? How many were not damaged?

Solution: Base × Rate = Amount

80   ×   1/4   = 20 Damaged
80   ×   3/4   = 60 Not damaged

● **Complete Assignment 10.1** ●

● **Complete Assignment 10.2** ●

ASSIGNMENT 10.1 Percentage Amount Applications

1. Convert each of the following percents to a decimal and a fraction. The first problem is completed as an example.

No.	Percent	Decimal Equivalent	Fractional Equivalent
	20%	.20 (or .2)	20/100, reduced to 1/5
1	30%	_____	_____
2	5%	_____	_____
3	8%	_____	_____
4	7%	_____	_____
5	15%	_____	_____

2. Compute the amount for each of the following problems. Round answers to two decimal places.

(a) 52% of $520   = $ _____   (e) 4 1/2% of $764 = $ _____

(b) 3% of $1,640   = $ _____   (f) 8% of $514.85   = $ _____

(c) 20% of $1,840 = $ _____   (g) 7% of $316.38   = $ _____

(d) 1/2% of $3,640 = $ _____   (h) 17 3/4% of $42 = $ _____

3. This year a musical production was attended by 15,500 persons. This was 92% of last year's attendance. How many attended last year?

_____

4. The Monroe City Council voted to place a 2% tax on personal incomes. If the average employee in Monroe had income of $14,514, how much average tax was levied on each employee?

$ _____

5. Binford Peeples made $820 per week. If he received a raise of 8%, find the amount of his (a) raise and (b) new salary.

(a) $ _____

(b) $ _____

6. Bert Brown and Clara Johnson were partners in a business with an annual profit of $64,500. Mr. Brown received 47% of the net profit, and Ms. Johnson received 53% of the net profit. How much did (a) Mr. Brown and (b) Ms. Johnson receive?

(a) $ _____

(b) $ _____

7. Randy Schwartz purchased a condominium for $85,500. The depreciation allowance for tax purposes was 5% per year. How much was the annual depreciation allowance for the condominium?

$ _____

8. Roxanne Adams owned a bond worth $2,000 that paid interest at 8 1/2% per year. How much interest did she earn each year on the bond?

$ _____

110

ASSIGNMENT 10.2 Percentage Amount Applications

1. The salaries and merit raise indexes for six employees are shown below. Multiply the salary amount by the raise index rate to compute the new salary amount.

(a) Salary $1,500.00
    Raise Index   108%

    New Salary $ _____

(b) Salary $1,450.00
    Raise Index   109%

    New Salary $ _____

(c) Salary $1,670.00
    Raise Index 110 1/2%

    New Salary $ _____

(d) Salary $1,548.00
    Raise Index 112 1/2%

    New Salary $ _____

(e) Salary $1,476.00
    Raise Index 104 3/4%

    New Salary $ _____

(f) Salary $1,950.00
    Raise Index 111%

    New Salary $ _____

2. Use the formula Rate × Base = Amount to find the following:

Rate × Base = Amount

(a) 9/10 of 650   = _____

(b) 4/5 of 785   = _____

(c) 3/8 of 248   = _____

Rate × Base = Amount

(d) 5/6 of 66   = _____

(e) 3/4 of 76   = _____

(f) 5/7 of 56   = _____

Rate × Base = Amount

(g) 2/3 of 780   = _____

(h) 1/12 of 144   = _____

(i) 1/9 of 162   = _____

3. Dr. Ernest Bishop had a gross earned income of $120,000. Of this amount, 42% represented income from patients who paid cash for their medical services, and 58% represented income from patients who charged their medical services. How much of the gross earned income was from (a) cash patients and how much was from (b) charge patients?

(a) $ _____

(b) $ _____

4. The building owned by Brodnex Jewelry Store had an assessed value of $220,000 for property tax purposes. Tax rates were as follows: city, 3.6%; county, 5.3%; and special business, 2.5%. How much tax was owed on the building for (a) city, (b) county, and (c) special business taxes?

(a) $ _____

(b) $ _____

(c) $ _____

5. Bill White owned a house valued at $120,000 and furniture valued at $25,000. The house was insured at 80% of its value, and the furniture was insured at 65% of its value. For how much was (a) the house insured and (b) the furniture insured? Assuming that the above amounts represented realistic values, (c) how much would Mr. White lose if the house and furniture were completely destroyed by fire?

(a) $ _____

(b) $ _____

(c) $ _____

6. Canty Importers had annual sales of $250,000 during the first year of operation. Second-year sales were projected to be 125% of first-year sales. Third-year sales were projected to be 130% of second-year sales. What are the projected sales for the (a) second year and (b) third year?

(a) $ _____

(b) $ _____

7. The Wilson Florist Shop used 2,600 liters of gasoline last year in its delivery truck. By purchasing a more fuel-efficient truck, an estimated 7% savings in gasoline could be realized next year. If this were true, (a) how much gasoline would be saved next year, and (b) how much gasoline would be used next year?

(a) _____

(b) _____

8. Connie Gaines had a monthly salary of $2,400. Deductions were made as follows: payroll taxes, 28%; credit union, 8%; and savings account, 12 1/2%. How much was deducted from her check for (a) payroll taxes, (b) credit union, and (c) savings account?

(a) $ _____

(b) $ _____

(c) $ _____

112

BASE AND RATE APPLICATIONS

Percentage amounts in business were introduced in Chapter 10. This chapter expands the discussion of percentage amounts to include computations for base and rate.

Overview of Base and Rate

The *amount* (A) is obtained by multiplying the base by the rate. The *rate* (R) is a percent, fraction, or decimal that indicates which part of the base is to be used in the calculation. The *base* (B) represents the entire amount and always has a value of 100%. Examples in this chapter show the relationships between the amount, base, and rate and how each is computed.

Review of Percentage

The formula *Base × Rate = Amount* was introduced in Chapter 10 and is always used to compute the percentage (amount). See Example 11.1.

EXAMPLE

11.1

Problem: The Novelty Shoppe estimates that 5% of its daily charge sales will be uncollectible. If the shop's daily charge sales today were $3,500, how much will be uncollectible?

Solution: Base × Rate = Amount
$3,500 × .05 = $175

Computing the Base

The same three elements needed to compute the amount are needed to compute the base. The following formula is used to compute the base: *Amount/Rate = Base*. See Example 11.2.

EXAMPLE

11.2

Problem: Emily Gomez earned $80 in commissions on her job. If the commission rate was 20%, how much in sales were required to provide the commission?

(Solution on following page)

CHAPTER 11

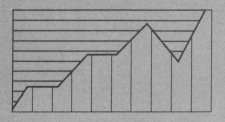

Solution: Amount / Rate = Base
$80 / .20 = $400

| • **Complete Assignment 11.1** • |

Computing the Rate

If the amount and base are known, the rate can be computed by using the following formula: *Amount/Base* = *Rate*. See Example 11.3.

EXAMPLE   **Computing the rate**

11.3

Problem: Emily Gomez received $80 in sales commission. If her daily sales were $400, what was her rate of commission?

Solution: Amount / Base =   Rate
$80   / $400 = .20 or 20%

When working with problems involving amount, base, and rate, the missing element can be computed if the other two elements are known. In these instances, analyze the problem carefully to determine which two elements are known so that the appropriate formula will be used to determine the element that is not known.

Rate of Percent Increase

The same basic formula can be used to determine the rate of increase, as shown in Example 11.4.

EXAMPLE   **Computing rate of increase**

11.4

Problem: Robert Newport earned $22,000 last year. His salary this year is $23,760. What was his rate of increase?

Solution: Step 1.   Find the *amount* of increase.

Current salary − Previous salary = Amount of increase
$23,760   − $22,000   = $1,760

Step 2.   Find the *rate* of increase.

Amount of increase/Previous salary = Rate of increase
$1,760/$22,000   =   .08 or 8%

Notice that the basic formula was used to compute the rate. The amount ($1,760) was divided by the base ($22,000) to compute the 8% rate (Amount/Base = Rate).

Rate of Percent Decrease

The rate of percent may represent an increase as shown in Example 11.4, or it may represent a decrease. In either case, the computations are similar. Example 11.5 illustrates computation of the rate of percent decrease.

Computing rate of decrease   EXAMPLE

11.5

Problem: The Easy Stop Grocery had 780 customers last week. This week, there were only 663 customers—a decrease of 117 customers (780 − 663 = 117). What was the rate of decrease from last week?

Solution:

Customer decrease	/	Customers last week	=	Rate of decrease
117	/	780	=	.15 or 15%

Aliquot Parts

Using aliquot parts can make some types of multiplication problems easier to solve and the solutions more accurate. An *aliquot part* of a number is any number (whole or mixed) that can be divided into the number evenly (that is, without leaving a remainder). For example, 2 is an aliquot part of 10, 5 is an aliquot part of 50, 7½ is an aliquot part of 15, and 8⅓ is an aliquot part of 25.

Aliquot Parts of $1

Using aliquot parts of $1 may make multiplication easier. For example, the purchase of 220 items at 25 cents each can be computed by mentally determining the cost of the same number of items at $1. Since 25 cents is an aliquot part (¼) of $1, the final computation can be made by multiplying $220 by ¼: $220 × ¼ = $55. Of course, the same result could be obtained by multiplying 220 by $0.25.

The commonly used aliquot parts of $1 are shown in Example 11.6.

EXAMPLE

11.6

Commonly used aliquot parts of $1

$\$\frac{1}{2} = 50$ cents

$\$\frac{1}{3} = 33\frac{1}{3}$ cents; $\frac{2}{3} = 66\frac{2}{3}$ cents

$\$\frac{1}{4} = 25$ cents; $\frac{3}{4} = 75$ cents

$\$\frac{1}{5} = 20$ cents; $\frac{2}{5} = 40$ cents; $\frac{3}{5} = 60$ cents; $\frac{4}{5} = 80$ cents

$\$\frac{1}{6} = 16\frac{2}{3}$ cents; $\frac{5}{6} = 83\frac{1}{3}$ cents

$\$\frac{1}{7} = 12\frac{1}{2}$ cents; $\frac{3}{8} = 37\frac{1}{2}$ cents; $\frac{5}{8} = 62\frac{1}{2}$ cents; $\frac{7}{8} = 87\frac{1}{2}$ cents

$\$\frac{1}{10} = 10$ cents; $\frac{3}{10} = 30$ cents; $\frac{7}{10} = 70$ cents; $\frac{9}{10} = 90$ cents

$\$\frac{1}{12} = 8\frac{1}{3}$ cents

$\$\frac{1}{15} = 6\frac{2}{3}$ cents

$\$\frac{1}{16} = 6\frac{1}{4}$ cents

$\$\frac{1}{20} = 5$ cents

Even if a calculator is used, using aliquot parts provides a more accurate answer when the price involves an odd part of $1, such as $8\frac{2}{3}$ cents in Example 11.7.

EXAMPLE

11.7

Problem: Marshall Office Supply purchased 1,800 tablets for $8\frac{1}{3}$ cents each. What was the cost of the order?

Solution: **Step 1:** Find the cost of the order at $1 per item.

No. of items $\times$ $1 = Cost at $1
$\qquad$ 1,800 $\quad\times$ $1 = $1,800

Step 2: Find the cost using the aliquot part of $1.

Cost at $1 $\times$ Aliquot part of $1 = Cost
$\qquad$ $1,800 $\quad\times\qquad$ 1/12 $\qquad$ = $150

Notice that $\frac{1}{12}$ was shown in the table in Example 11.6 to be the aliquot part of $1 based on a price of $8\frac{1}{3}$ cents. This answer is easy to compute and more accurate than multiplying 1,800 by $0.0833333, which will yield an answer of $156 ($6 too much).

● Complete Assignment 11.2 ●

ASSIGNMENT 11.1 Base Applications

1. Compute the base for each of the following problems. The first problem is completed as an example.

No.	Amount	Rate	Base
	$ 35.63	7%	$509.00
1	96.48	8%	1,260
2	45.11	10%	451.10
3	21.60	6%	360
4	180.00	120%	_____
5	500.00	125%	_____

2. Compute the base *or* amount for each of the following problems. The first problem is completed as an example.

No.	Amount	Rate	Base
	$ 3.93	6%	$ 65.60
1	$360.81	9%	$_____
2	$_____	4.6%	$565.00
3	$_____	6%	$720.00
4	$ 37.80	4.5%	$_____
5	$ 31.36	4%	$_____

3. Harry Summer earned 8.5% on a savings account. His annual interest was $382.50. How much money did he have in his savings account?

$ _____

4. Sales of stereo equipment at Berclair Electronics for one year were $250,000, which was 25% more than sales for the previous year. How much were the company's sales for the previous year?

$ _____

5. John Eastridge earned $138 during the week on his part-time job. This was 15% more than Bill Randal earned. How much did Bill earn?

$ _____

6. The Smithson family spent $31.20 during the week on entertainment. This represented 6.5% of their weekly income. How much was their weekly income?

$ _____

7. The Dayton Furniture Store sold a bedroom suite for $1,500. This was 80% of its regular price. What was the regular price of the bedroom suite?

$ _____

8. The Barker Real Estate Company earned $5,950, which represented a 7% commission based on the selling price of a house. What was the selling price of the house?

$ _____

9. Josephine Higginbottom bought a used car by making a down payment of $1,465, which represented 25% of the price of the car. What was the price of the car?

$ _____

10. Anne Mabry donated $480 to the church building fund. This represented 1.6% of the donations received. How much had been donated so far?

$ _____

118

ASSIGNMENT 11.2 Rate/Base/Amount Applications

1. Supply the missing information for each of the following problems. The first problem is completed as an example.

No.	Amount	Base	Rate
	$50.00	$200.00	25%
1	$ _____	$360.00	12%
2	$32.00	$ _____	8%
3	$45.00	$500.00	_____
4	$ _____	$850.00	14%
5	$25.03	$ _____	5%

2. Wanda Rockford earned $50 on her savings account on a balance of $400. What was her rate of interest?

_____

3. The East Auto Shop sold 40 cars this week and sold 32 cars last week. What was the rate of increase in number of cars sold this week over last week?

_____

4. Harry Yong loaned $2,000 to a customer who agreed to pay back $2,250 one year later. What was the rate of interest on the loan?

_____

5. Henri Lee purchased a car for $400 and sold the car for $520. What percent of profit did Mr. Lee make based on the original price of the car?

_____

6. Bill Anderson missed 10 days of work last year. He missed 12 days this year. What was the rate of increase this year?

_____

7. A furniture store sold a sofa for $800. The sofa was regularly priced at $1,000. What was the rate of discount?

_____

8. A store had 85 TV sets in inventory last week. During the past week, 20% of the sets were sold. How many were sold during the week?

_____

9. A business decided that 4% of its total sales of $84,500 was uncollectible. How much in sales was uncollectible?

$ _____

10. An engineering firm had revenue of $450,000 with profits of $11,250. What percent of its sales were its profits?

_____

11. A firm had 25 non-union members. This represented 4% of its total workers. How many persons were employed by the firm?

_____

12. Reigel Management Services owned 1,725 apartments. An additional 4% were purchased. (a) How many apartments were purchased, and (b) how many did the company own?

(a) _____

(b) _____

13. The Crowe Manufacturing Company produced 27,400 chair frames last year and 28,085 chair frames this year. What was the rate of increase in production this year?

_____

14. Ralph Flannary's weekly salary was $450.00 before deductions and $337.50 after deductions. What percent of his salary was deducted?

_____

120

FINANCE CHARGES

Many retail businesses permit customers to purchase merchandise and pay for the purchase over a period of time. This method is called a *credit purchase* or *charge purchase*. On credit purchases, the business charges extra for allowing the customer to pay for the purchase over a period of time. This *finance charge* is the amount the customer pays for this use of credit.

There are several legal methods that businesses may use to compute finance charges. The method used can make a big difference in the amount of finance charge that the customer will eventually pay, so it is important to develop a good understanding of these methods of computing finance charges.

The Truth-in-Lending Act

The Truth-in-Lending Act was passed by Congress in 1969 to protect consumers from companies that try to hide the true rate of finance charges being assessed. This law requires businesses to reveal (a) the exact amount of finance charge and (b) the *annual percentage rate* (APR) of the total finance charge. The Act does not specify the maximum amount of interest that can be charged, but it requires that the rate be revealed to the customer. Some states set a maximum finance rate charge. Regardless, the APR must be stated for *all* credit purchases. Therefore, ask the company to indicate the APR prior to making a purchase. Use this rate to compare rates provided by various businesses offering the same product.

If you were employed by a business that charged more than the maximum APR allowed by law, should you report the employer? This is an ethical issue faced by some employees.

The APR is usually stated as an annual or monthly rate. If the rate is stated as a monthly rate, simply multiply the rate by 12 (12 months in a year) to obtain the annual rate, as shown in Example 12.1.

EXAMPLE   Computing annual percentage rates

12.1

Problem: Ted Jones decided to purchase a sofa. Various department stores quoted the following monthly finance rates: 1½%, 1⅔%, and 1.575%. What is the APR for each of these rates?

Solution:

Monthly rate			Annual percentage rate
1 1/2%	× 12	=	18%
1 2/3%	× 12	=	20%
1.575%	× 12	=	18.9%

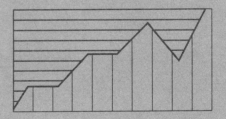

Credit Card Finance Charges

Many department stores and oil companies offer credit cards for use in purchasing their products. General purpose credit cards such as American Express, MasterCard, and VISA cards are also available. Most of these cards are usually offered on a *revolving charge* basis whereby the finance charge is based on either the *balance from the previous month* or the *average daily balance* during the month. Regardless, the Truth-in-Lending Act requires the credit card company to inform all customers of the annual percentage rate charged.

EXAMPLE

12.2

Credit card statement

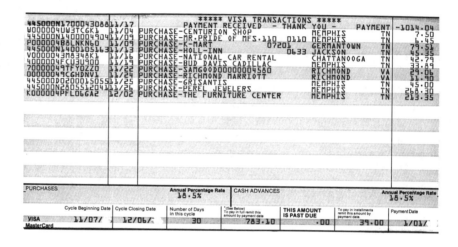

Finance Charges Based on Previous Balance

The finance rate must be stated on the application for the credit card and on each account statement the customer receives. If the balance is based on the previous month's balance, computation is fairly easy, as shown in Example 12.3.

Results should be carried to four decimal places and rounded to two decimal places (the nearest cent). Customers usually have the option of paying the entire balance at any time without further finance charges.

EXAMPLE

12.3

Computing account balances and finance charges

Problem: Juan Perez purchased clothes on May 1 while using his credit card. Terms are that unpaid balances will be assessed a 1½% monthly finance charge. He made a $50 payment on June 8 and another $50 payment on July 8. What are his account's balances and finance charges?

Solution:

Balance Subject to Finance Charge after June 1	$ 350.00
Finance Charge = $350 × .015 (1½%)	+ 5.25
Amount Due after Finance Charge	355.25
Less Payment (June 8)	− 50.00
Balance after Payment	305.25
Finance Charge after July 1 ($305.25 × .015)	+ 4.58
Amount Due after Finance Charge	309.83
Less Payment (July 8)	− 50.00
Balance after Payment	$ 259.83

Companies that provide credit cards normally permit customers a specified period of time (such as 30 days) to pay the balance with no additional interest charges. Under these terms, additional purchases may not be subjected to a finance charge until 30 days have elapsed. See Example 12.4.

Computing account balances and finance charges   EXAMPLE

12.4

Problem: Bill Smothers purchased furniture for the following amounts: $500 on January 1 and $800 on February 10. Finance charges are 1% per month, with a $100 minimum payment each month. Bill made $100 payments on February 8, March 8, and April 8. No finance charges are assessed if payments are received within 30 days of purchase. What were his balances and finance charges for the three months?

Solution:

Balance Subject to Finance Charge on February 1	$ 500.00
Finance Charge ($500 × .01)	+ 5.00
Amount Due after Finance Charge	$ 505.00
Less Payment (February 8)	− 100.00
Balance after Payment	405.00
Additional Purchase on February 10	+ 800.00
Balance after Additional Purchase	1,205.00
Finance Charge after March 1	+ 4.05
($405 × .01)	
Balance after Finance Charge	1,209.05
Less Payment (March 8)	− 100.00
Balance after Payment	1,109.05
Finance Charge after April 1	
($1,109.05 × .01)	+ 11.09
Balance after Finance Charge	$ 1,120.14

Notice that the finance charge after March 1 was based on the previous balance ($405) and *not* on the current balance ($1,205) because the purchase ($800) was not subject to a finance charge until after 30 days elapsed. Some companies base the finance charge on the unpaid balance at the end of the month (rather than the previous month's balance). In this case, the finance charge would have been based on the unpaid balance ($1,205). This points out another reason why the terms of the credit agreement should be read carefully.

● **Complete Assignment 12.1** ●

Finance Charges Based on Average Daily Balance

Many department stores, as well as other credit card finance companies, compute the finance charge based on the actual number of days that an amount was owed during the month. For example, a purchase made 10 days prior to the end of the month will draw finance charges for 10 days. Although this computation is fairly simple, the number of computations is large. Therefore, a computer is used for this type of computation using the steps shown in Example 12.5.

EXAMPLE   Computing average daily balance and finance charges

12.5

Problem: Ted Swanson made a $400 purchase on February 8 and a $500 purchase on February 18. Using the average daily balance method, what are the average daily balance and finance charges? The finance rate is 1%.

Solution: Step 1. Determine the number of equivalent dollar days that the credit was used for each amount by multiplying each amount by the number of days the amount was used.

$400 × 20 = $8,000 (equivalent dollar days for first purchase, February 8 to February 28)
$500 × 10 = $5,000 (equivalent dollar days for second purchase, February 18 to February 28)

Step 2. Determine the total dollar days by adding the amounts obtained in Step 1.

$8,000 + $5,000 = $13,000 (total equivalent dollar days)

Step 3. Determine the average daily balance by dividing the total dollar days obtained in Step 2 by the number of days in the month (28 for February).

$13,000/28 = $464.28 (average daily balance, 28 days in February)

(Continued on following page)

Step 4. Multiply the average daily balance by the monthly finance rate to determine monthly finance charge.

$464.28 × .01 = $4.64 (monthly finance charge)

Minimum Payments

Companies usually base minimum monthly payments on the account balance. The larger the balance, the larger the minimum payment required will be. A schedule used by one financial institution is shown in Example 12.6 and utilized in Example 12.7.

Minimum monthly payment schedule   EXAMPLE

12.6

MINIMUM MONTHLY PAYMENT SCHEDULE. Your minimum monthly payment will change only at the time of a later advance.

BALANCE: (immediately after latest advance)	REGULAR MINIMUM MONTHLY PAYMENT	BALANCE: (immediately after latest advance)	REGULAR MINIMUM MONTHLY PAYMENT
$ .01 - 1,500.00	$ 50	$ 5,400.01 - 5,700.00	$ 140
1,500.01 - 1,800.00	55	5,700.01 - 6,000.00	145
1,800.01 - 2,000.00	60	6,000.01 - 6,300.00	150
2,000.01 - 2,150.00	65	6,300.01 - 6,500.00	155
2,150.01 - 2,300.00	70	6,500.01 - 6,700.00	160
2,300.01 - 2,450.00	75	6,700.01 - 6,900.00	165
2,450.01 - 2,600.00	80	6,900.01 - 7,200.00	170
2,600.01 - 2,750.00	85	7,200.01 - 7,400.00	175
2,750.01 - 2,900.00	90	7,400.01 - 7,700.00	180
2,900.01 - 3,300.00	95	7,700.01 - 8,000.00	185
3,300.01 - 3,600.00	100	8,000.01 - 8,300.00	190
3,600.01 - 3,900.00	105	8,300.01 - 8,600.00	195
3,900.01 - 4,200.00	110	8,600.01 - 8,900.00	200
4,200.01 - 4,440.00	115	8,900.01 - 9,100.00	205
4,440.01 - 4,600.00	120	9,100.01 - 9,400.00	210
4,600.01 - 4,800.00	125	9,400.01 - 9,800.00	215
4,800.01 - 5,100.00	130	9,800.01 - 10,200.00	220
5,100.01 - 5,400.00	135	10,200.01 - 11,000.00	225

% OF BALANCE ROUNDED
TO NEXT HIGHER $5.00

$11,000.01 – and over	2.05%

EXAMPLE

12.7

Problem: Don Fogelman received a credit card statement showing a $2,798 balance. What is the minimum monthly payment due?

Solution: First, find the range containing the balance (in this example, $2,750.01 − $2,900.00).
Second, find the corresponding regular minimum monthly payment due (in this example, $90).

Installment Purchases and APR

Many companies add finance charges to the purchase price to determine the amount due. The amount due is then spread evenly over the number of months for paying for the purchase.

EXAMPLE **Advertisement of installment purchase plan**

12.8

$99⁹⁹ PER MO.

PLUS: FREE RUST PROOFING, CHROME & PAINT SEALER — FREE GIFT WHEN YOU BUY — ASK FOR DETAILS. *60 mos. w/$633 dn., 9.85 APR, plus tax, title, fee & freight with approved credit. Total of payments $5999.40

EXAMPLE **Calculating finance charges**

12.9

Problem: Joe Wright purchased an automobile for $15,000. A finance charge of 6% per year was added to the purchase price. What are the finance charges and monthly payments if payments are made over 48 months (4 years)?

Solution: **Step 1.** Find the finance charge amount.

Purchase price	×	Interest rate	×	Number of years	=	Finance charge
$15,000	×	.06	×	4	=	$3,600

Step 2. Find the total amount due.

Purchase Price	+	Finance Charge	=	Total Due
$15,000	+	$3,600	=	$18,600

Step 3. Find the monthly payment amount.

Total Due	/	Number of Payments	=	Monthly Payment
$18,600	/	48 (4 × 12)	=	$387.50

Notice that the interest rate stated is 6%. However, 6% is not the APR or true interest rate because the interest rate was applied to the full amount ($15,000) of the purchase. This could be misleading because the full amount was not owed for the full term. Actually, $15,000 was owed only until the time of the first payment. During the last month, only $387.50 was owed. As a general rule, the APR will be approximately double the interest rate stated for this type of finance plan.

The following formula can be used to compute the actual APR:

$$\text{APR} = \frac{2 \times \text{Number of payments per year} \times \text{Interest charge}}{\text{Amount financed} \times (\text{Total number of payments} + 1)}$$

Computing annual percentage rate   EXAMPLE

12.10

Problem: In the previous example, Joe Wright purchased an automobile for $15,000. While paying for the automobile on an installment basis, his finance charges will be $3,600. His monthly payments will be $387.50 for 48 months. What is the APR?

Solution: Note: Amounts from the example are substituted for parts in the above formula to compute the APR.

$$\text{APR} = \frac{2 \times 12 \times \$3,600}{\$15,000 \times 49(48 + 1)}$$

$$\text{APR} = \frac{86,400}{735,000} = 0.117551 \text{ or } 11.76\%$$

Rule of 78

Purchase agreements on installment credit usually offer the buyer the option of paying off the loan early. For example, if the purchaser of an automobile under a 48-month agreement decides to pay the remaining balance in less than 48 months, the lender must decide on the amount of interest that is canceled, or which will not be paid. A common method to compute this amount is the *Rule of 78*. Under this method, the amount of finance charge assessed is greatest during the early months and decreases each subsequent month. Under this method, paying off the loan halfway through the finance period will not result in having half of the interest amount canceled.

The following formula is used to compute the amount of finance charge that is considered unearned:

$$\frac{\text{Canceled finance}}{\text{charge}} = \frac{\text{Sum of digits of remaining months}}{\text{Sum of digits in life of contract}} \times \frac{\text{Total}}{\text{finance}}_{\text{charges}}$$

The sum of digits is defined in Example 12.11.

EXAMPLE   Computing canceled finance charges

12.11

Problem: The Burkhart Furniture Company sold a sofa with payments to be made for 12 months. Computed total finance charges were $312. After making 8 payments, the customer decided to pay the balance. What finance charge should be canceled?

Solution: **Step 1.**   Find the sum of digits of remaining months.
$$1 + 2 + 3 + 4 = 10 \text{ (four months remaining)}$$

Step 2.   Find the sum of digits in life of contract.
$$1 + 2 + 3 + 4 + 5 + 6 + 7 + 8 + 9 + 10 + 11 + 12 = 78 \text{ (twelve months in contract)}$$

Step 3.   Compute the amount of canceled finance charge.
$$\frac{10}{78} \times \$312 = \$40$$

Therefore, $40 of the original $312 finance charge will be cancelled because of early payment.

A shortcut method to determine the numbers to use in Steps 2 and 3 is to use the formula $N \times (N + 1)/2$, where N equals the number of periods. For example, 12 periods using this formula will be $(12 \times 13)/2$, or 78. The formula used for 4 periods will be $(4 \times 5)/2$, or 10. Notice that these are the same values as were computed in the example, but the shortcut method saves time.

EXAMPLE   Computing canceled finance charges

12.12

Problem: Joe Roth purchased a lawnmower under a 6-month installment plan with $12.60 total finance charges. After four months, he decided to pay the balance. Using the Rule of 78 and the shortcut method, how much finance charge should be canceled?

Solution:
$$\frac{2 \times (2 + 1)/2}{6 \times (6 + 1)/2} = \frac{3}{21}$$
$$\frac{3}{21} \times \$12.60 = \$1.80$$

● **Complete Assignment 12.2** ●

ASSIGNMENT 12.1   Finance Charges

1. Jin Cheng purchased a stereo using a credit card with a 1.75% monthly finance charge. What is the annual percentage rate?

_____

2. Bill Barksdale purchased a television set for $900 with monthly finance charges of 1½% based on the previous balance. He decided to pay $50 after the first month. How much of the payment would apply to the (a) balance, and how much would apply to the (b) finance charge?

(a) $ _____

(b) $ _____

3. Sarah Brown purchased a new office safe for $1,240 with monthly finance charges of 1% based on the previous balance. She decided to pay $63 after the first month. How much of the payment will apply to the (a) balance, and how much will apply to the (b) finance charge? (c) What will the balance be after the payment?

(a) $ _____

(b) $ _____

(c) $ _____

4. Jerry Sellers purchased a new watch for a $180 cash price. The amount can be financed for 12 monthly payments of $15 plus a down payment of $50. If he decided to buy the watch on credit, (a) how much will the total finance charge equal? (b) How much will the credit price of the watch equal? (c) How much can be saved by paying cash for the watch?

(a) $ _____

(b) $ _____

(c) $ _____

5. James Fung can purchase a used car for a base price of $6,000 plus sales taxes of $360. A down payment of $1,200 will be required to purchase the car at this price. Finance charges equal 2% of the previous balance. (a) What is the total cost of the car? (b) How much will Mr. Fung borrow to finance the car? (c) How much will the finance charge be for the first month?

(a) $ _____

(b) $ _____

(c) $ _____

6. Pearline Bronger purchased merchandise from the Bestway Specialty Shop totaling $400. Finance charges are 1% per month based on the previous balance. She decided to pay $30 per month. Compute the finance charge for (a) the first month and (b) the second month.

(a) $ _____

(b) $ _____

7. Jim Munice purchased merchandise totaling $300 on February 10 and merchandise totaling $520 on March 10. Terms are 1% per month based on the balance from the previous month with no finance charge assessed for 30 days after purchase. Statements are issued on the first day of each month. Payments were made on April 1 ($100) and on May 1 ($100). Compute the balance due on (a) April 1 and (b) May 1 and the finance charges on (c) April 1 and (d) May 1.

(a) $ _____

(b) $ _____

(c) $ _____

(d) $ _____

8. Wanda Rodriguez purchased a ring for $1,500 on August 8 and a necklace for $160 on September 9. She made a 10% down payment at the time of each purchase. Statements are issued on the first day of each month with a 1½% finance charge based on the balance from the previous month with no finance charge if the account is paid during the first 30 days. She made a $100 payment on October 2 and another $100 payment on November 2. Compute the balance due on (a) September 1, (b) October 1, and (c) November 1 and finance charges on (d) September 1, (e) October 1, and (f) November 1. (Round all finance charges to 2 decimal places.)

(a) $ _____   (d) $ _____

(b) $ _____   (e) $ _____

(c) $ _____   (f) $ _____

9. Carl Jorgenson bought a camera for $360 on May 15 with terms of 10% cash down payment and a finance charge of 1½% based on the balance from the previous month. No finance charges are assessed if full payment is received within 30 days after the sale is made. He decided to pay $30 for each month *plus* the finance charge for the month. How much will his payment be for the (a) July 1 and (b) August 1 statements?

(a) $ _____

(b) $ _____

130

ASSIGNMENT 12.2 Consumer Credit

1. The Discount Furniture Store makes finance charges of 1% per month based on the average daily balance during the month. Ysing Inertz bought a chair on June 10 costing $420 and an end table for $210 on June 15. Compute the following amounts:

    (a) Equivalent dollar days, first purchase $ _____

    (b) Equivalent dollar days, second purchase $ _____

    (c) Equivalent dollar days, combined purchases $ _____

    (d) Average daily balance $ _____

    (e) Monthly finance charge $ _____

2. Botter Distributors sold automotive parts to John Collier. There was no beginning balance as of September 1. A sale for $170 was made on September 5, and a sale for $60 was made on September 20. Finance charges are based on 1½% of the average daily balance. Compute the following amounts:

    (a) Equivalent dollar days, first purchase $ _____

    (b) Equivalent dollar days, second purchase $ _____

    (c) Equivalent dollar days, combined purchases $ _____

    (d) Average daily balance $ _____

    (e) Monthly finance charge $ _____

3. Using the Rule of 78, compute the amount of finance charge that will be canceled under each of the following conditions:

Total Finance Charge	Total in Contract Months	Early Payoff	Finance Charge Canceled
$ 420.00	6	End of Month 3	$ _____
1,260.00	6	End of Month 4	$ _____
2,379.00	12	End of Month 8	$ _____
427.50	18	End of Month 15	$ _____
3,727.50	20	End of Month 10	$ _____

4. John White's credit card balance was $4,725. Using the Minimum Monthly Payment Schedule in Example 12.6, what is the amount of his minimum monthly payment?

$ _____

5. Florence Robertson's credit card balance was $2,424.89. Using the Minimum Monthly Payment Schedule in Example 12.6, what is the amount of her minimum monthly payment?

$ _____

6. A customer purchased a used car for a $5,600 cash price or twelve monthly payments of $550. (a) What is the amount of the finance charge? (b) How much of the finance charge will be cancelled if the balance is paid after the seventh month using the Rule of 78? (Round your answer to two decimal places.)

(a) $ _____

(b) $ _____

7. A dinette set was sold for an $800 cash price. The customer can pay a 20% finance charge added to the cash price and make 12 equal monthly payments. (a) What is the amount of the finance charge? (b) How much of the finance charge will be cancelled if the balance is paid after the tenth month using the Rule of 78?

(a) $ _____

(b) $ _____

8. Ginny Runyan purchased a television for $800. She agreed to make 24 payments of $38 each over a 2-year period. What were her (a) interest charge and (b) annual percentage rate (APR) for the finance charges?

(a) $ _____

(b) _____

DISCOUNTS ON PURCHASES

Businesses take advantage of discounts on purchases for many reasons. The major reason is to save money on the purchase by taking advantage of a discount to reduce the purchase price. Several additional ways that businesses take advantage of discounts on merchandise purchases will be discussed in Chapter 14.

EXAMPLE Sales discounts

13.1

Compact Disc Digital Audio Player

Save $110 **149⁹⁵**
Reg. 259.95
Low As $20 Per Month ★
Discover digital audio! Programmable memory plays up to 15 cuts in any order you choose. #42-5001

33-Number Memory Auto-Dialing Phone

Cut 29% **49⁹⁵**
Reg. 69.95
Auto-dials 30 often-called numbers plus three emergency numbers. Tone/pulse dialing†. #43-605

Full-Size Stereo Headphones Cut $10

Cut 40% **14⁹⁵**
Reg. 24.95
Big 3½" drivers deliver full-range stereo sound. Cushioned earcups and adjustable headband. #33-993

Seven-Band Auto Equalizer/Booster

33% Off **39⁹⁵**
Reg. 59.95
Add 40 watts of power and complete tonal control! 4-speaker fader. #12-1871

Quantity Discounts

Businesses may be encouraged to make larger purchases if quantity discounts are offered. To determine the best alternative, however, the cost of warehouse space to store the purchases must be compared

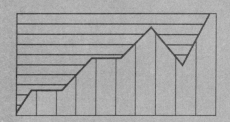

to the savings in purchase price. One wholesaler offers goods according to the following schedule:

DISCOUNT SCHEDULE

Items Purchased	Discount
0–20	0%
21–40	1%
41–60	2%
61–80	3%
81–100	4%
100 or more	5%

Use this schedule to solve the problem in Example 13.2.

EXAMPLE 13.2   Computing discounted cost

Problem: Novelties of Distinction purchased 87 items consisting of calendars for sale during the Christmas season. The normal cost of these items is $1.25. What is the total discounted cost of the order if the quantity discount schedule is used?

Solution: **Step 1.** Find the cost of the order at the regular price.

Number of items × Cost per item = Normal cost
       87   × $1.25   = $108.75

Step 2. Find the amount of the discount.

Normal cost × Discount rate = Discount
 $108.75   ×   0.04   = $4.35

Step 3. Find the discounted cost.

Normal cost − Discount = Discounted cost
 $108.75   − $4.35   = $104.40

Cost Based on Time

Many construction bids are based on project completion time. For example, a company may offer a construction company a bonus to the bid price if a building is completed by a certain date that is earlier than the bid date. This bonus may permit the construction company to hire additional personnel or to pay employees overtime to finish the project early.

EXAMPLE

13.3

Problem: The Acme Construction Company bid on a project to pave two miles of city streets for a total price of $2,225,000. The bid contract stipulated that a 17% bonus will be awarded if the project is completed by August 31. The project was completed on August 15. What is the amount of the bonus?

Solution: Project amount × Bonus rate = Bonus amount
   $2,225,000   ×   0.17   = $378,250

The bid contract may also include penalties if the project is delayed beyond a specified date, as shown in Example 13.4.

EXAMPLE

13.4

Problem: Benson and Associates, a construction company, offered a $12,540,000 bid on an office building. The bid contract stipulated that a penalty of 1.5% would be assessed if the project was not completed by March 31. The project was completed on April 20. What is the amount of the penalty? How much will the company receive for the project?

Solution: **Step 1.** Find the amount of the penalty.

Original amount × Penalty percent = Penalty
   $12,540,000   ×   0.015   = $188,100

Step 2. Find the amount received for the project.

Original amount − Penalty = Amount received
   $12,540,000   − $188,100 = $12,351,900

Special Sales Discounts

Many retail stores offer special sales discounts during certain holiday periods or to reduce their inventory of specific merchandise items. Advertising notices similar to the one in Example 13.5 are published in newspapers to promote special sales.

EXAMPLE   Advertisement of sales discount

13.5

SALE!! MUST CLEAR!
CHRISTMAS MERCHANDISE
50% off
- **SILK FLOWERS 50% off**
- **GIFT ITEMS 20% off**
- **SILK TREES 40% off**

OPEN DAILY 8-5   SUN 9:30-5

EXAMPLE   Computing discounted cost

13.6

Problem: The Brookview Sports Center offered a special 35% discount on a discontinued line of sportswear. How much will a $125 jogging suit cost after the discount?

Solution: **Step 1.**   Find the discount.

Original price × Discount rate = Discount
     $125   ×   0.35   = $43.75

Step 2.   Find the discounted price.

Original price − Discount = Discounted price
     $125   − $43.75   = $81.25

• Complete Assignment 13.1 •

ASSIGNMENT 13.1 Discount Applications

1. The Franklin Book Store offers a 17.5% discount on all purchases over $30. Norman Marichial made a purchase totaling $46.25. How much is his discount?

   $ _____

2. The Benton House of Fashion offers a 15% discount on purchases of $100–$200, a 20% discount on purchases of $201–$300, and a 25% discount on purchases of $301–$400. On a $275 sale, how much is the discount?

   $ _____

3. The City Card Center offers a 5% discount on the purchase of 5–10 items, a 9% discount on the purchase of 11–15 items, and a 12% discount on all purchases of more than 15 items. Harry Jacobs purchased 12 cards at $2.50 each. How much is his total discount?

   $ _____

4. Distinctive Fashions offered a special sale on shoes by offering the second pair of shoes at one-half price if the first pair were purchased at the regular price. What is the cost of 2 pairs of shoes if each pair normally sells for $49.80?

   $ _____

5. The Best Construction Co. won a $345,500 construction contract with a stipulation that a 1% bonus would be awarded for each day that the job is finished ahead of schedule. The job was finished 13 days ahead of schedule. How much were the (a) bonus and (b) total amount received?

   (a) $ _____

   (b) $ _____

6. The Best Construction Co. won a $298,700 construction contract with a stipulation that a 1.75% penalty would be assessed if the job was not finished on time. The job was finished 12 days late. How much were the (a) penalty and (b) total amount received?

   (a) $ _____

   (b) $ _____

7. The Roane Ready Mix Concrete Co. won a highway paving contract amounting to $3,498,500. If they finish by the deadline, they will receive a 2.5% bonus. If they finish later than the deadline, they will be assessed a 2.5% penalty. How much is the (a) most and (b) least that they can receive from the contract?

(a) $ _____

(b) $ _____

8. The Roane Ready Mix Concrete Co. won a highway paving contract amounting to $2,546,800. There will be a $975-per-day penalty for each day the contract is not finished after April 3. If they finish the job on May 8, how much will the (a) penalty and (b) final amount received be?

(a) $ _____

(b) $ _____

9. The Oslow Book Store offered a special sale on selected books by providing a 28% discount. On a $187.50 order, how much was the (a) discount and (b) amount due for the order?

(a) $ _____

(b) $ _____

10. The Video Scene offered a 15% discount if total sales are above $57. Harold Robbins purchased 5 video tapes for a total cost of $122.40. How much was the (a) discount and (b) amount due?

(a) $ _____

(b) $ _____

11. Kiddie Korner offered a promotional sale by selling the second pair of shoes at one-half price if the first pair was purchased at the regular price. Sarah Hughes purchased two pairs of shoes with a price of $39.50 each. What was the total price of the shoes?

$ _____

12. Joan Diaz decided to purchase several toys costing $12.37 each. She has $287. How many toys could she purchase if a 20% discount was offered on each toy?

• **Complete Unit 3 Spreadsheet Applications** •

138

UNIT 3 SPREADSHEET APPLICATION 1: Discount Listing

The following spreadsheet is used to compute the discount amount and final price for each item. It also computes the total cost for the number of units purchased for each item. Totals are computed for the number purchased and total cost columns. The original price is multiplied by the discount rate to compute the discount amount. The discount amount is then deducted from the original price to compute the final price of each item. The final price is multiplied by the number purchased to compute the total cost for each item. Amounts for Product Number B-217 are computed as an example for checking the logic of your computations.

```
         A          B        C        D        E        F          G       H
 1John's Shoppe                 DISCOUNT LISTING
 2================================================================================
 3  Product    Original Discount Discount    Final     Number       Total
 4  Number      Price     Rate   Amount     Price    Purchased       Cost
 5================================================================================
 6  B-217        2.33     .25      .58       1.75        20          34.95
 7  B-218        4.59     .25                            15
 8  C-243        3.67     .20                            12
 9  C-316       14.75     .20                            25
10  R-345        3.89     .18                            27
11  R-349        4.52     .18                            25
12  R-364        3.74     .23                             8
13  T-008       10.25     .15                            35
14  T-111        2.17     .25                            12
15  T-113        2.43     .25                            50
16  T-426        8.43     .15                            27
17  T-457        6.30     .35                            25
18================================================================================
19Total          xxxxxxxxxxxxxxxxxxxxxxxxxxxxxxxxxxxxxxx
20================================================================================
```

Refer to the spreadsheet above to answer the following questions:

1. What is the discount amount for Product Number C-243? $ _____

2. What is the final price for Product Number R-349? $ _____

3. What is the final price for Product Number T-111? $ _____

4. What is the total cost for Product Number T-426? $ _____

5. What is the total number purchased? _____

6. Which product number had the highest total cost? _____

7. Which product number had the lowest final cost? _____

8. How many product numbers had a discount amount greater than $1.00? _____

9. How many product numbers had a total cost greater than $100.00? _____

10. What is the average total cost for all items (the sum of the total cost column divided by the sum of the number purchased column)? $ _____

UNIT 3 SPREADSHEET APPLICATION 2: Finance Charges

The following spreadsheet is used to determine the finance charge, total due, monthly payment, and annual percentage rate (APR) for a series of purchases. Sums of the finance charge and total due columns are also computed. The finance charge is computed by multiplying the purchase price times the interest rate times the years financed. The total due is computed by adding the purchase price to the finance charge. The monthly payment is computed by dividing the total due by the number of payments. The APR is computed by using the following formula:

$$APR = \frac{2 \times \text{Number of payments per year} \times \text{Interest charge}}{\text{Amount financed} \times (\text{Total number of payments} + 1)}$$

The computed amounts for the first purchase are shown in the spreadsheet to permit you to determine whether or not your logic is correct.

```
        A         B         C         D         E        F          G          H
 1City Savings Bank                FINANCE CHARGES
 2================================================================================
 3 Purchase Interest    Years    Finance    Total  Number of  Monthly
 4    Price   Rate Financed    Charge      Due   Payments  Payment           APR
 5================================================================================
 6  15,000    .06        4     3,600    18,600        48   387.50       11.76%
 7  17,000    .08        5                            60
 8  12,000    .05        4                            48
 9  10,000    .09        3                            36
10   9,000    .06        4                            48
11     600    .10        5                            60
12   2,000    .08        4                            48
13   3,000    .12        3                            36
14   4,000    .08        4                            48
15   5,000    .06        3                            36
16     400    .09        5                            60
17   3,000    .07        5                            60
18================================================================================
19Total   xxxxxxxxxxxxxxxxx              xxxxxxxxxxxxxxxxxxxxxxxxxxxxxx
20================================================================================
```

Refer to the spreadsheet above to answer the following questions:

1. What is the finance charge for the $12,000 purchase price? $ _____

2. What is the finance charge for the $3,000 purchase price? $ _____

3. What is the total due for the $600 purchase price? $ _____

4. What is the total due for the $400 purchase price? $ _____

5. What is the monthly payment for the $17,000 purchase price? $ _____

6. What is the monthly payment for the $4,000 purchase price? $ _____

7. What is the APR for the $10,000 purchase price?   _____

(Continued on following page)

8. What is the APR for the $4,000 purchase price? _____

9. How much are the total finance charges? $ _____

10. How many purchases had monthly payments greater than $225.00? _____

● Complete Unit 3 Self-Test ●

142

UNIT 3 SELF-TEST   Percentage Amounts in Business

1. Compute each of the following amounts (Rate $\times$ Base = Amount):

    (a) 15% of $720   = _____   (d) 12¾% of $1,200 = _____

    (b) 8% of $120.30 = _____   (e) 8% of $675   = _____

    (c) 16½% of $320 = _____   (f) 25% of $680.48 = _____

2. Carl Swift contributed 12% of his salary to foundations. If his salary was $18,360, how much did he contribute?

    $ _____

3. Joy Carlisle spent $191.21 for a new radio for her car. If this amount represented 8.5% of her savings account, how much savings did she have?

    $ _____

4. The Crocker Auto Service offered to repair a car for $276. This was 15% more than the repair estimate by The Auto Shoppe. How much was the estimate by The Auto Shoppe?

    $ _____

5. The Dolly Furniture Store ran a special sale with items selling at 60% of their regular price. If the sale price of an item is $750, what was the regular price for the item?

    $ _____

6. Bill Brock had sales of $2,800 this month. This was 12% more than his sales last month. How much were his sales last month?

    $ _____

7. Turner Auto Sales bought a car for $800 and sold it for $1,000. What was the percent of profit based on the original price of the car?

    _____

8. Carl Johnson missed 10 days of work last year. He missed 14 days of work this year. What was the rate of increase this year?

    _____

9. Carla Brower answered 80 questions correctly on an exam. On a second exam, she answered 100 questions correctly. What was the percent of increase in her performance?

_____

10. Brad Simpson had a monthly salary of $1,200. He spent $300 during the first week. What percent of his salary did he spend during the first week of the month?

_____

11. Use an aliquot part of $1.00 to compute the following:

(a) 78 items @ 16⅔ cents = _____

(b) 45 items @ 6⅔ cents = _____

(c) 150 items @ 33⅓ cents = _____

(d) 48 items @ 12½ cents = _____

12. Inez Anderson bought a new car for $12,000 and made a down payment of 12½%. How much was her down payment?

$_____

13. A grain bin holds 624 tons. It appears to be 33 1/3% full. How much grain is in the bin?

_____

14. Jennie Sue Runyan makes $12 per hour. If she received an 8 1/3% raise, how much would her raise be?

$_____

15. Juan Ramos bought a new watch for $650. If the first monthly finance charge was 1 1/2% of the purchase price, how much was the first month's finance charge?

$_____

16. Meryl Studebaker bought a new television for $900 with monthly finance charges of 1 1/2%. If a payment of $60 was made at the end of one month, how much of the payment applied to the (a) balance and how much applied to the (b) finance charge?

(a) $_____

(b) $_____

144

UNIT 3 SELF-TEST (continued)

17. Craig Humphreys bought a camera for $500 on June 15 with a cash down payment of 10% and a monthly finance charge of 1% per month. He decided to pay $40 per month, plus the finance charge for the month. How much was his payment at the end of (a) the first month and (b) the second month?

    (a) $ _____

    (b) $ _____

18. The Value Furniture Company calculates finance charges of 1% per month based on the average daily balance during the month. Chuck Cotter bought a table on October 10 costing $360 and a lamp on October 20 costing $100. Compute the following amounts:

    (a) Equivalent dollar days, first purchase   = $ _____

    (b) Equivalent dollar days, second purchase   = $ _____

    (c) Equivalent dollar days, combined purchases = $ _____

    (d) Average daily balance   = $ _____

    (e) Monthly finance charge   = $ _____

Note: Use a calculator, if one is available, to solve Problems 19–24.

19. $348.2 + 34.06 + 14 =$ _____   22. $499.5225 \times 2.05 =$ _____

20. $45.2 - 8.95 + 13.41 =$ _____   23. $1,765.50 \times 20\% =$ _____

21. $17.3 / 3 + 4.56 - 2 =$ _____   24. $45.38 \times 0.005 =$ _____

25. Karl Rodoski purchased an automobile for $15,000. A finance charge of 8% per year was added to the purchase price. What are the (a) finance charges, (b) monthly payments, and (c) annual percentage rate (APR) if payments are made over 36 months (3 years)?

    (a) $ _____

    (b) $ _____

    (c) _____

Marketing Mathematics

Most companies are involved in selling a product or service. Companies attempt to price the product or service at a price that covers expenses and still provides an adequate return to the owners. This unit shows how prices of merchandise are computed and how commissions paid to salespersons are computed. Discounts commonly offered by manufacturers and wholesalers to retailers are presented.

Some skills you can achieve in this unit include the following:

- **Computing cash discounts on merchandise sales and purchases.**
- **Determining cash discount dates.**
- **Computing a single trade discount from list price.**
- **Computing net price after allowing for trade discount.**
- **Computing a single trade discount figure equivalent to a series of trade discount terms.**
- **Using shortcut methods for computing trade discount amounts.**
- **Computing markup and markdown percents on merchandise when the cost or selling price is known.**
- **Computing markdown amount and sale price for merchandise.**
- **Computing sales commission for merchandise sold.**
- **Computing consignment sales commission amounts and net proceeds.**

UNIT 4

CASH DISCOUNTS

Companies selling merchandise like to receive payment for the merchandise as soon as possible after delivery to keep cash flowing back to the business. To encourage buyers to pay by a specified date, the seller often offers a *cash discount* or reduction from the net price of the invoice. This chapter will show you how cash discounts and specified dates are determined.

Overview of Cash Discounts

Many companies offer cash discounts for prompt payment of accounts for merchandise sold. This can benefit both the buyer and the seller because the seller receives early payment and the buyer does not have to pay the full amount for the purchase. Costs and quantities of items purchased are listed on an *invoice.* The customary procedure is to allow a cash discount only if payment is received by a specified date, as indicated by the seller on the invoice. After the specified date, the buyer must pay the full price for items listed on the invoice.

Typical Cash Discount Terms

Both buyer and seller must abide by the terms of the cash discount, as indicated on the invoice. However, payment must be made by the specified due date to qualify for the cash discount, if any. For example, terms such as 2/10, n/30 (read *two ten, net thirty*) mean that a 2% discount will be allowed if payment is made within 10 days from the date of the invoice, and the full amount must be paid within 30 days. No cash discount will be allowed from Day 11 to Day 30. Other typical discount terms are expressed as follows:

   5/15, n/45. This means that the full amount is due within 45 days from the date of the invoice. However, a 5% discount will be given if the bill is paid within 15 days from the date of the invoice. (Read *five fifteen, net forty-five.*)

   3/10 EOM, n/30 EOM. The full amount is due within 30 days after the end of the month (EOM). However, a 3% discount will be given if the bill is paid within 10 days after the end of the month. (Read *three ten end of month, net thirty end of month.*)

   n/30. The full amount is due within 30 days from the date of the invoice. No discount is given for early payment. (Read *net thirty.*)

   3/20, 1/45, n/90. The full amount is due within 90 days from the date of the invoice. However, a 3% discount will be given if the bill is paid within 20 days, or a 1% discount will be given if payment is received later than 20 days but within 45 days after the date of the invoice. (Read *three twenty, one forty-five, net ninety.*) A sample invoice form is shown in Example 14.1.

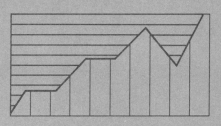

EXAMPLE Typical invoice form
14.1

Invoice

THE Computer Center, Inc.
5512 Poplar Ave.
Memphis, TN 38119
901-685-0009

No. **B 4610**

Date

Your
Order No.

Sold To

Shipped to

Our Order No.	Salesman	Terms 10 Days Net	F.O.B.	Date Shipped	Shipped Via

Quantity Ordered	Quantity Shipped	Stock Number/Description	Unit Price	Unit	Amount

PLEASE REMIT FROM THIS INVOICE
NO STATEMENT WILL BE SENT

A FINANCE CHARGE OF 1.5%
PER MONTH OR 18% PER YEAR
WILL BE ADDED TO INVOICES OVER
30 DAYS.

Received by _____

SUBTOTAL

SALES TAX

TOTAL

All merchandise returned for credit, refund or exchange must be in new and re-saleable condition, in original cartons with original packing, accessories, guarantees and instructions, and must be accompanied by this sales slip, within 10 days. No returns, refunds or exchanges of software, books or used equipment. All goods are sold without warranties, express or implied, including warranties of merchantability or fitness for a particular purpose, except for those warranties given by the manufacturer of the goods. Used equipment is sold "As Is" and has no warranty.

Determining the Cash Discount and Due Dates

The exact date that is the last date for taking the cash discount must be determined to ensure that both the buyer and seller will know about this date. For this reason, exact calendar days are used based on the number of days that elapse from the date of the invoice.

The spreadsheet table in Example 14.2 can be used to compute the last date for taking the cash discount and/or the due date. The values in the table represent the number of days that elapse after January 1 each year. The steps for using this table are shown in Example 14.3.

Exact days-in-a-year calendar spreadsheet   EXAMPLE

14.2

```
       A    B  C    D    E    F    G    H    I    J    K    L    M    N  O
   1Spreadsheet Table to Compute Exact Days-in-a-Year (excluding leap year)
   2------------------------------------------------------------------------
   3 Day of|Jan.  Feb. Mar. Apr.  May  June July Aug. Sept. Oct. Nov. Dec.
   4 Month | 31    28   31   30   31    30   31   31   30    31   30   31
   5------ | ---------------------------------------------------------------
   6     1 |  1    32   60   91   121   152  182  213  244   274  305  335
   7     2 |  2    33   61   92   122   153  183  214  245   275  306  336
   8     3 |  3    34   62   93   123   154  184  215  246   276  307  337
   9     4 |  4    35   63   94   124   155  185  216  247   277  308  338
  10     5 |  5    36   64   95   125   156  186  217  248   278  309  339
  11     6 |  6    37   65   96   126   157  187  218  249   279  310  340
  12     7 |  7    38   66   97   127   158  188  219  250   280  311  341
  13     8 |  8    39   67   98   128   159  189  220  251   281  312  342
  14     9 |  9    40   68   99   129   160  190  221  252   282  313  343
  15    10 | 10    41   69  100   130   161  191  222  253   283  314  344
  16    11 | 11    42   70  101   131   162  192  223  254   284  315  345
  17    12 | 12    43   71  102   132   163  193  224  255   285  316  346
  18    13 | 13    44   72  103   133   164  194  225  256   286  317  347
  19    14 | 14    45   73  104   134   165  195  226  257   287  318  348
  20    15 | 15    46   74  105   135   166  196  227  258   288  319  349
  21    16 | 16    47   75  106   136   167  197  228  259   289  320  350
  22    17 | 17    48   76  107   137   168  198  229  260   290  321  351
  23    18 | 18    49   77  108   138   169  199  230  261   291  322  352
  24    19 | 19    50   78  109   139   170  200  231  262   292  323  353
  25    20 | 20    51   79  110   140   171  201  232  263   293  324  354
  26    21 | 21    52   80  111   141   172  202  233  264   294  325  355
  27    22 | 22    53   81  112   142   173  203  234  265   295  326  356
  28    23 | 23    54   82  113   143   174  204  235  266   296  327  357
  29    24 | 24    55   83  114   144   175  205  236  267   297  328  358
  30    25 | 25    56   84  115   145   176  206  237  268   298  329  359
  31    26 | 26    57   85  116   146   177  207  238  269   299  330  360
  32    27 | 27    58   86  117   147   178  208  239  270   300  331  361
  33    28 | 28    59   87  118   148   179  209  240  271   301  332  362
  34    29 | 29   -----  88  119   149   180  210  241  272   302  333  363
  35    30 | 30   -----  89  120   150   181  211  242  273   303  334  364
  36    31 | 31   -----  90  ----- 151  ------ 212  243 ------ 304 ----- 365
```

As an introduction to using the table, assume that the current date is July 14. How many days remain until Christmas (December 25)? Subtract the value in the table for July 14 (195) from the value in the table for December 25 (359); the result is 164 days. You may want to practice with other dates, such as the number of days until your birthday or the number of days until your next college break from classes.

Example 14.3 shows how to use the table to solve cash discount problems and find due dates.

Using the spreadsheet table to determine a due date   EXAMPLE

14.3

Problem: The date of an invoice is February 26 with terms of 2/10, n/45. What are the (a) last day to take the cash discount and (b) due date?

Solution: Step 1. Move down Column A until you locate the day of the month representing the date of the invoice: in this example, 26 on Row 31.

Step 2. Move across the row to the column representing the month for the invoice date: in this example, February in Column D (Row 31). The value *57* is in this location.

(Continued on following page)

Step 3. Find the last date for the cash discount by adding 10 to this value (57 + 10) = 67. Find the month above this value (located in Column E, Row 13: March). Find the day in Column A that is to the left of this value: 8. Therefore, the date is March 8.

Step 4. Find the due date in the table by adding 45 to the value located in Step 2 (57 + 45) = *102*. Find the month above this value (located in Column F, Row 17: April). Find the day in Column A that is to the left of this value: 12. Therefore, the due date is April 12.

With practice, you will find this table easy to use. The cash discount and due dates are given for Examples 14.4 and 14.5. For practice, use the table to determine the dates and see if you arrive at the same dates as the ones provided.

EXAMPLE
14.4

Finding cash discount dates and due dates

Problem: Find the cash discount and due dates for invoices with the following terms: (a) 3/10, n/30, (b) 3/10 EOM, n/30 EOM, (c) n/30, (d) n/EOM, and (e) 3/15, 2/30, n/45.

Solution:

Terms	Last Cash Discount Date	Due Date
3/10, n/30	August 20	September 9
3/10 EOM, n/30 EOM	September 10	September 30
n/30	None	September 9
n/EOM	None	August 31
3/15, 2/30, n/45	August 25 or September 9	September 24

Computing the Cash Discount

You must determine whether the *date of payment* is on or before the cash discount date in order to qualify for the cash discount. If the date of payment qualifies the buyer for a cash discount, compute the cash discount using the steps shown in Example 14.5. Computation of cash discount for an invoice with no freight charges or returns bases the discount rate on the net invoice price. Returns represent merchandise that comes back to the seller due to damage or other reasons. Amounts should be rounded to the nearest cent for each computation.

Computing cash discount and cash price   EXAMPLE

14.5

Problem: The Bullhart Equipment Center purchased merchandise totaling $656.50 with terms of 2/10, n/30. The invoice, dated January 28, was paid on February 3. What are the cash discount and cash price?

Solution: **Step 1.** Find the cash discount.

Net price × Cash discount rate = Cash discount
$656.50 ×   .02 (2%)   = $13.13

Step 2. Find the cash price.

Net price − Cash discount = Cash price
$656.50 − $13.13   = $643.37

Freight Terms

Freight charges are necessary when merchandise is shipped to the buyer. These charges may be paid by the seller or the buyer depending on the terms of the sales invoice. *FOB* (Free On Board) *shipping point* means that the buyer pays the shipping costs. *FOB destination* means that the seller pays the shipping costs. Regardless of who pays the shipping costs, any cash discount does not apply to the portion of the invoice relating to shipping costs. Freight charges and returns, if any, should be deducted from the net invoice amount prior to computing the cash discount, as shown in Example 14.6.

Computing net price subject to the cash discount   EXAMPLE

14.6

Problem: The City Sports Center purchased goods with a net invoice amount of $324.52, including $16.37 freight charges and $14.00 in returns. What is the net price subject to the cash discount?

Solution: Net invoice   Freight   Purchase
amount   − charge − returns = Net price
$324.52   − $16.37 − $14.00   = $294.15

After deducting the cash discount, these amounts are then included in the final amount due, as shown in Example 14.7.

EXAMPLE

14.7

Problem: The Culver Shoppe purchased goods with a net invoice amount of $750.56, including $12.38 for freight charges and $26.00 in returns. The invoice, dated August 18 with terms of 3/15, n/45, was paid on September 1. What are the net price subject to discount, cash discount, and final cash price for the invoice?

Solution: **Step 1.**

Net invoice amount =		$750.56
Less prepaid freight charges	$12.38	
and returns	+26.00	− 38.38
Net price subject to discount =		$712.18

Step 2. Cash discount = $712.18 × .03 = 21.3654   − 21.37

Step 3.

Net price =	690.81
Plus freight charges	+ 12.38
Cash price =	$703.19

● **Complete Assignment 14.1** ●

● **Complete Assignment 14.2** ●

ASSIGNMENT 14.1 Computing Cash Discount

1. Determine the cash discount date and due date for each of the following invoices. The first entry is completed as an example.

Invoice No.	Invoice Date	Terms	Cash Discount Date(s)	Due Date
	May 25	2/10, n/30	April 4	April 24
1	January 18	2/10, n/30	_____	_____
2	April 17	3/15, n/45	_____	_____
3	July 19	3/20, n/40	_____	_____
4	August 10	2/15 EOM, n/30 EOM	_____	_____
5	September 9	n/EOM	_____	_____
6	October 10	2/10, 1/20, n/30	_____	_____
7	March 23	5/10, n/30	_____	_____
8	December 8	3/10, n/10 EOM	_____	_____
9	February 28	2/15, n/60	_____	_____
10	June 30	1/10, n/20	_____	_____

2. Assume that the following invoices are paid within the cash discount periods. Compute the cash discount and the cash price for each invoice. The first entry is completed as an example.

Invoice No.	Net Price	Discount Terms	Cash Discount	Cash Price
	$ 354.17	2/10, n/30	$7.08	$347.09
1	750.50	2/10, n/30	$ _____	$ _____
2	296.18	3/15, n/30	$ _____	$ _____
3	641.76	3/20, n/45	$ _____	$ _____
4	711.80	4/15, n/40	$ _____	$ _____
5	2,716.58	5/10, n/30	$ _____	$ _____

3. The following invoice is for merchandise from Lanko Wholesalers. Complete the extensions for each item, total the extensions to compute the net price, compute the cash discount, and compute the cash price if the invoice is paid on October 5.

Invoice No. 1820

Sold to: Harrah's Shop
2800 Kirby Parkway
Memphis, TN 38119

Date: September 15, 19---
Terms: 4/10 EOM, n/60
Acct.: No. 28–9732
Via: Truck

Catalog No.	Quantity	Unit Price	Amount
A-341	18	$19.85	$
A-362	12	16.34	$
B-681	9	32.14	$
F-111	18	14.18	$
Z-819	7	21.36	$
		NET PRICE	$
		CASH DISCOUNT	$
		CASH PRICE	$

4. An invoice for merchandise from Fay's Fashions is shown below. Complete the extensions for each item, total the extensions to compute the net price, compute the cash discount, and compute the cash price if the invoice is paid on April 4.

Invoice No. 2945

Sold to: Distinctive Shop
1 Office Park Circle
Birmingham, AL 15223

Date: March 27, 19--
Terms: 2/15, n/30
Acct.: No. 34-2845
Freight: FOB Destination

Catalog No.	Quantity	Unit Price	Amount
C-423	17	89.45	$
B-679	13	115.75	$
GG-98	14	78.35	$
H-562	8	35.98	$
		NET PRICE	$
		CASH DISCOUNT	$
		CASH PRICE	$

156

ASSIGNMENT 14.2 **Computing Cash Discount**

1. Roberts Electronics sold merchandise to Simon's Shop on March 4 with a net price of $384.76. Cash discount terms were 3/10, n/30. If the invoice is paid on March 9, how much will Roberts Electronics receive as the cash price for the invoice?

$ _____

2. Rembrook and Associates received an invoice dated August 8 with a net price of $312.80 and cash discount terms of 2/10 EOM, n/90. (a) What was the last day that the invoice could have been paid and still have been subject to the cash discount? (b) What was the due date for the invoice? (c) If the invoice was paid on September 3, what was the cash price? (d) If the invoice was paid on September 15, what was the cash price?

(a) _____

(b) _____

(c) $ _____

(d) $ _____

3. Maple Products purchased merchandise with a net price of $478.24 (including freight charges of $36.00). The invoice date was October 29 with terms of 3/10, 2/30, n/45 EOM. What was the cash price to be paid if the invoice was paid on each of the following dates? (a) November 3, (b) November 7, and (c) November 20.

(a) $ _____

(b) $ _____

(c) $ _____

4. Fulmer Enterprises ships merchandise to customers in the United States and several foreign countries. A discount of 7 1/2% is offered to customers who pay within 30 days from the date of the invoice. A recent invoice dated February 11 was received by the Ramrod Corporation with a net price of $1,760.80, including freight charges of $30.00. Assume that the invoice was paid on March 1. (a) How much was the cash discount? (b) How much was the cash price including freight charges? (c) What was the last date that the invoice could be paid and still be subject to the cash discount?

(a) $ _____

(b) $ _____

(c) _____

5. Beacon Unlimited has cash discount terms of 3/10, 2/20, n/45. On an invoice to Abel Co. dated June 16 for $2,340.20, how much will be due if the invoice is paid on (a) June 22, (b) June 30, and (c) July 31?

(a) $ _____

(b) $ _____

(c) $ _____

6. Ramsey's Chair Factory sent merchandise to the Freemore Furniture Store with an invoice date of April 15, cash discount terms of 3/10, n/30, and a net price of $2,986.40. Freight charges of $50 were included in the net price. They returned merchandise costing $175 to Ramsey's on April 20. Compute the (a) cash discount on April 23 and (b) amount of the check that should have been written on April 23.

(a) $ _____

(b) $ _____

7. Bardow's Department Store sent an invoice with an October 13 date and a total net price of $12,713.48 to Wade Bargers. Terms were 11/10 EOM, 7/30 EOM. The bill was paid on November 23. Compute the (a) last date to receive the 11% discount, (b) last date to receive the 7% discount, (c) amount of the cash discount on November 23, and (d) cash price on November 23.

(a) _____

(b) _____

(c) $ _____

(d) $ _____

8. The House of Dave sent an invoice dated January 23 for $85.20 with terms of 3/10, n/30. (a) What would the cash discount price be if the bill was paid on February 1? (b) What amount will be due if the invoice is paid on February 5?

(a) $ _____

(b) $ _____

158

TRADE DISCOUNTS

Many manufacturers and suppliers of merchandise provide a catalog that includes a description and list or catalog price for each item. This price is often the suggested retail or selling price. Stores buying the merchandise for resale are provided a separate discount sheet showing a *trade discount* from the list price. In this chapter, you will learn how to compute the trade discount and how to determine the price that retailers are charged for merchandise purchased from manufacturers and suppliers.

Overview of Trade Discounts

Manufacturers, wholesalers, and other suppliers provide a catalog that lists information about the various products they have available for sale. The *trade discount* is a reduction in list price allowed to dealers in the same line of business or trade. The amount to be paid after the trade discount is deducted is the *net price*. A *cash discount* may be provided in addition to the trade discount to encourage prompt payment.

Owners and managers should be aware of suppliers that offer large trade discounts. The trade discount decreases the amount actually required to purchase the merchandise. Trade discounts may be stated as single discount rates or as a chain or series of two or more discount rates. Trade discounts are based on the list price of merchandise. Freight charges, if any, should be deducted from the invoice before computing the trade discount.

Computing a Single Trade Discount

The trade discount may be quoted as a single rate. The base list price is then reduced by the amount of the discount to compute the final net price. The basic formula (*Base* × *Rate*) = *Amount* can be used here, as shown in Example 15.1.

EXAMPLE Computing trade discount and net price

15.1

Problem: Merkle Wholesale Distributors sells merchandise with a $1,200 list price and a single trade discount of 40%. What will be the trade discount and net price for this order?

Solution: **Step 1.** Find the trade discount.

$$\text{(Base)} \times \text{(Rate)} = \text{(Amount)}$$
$$\text{List price} \times \text{Trade discount rate} = \text{Trade discount}$$
$$\$1,200.00 \times 0.40\ (40\%) = \$480.00$$

Step 2. Find the net price.

$$\text{List price} - \text{Trade discount} = \text{Net price}$$
$$\$1,200.00 - \$480.00 = \$720.00$$

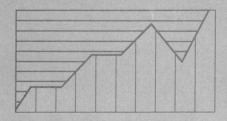

Computing Net Price: Complement Method

The *complement method* provides an alternative computation for finding the net price. In percentage terms, list price represents the whole or base (100%), and the net price represents the amount left after the trade discount rate has been subtracted. In other words, after deducting a trade discount of 40%, the net price (60%) equals the rate charged. To illustrate this method, merchandise with a list price of $1,200.00 and a trade discount of 40% will leave a net price of $720 as computed by the steps shown in Example 15.2.

EXAMPLE   **Computing complement trade discount rate**

15.2

Problem: Merkle Wholesale Distributors sells merchandise with a $1,200 list price and a single trade discount of 40%. What will be the complement trade discount rate and net price for this order?

Solution: **Step 1.** Find the complement trade discount rate.

1.00 − Trade discount rate = Net price rate
1.00 −   0.40   =   0.60 (60%)

Step 2. Find the net price.

List price × Net price rate = Net price
$1,200   ×   0.60   = $720.00

Notice that the same net price amount ($720.00) was obtained using either the regular method in the previous example or the complement method used in this example.

Computing Net Price Using a Series of Trade Discounts

Suppliers may decide to offer two or more trade discounts to encourage companies to purchase slow-moving items, for promotional purposes, or to sell larger orders. Trade discounts are often written as a series, such as 25/20/5, or 25% less 20% less 5%. The first discount is deducted from the list price to compute the first net price. The second discount is deducted from the first net price to obtain the second net price. The third discount is deducted from the second net price to obtain the third or final net price in this example. Assume a list price of $180 and 25/20/5 as the trade discount series being offered. The final net price should be rounded to the nearest cent. However, calculations made before the final net price should be rounded to four places. See Example 15.3.

EXAMPLE

15.3

Problem: An invoice shows a $180.00 list price with 25/20/5 as the trade discount series being offered. What is the final net price, rounded to the nearest cent?

Solution:

List Price	$180.00
First Trade Discount ($180 × 0.25 (25%))	− 45.00
First Net Price	135.00
Second Trade Discount ($135 × 0.20 (20%))	− 27.00
Second Net Price	108.00
Third Trade Discount ($108 × 0.05 (5%))	− 5.40
Third and Final Net Price	$102.60

In Example 15.3, $102.60 is the amount due after the series of three trade discounts has been given. Suppliers often offer both trade and cash discounts. Cash discounts, if any, are based on the final net price ($102.60 in this example) and provide an additional deduction for prompt payment.

To illustrate, the trade discounts of 25/20/5, plus a cash discount of 5%, will result in an additional discount of $5.13 ($102.60 × 0.05).

● **Complete Assignment 15.1** ●

Computing an Equivalent Single Discount

In the preceding example, three trade discounts were applied, one at a time, to determine the final net price. Several methods can be used to compute a single discount rate that is equivalent to the series of discounts. Three of these methods are discussed in this section. A procedure similar to the one used above can be used, except the value 1.00 always replaces the list price in the computation. The final percent computed represents the final *net price*. To obtain the equivalent single discount rate, the final percent must be subtracted from 1.00.

EXAMPLE

15.4

Problem: An invoice offers 25/20/5 as the series of trade discounts. What is the single equivalent discount for this series?

(Solution on following page)

Solution: **Step 1.**   Find the net price equivalent percentage.

List Price (always use 1.00)	1.00
First Discount (1.00 × 0.25)	−0.25
First Reduced Percentage (1.00 − 0.25)	0.75
Second Discount (0.75 × 0.20)	−0.15
Second Reduced Percentage (0.75 − 0.15)	0.60
Third Discount (0.60 × 0.05)	−0.03
Net Price Equivalent Percentage (0.60 − 0.03)	0.57

Step 2.   Find the single equivalent discount of the series, 25/20/5.

	Net price equivalent		Single equivalent
1.00 −	percentage	=	discount
1.00 −	0.57	=	0.43 (43%)

After the single equivalent discount rate has been determined, computations for the trade discount and final net price are fairly easy, as shown in Example 15.5.

EXAMPLE

15.5

Problem: Assume that the above trade discount series (25/20/5) is offered for a $180.00 list price. What are the trade discount and net price?

Solution: **Step 1.**   Find the single equivalent discount.
Note: Use the steps shown in Example 15.4. Based on that example, 0.43 was computed as the single equivalent discount.

Step 2.   Find the trade discount.

		Single equivalent		
List price	×	discount rate	=	Trade discount
$180	×	0.43	=	$77.40

Step 3.   Find the final net price.

List price	−	Trade discount	=	Net price
$180	−	$77.40	=	$102.60

The following example provides extra practice for computing a single equivalent discount rate. Although this series contains only two rates, the same procedures shown earlier are used.

EXAMPLE

15.6

Problem: The Usterholf Company offers a 30/15 trade discount series for an invoice with a $1,200 list price. What are the single equivalent discount percent, trade discount, and final net price?

Solution:

List Price Equivalent (always use 1.00)	1.00
First Discount (1.00 × 0.30)	−0.30
First Reduced Equivalent Rate (1.00 − 0.30)	0.70
Second Discount (0.70 × 0.15)	−0.105
Net Price Equivalent Rate (0.70 − 0.105)	0.595 (59.5%)
Equivalent Trade Discount Rate (1.00 − 0.595)	0.405 (40.5%)
Final Net Price Amount ($1,200 × 0.595)	$714.00
Trade Discount Amount ($1,200 × 0.405)	$486.00

Note: The equivalent single discount for 30% and 15% is 40.5%.

Shortcut Methods for Computing an Equivalent Single Discount

Two basic shortcut methods for computing an equivalent single discount rate are discussed below. The first is for trade discount series with only two rates, and the second is for trade discount series with two, three, or more rates.

Shortcut Method 1

This shortcut method can be used to find the equivalent single discount when the series of discounts contains *only two* rates of discount.

EXAMPLE

15.7

Problem: Robertson Suppliers offers a 25/15 trade discount series. Using the shortcut method, what is the single equivalent trade discount rate?

Solution: **Step 1.** Find the sum of the two rates.

$$.25 + .15 = .40$$

Step 2. Find the product of the two rates.

$$.25 \times .15 = .0375$$

(Continued on following page)

Step 3. Subtract the product in Step 2 from the sum in Step 1 to compute the single equivalent trade discount rate.

$$.40 - .0375 = .3625 \ (36.25\%)$$

Shortcut Method 2

A fairly simple shortcut method to obtain the single equivalent discount rate is outlined in Example 15.8. This method can be used with a series of two, three, or more discount rates.

EXAMPLE

15.8

Problem: Pyum Exporters offers a 25/15/10 trade discount series. Using the shortcut method, what is the single equivalent trade discount rate and the trade discount amount for an invoice with a $600 list price?

Solution: **Step 1.** Subtract each rate in the series from 1.00.

$$1.00 - 0.25 = 0.75$$
$$1.00 - 0.15 = 0.85$$
$$1.00 - 0.10 = 0.90$$

Step 2. Find the rate representing the net price by multiplying the values obtained in Step 1.

$$0.75 \times 0.85 \times 0.90 = 0.57375 \text{ or } 57.375\%$$

Step 3. Find the single equivalent discount rate.

$$1.00 - \text{Rate from Step 2} = \text{Single equivalent rate}$$
$$1.00 - \qquad 0.57375 \qquad = \qquad 0.42625 \text{ or } 42.63\%$$

Step 4. Find the trade discount amount.

(Base)	×	(Rate)	=	(Amount)
List price	×	Equivalent rate	=	Trade discount
$600	×	0.42625	=	$255.75

Shortcut methods are designed to save time and reduce errors. The longer methods introduced in the first part of this chapter give the same results. The shortcut methods are much easier when working with computers, however, because a single formula can be designed to make desired computations.

● **Complete Assignment 15.2** ●

● **Complete Assignment 15.3** ●

ASSIGNMENT 15.1 Trade Discount Applications

1. Compute the trade discount and the net price amounts for each of the following invoices. The first item is completed as an example.

Invoice No.	List Price	Trade Discount Rate	Trade Discount Amount	Net Price Amount
	$ 850.00	.09	$76.50	$773.50
1	650.00	.08	$ _____	$ _____
2	1,600.00	0.125	$ _____	$ _____
3	960.00	0.30	$ _____	$ _____
4	545.00	0.20	$ _____	$ _____
5	675.00	0.35	$ _____	$ _____

2. Use the complement method to compute the net price for each of the following invoices. The first item is completed as an example.

Invoice No.	List Price	Trade Discount Rate	Net Price Complement Percent	Net Price Amount
	$ 850.00	0.09	91%	$773.50
1	860.00	0.20	80%	$ 688.00
2	1,640.00	0.35	45%	$ 416.00
3	4,875.00	0.40	61%	$ 2,925.00
4	1,583.00	0.25	75%	$ 1,187.25
5	855.00	0.30	70%	$ 598.50

3. Compute the net price for the following invoice for which a series of discounts was provided. Use the method discussed in Example 15.3. The Baker Company allows trade discounts of 25/20/5 on all purchases above $1,000. Complete the following schedule for a purchase with a list price of $1,600 to determine the net price.

List Price $ _____

First Trade Discount $ _____

First Net Price $ _____

Second Trade Discount $ _____

Second Net Price $ _____

Third Trade Discount $ _____

Final Net Price $ _____

4. A new discount sheet from Unique Products Unlimited shows that the company's new policy is to offer trade discounts of 40/20/10. How much will the net price be for an anticipated purchase of $6,000?

$ _____

5. Assume that you determine that another supplier, Paradise Importers, offers the same merchandise as Unique Products Unlimited in the above problem. The merchandise also has a list price of $6,000, but a trade discount series of 20/40/10 is offered by Paradise Importers. (a) How much will the net price be if the merchandise is purchased from Paradise Importers? (b) How much can be saved by purchasing the merchandise from Unique Products Unlimited?

(a) $ _____

(b) $ _____

6. Marshall Wholesalers offers merchandise with trade discounts of 20/10. In addition, customers with list price amounts over $1,000 receive an additional 10% discount on the amount exceeding $1,000. An invoice has a list price of $1,600. (a) Compute the amount of the trade discount based only on the 20/10 trade discount series. (b) Compute the amount of the extra cash discount provided for the amount over $1,000. (c) Compute the amount of the total trade discount. (d) Compute the net price.

(a) $ _____

(b) $ _____

(c) $ _____

(d) $ _____

166

ASSIGNMENT 15.2 Computing Trade Discounts: Equivalent Rates

1. Compute the net price equivalent discount rate and single equivalent discount rate for each of the following series of trade discounts. Use the method that is explained in Example 15.4. The first item is completed as an example.

Invoice No.	Trade Discount Series	Net Price Equivalent Rate	Single Equivalent Discount Rate
	30/10/10	56.7	43.3
1	40/20/10	_____	_____
2	40/30/5	_____	_____
3	40/15/10	_____	_____
4	20/20/10	_____	_____
5	30/10	_____	_____

2. The Brossnax Jewelry Supply Company offered merchandise with a trade discount of 30/20/10. An invoice had a list price of $6,300. (a) Compute the single equivalent trade discount rate. (b) Compute the amount of the net price. (c) Compute the amount of the trade discount.

(a) _____

(b) $ _____

(c) $ _____

3. Use one of the shortcut methods to compute the single equivalent discount rate in Problem 2 above. If your rates are not the same, make computations for both methods again to determine which one is correct.

4. The Austin Automotive Parts Store offers merchandise with trade discount terms of 20/10 and cash discount terms of 2/10, n/30. The list price for Invoice No. 2688, dated October 11, showed merchandise purchases of $648 plus $16.22 for freight charges. Payment was made on October 20. Compute the (a) amount of the trade discount, (b) amount of the cash discount, and (c) amount needed to pay the bill.

(a) $ _____

(b) $ _____

(c) $ _____

5. The spreadsheet format shown below can be used to compute the single discount equivalent rate for a trade discount series, trade discount amount, and final net price. Totals for trade discount amount and final net price (Columns E and F) should also be computed. As with other spreadsheet problems, you can use manual methods, an electronic calculator, or microcomputer spreadsheet software depending on resources available and directions from your instructor. Regardless, compute the needed values and enter the answers in the appropriate cell addresses on the spreadsheet. The first set of answers (Row 7) has been computed for you.

	A	B	C	D	E	F	G
1	Aschew and Associates		TRADE	DISCOUNT	COMPUTATIONS		
2	==						
3			Trade	Single	Trade	Final	
4	Invoice	List	Discount	Discount	Discount	Net	
5	No.	Price	Terms	Equivalent	Amount	Price	
6	==						
7	1021	850.00	10/20	.28	238.00	612.00	
8	1022	1,000.00	10/10				
9	1023	600.00	5/10				
10	1024	350.00	30				Spreadsheet
11	1025	400.00	25				Analysis
12	1026	1,200.00	10/25				
13	1027	600.00	5/10/10				
14	1028	800.00	5/10/10				
15	1029	900.00	10/5				
16	1030	740.00	35				
17	--						
18	Total	7,440.00	xxxxxxxxxxxxxxxxxxxxxxxxx				
19	==						
20	!!						

ASSIGNMENT 15.3 Computing Trade Discounts: Complete Invoice

1. Rogue Wholesale Suppliers offers merchandise for resale in retail outlets. Complete the following invoice to show payment of the bill on April 11. (Round all amounts to 2 decimal places.)

Invoice No. 87

To: Winston Department Store
5993 Elmore Avenue   Date: April 5, 19—
Paducah, KY 42001   Terms: 2/10, n/30

Quantity	Description	Unit Price	Amount	Net Amount
18	Delta Air Pumps	$17.28	$ 311.04	
15	Misong Automatic Air Pumps	34.16	$ 512.40	
10	Beta Air Jackets	15.28	$ 152.80	
	TOTAL		$ 976.24	
	LESS 20/10 TRADE DISCOUNTS		$ -274.24	
	NET PRICE			$ 702.00
16	Gloss-More Reading Lamps	41.48	$ 663.68	
18	Teak Floor Lamps	92.46	$ 1,664.28	
15	Brass Table Lamps	78.60	$ 1,170.00	
	TOTAL		$ 3,497.96	
	LESS 30/20 TRADE DISCOUNTS		$ 1,539.00	
	NET PRICE			$ 1,959.00
	INVOICE NET PRICE TOTAL			$ 2,661.00
	LESS CASH DISCOUNT			$ 53.22
	CASH PRICE			$ 2,607.78

2. Daniel's of California sells health and beauty products to retail outlets around the country. Compute the following invoice to show payment of the invoice on November 8. (Round all amounts to 2 decimal places.)

Invoice No. 683–8732

To: Ashley Drug Store
1839 Wyman Street
Dallas, TX 79402

Date: October 10, 19—
Terms: 2/10 EOM, n/60
Ship via: Truck

Quantity	Catalog No.	Description	Unit Price	Amount	Net Amount
18 dozen	X-711	Hold-It Hair Spray	$12.50	$	
15 dozen	X-815	Jet Conditioner	12.60	$	
16 dozen	X-910	Klean Soft Shampoo	12.75	$	
		TOTAL		$	
		LESS 5/10/10 TRADE DISCOUNT		$	
		NET PRICE			$
20	P-016	Super-P Blow Dryer	$32.75	$	
15	P-112	Perk Curling Iron	25.80	$	
		TOTAL		$	
		LESS 5/10 TRADE DISCOUNT		$	
		NET PRICE			$
6	D-172	Exercise Belt	$15.50	$	
8	D-184	Power Pull Exerciser	28.75	$	
10	D-192	Strength Tester	17.00	$	
		TOTAL		$	
		LESS 20/10/5 TRADE DISCOUNT		$	
		NET PRICE			$
		INVOICE NET PRICE TOTAL			$
		LESS CASH DISCOUNT			$
		CASH PRICE			$

170

MARKUP ON PURCHASES

Many companies are engaged in a business that buys merchandise at one price and sells the merchandise for a higher price. The difference between the selling price and the cost price is the *markup*. Computation of markup is important because markup must be sufficient to pay expenses such as salaries, rent, and utilities while making a profit and yet remain low enough to be competitive with similar businesses offering the same type of merchandise. Material in this chapter shows you how markup is computed.

Overview of Markup

Whether the business concern is a *retail store* selling merchandise to the general public or a *wholesale business* selling merchandise to other businesses for resale, the goal is to maintain markup sufficient to cover cost of the product, related expenses, and desired profit. *Markup*, the difference between the cost of purchasing or manufacturing the product and the sales price of the product, is also called *gross profit* or *markon*. The relationship between selling price, cost, and markup is expressed in the equations in Example 16.1.

EXAMPLE   **Selling price, cost, markup relationship**
_____

16.1

> 1. Selling price − Cost = Markup (Gross profit)
> 2. Cost + Markup = Selling price
> 3. Selling price − Markup = Cost

Example 16.2 illustrates each of these three equations.

EXAMPLE   **Computation of markup, selling price, and cost**
_____

16.2

1. Assume that a product costing $30 sells for $45. Markup is computed as follows:
   $45 − $30 = $15

2. Assume that a company desired a markup of $15 on a product costing $30. Selling price is computed as follows:
   $30 + $15 = $45

3. Assume a selling price of $45 and a markup of $15. Cost is computed as follows:
   $45 − $15 = $30

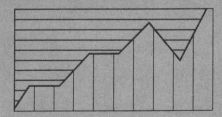

For computational purposes, markup is usually stated as a decimal or percent rate. Businesses may base the markup rate on the *cost price* or the *selling price.* Both types of computations are illustrated in the following section.

Computing Markup Based on Cost

Computing markup based on the cost price is fairly easy because the seller knows the cost of the product. The markup rate must be sufficient to cover the cost plus related expenses (salaries, rent, and similar items), make a profit, and still be competitive with prices offered by similar businesses.

When using cost price as a basis for markup computation, cost is the base (100%). Markup is added to the cost to determine the selling price. Stated in percentage terms with a markup of 20%, cost equals 100%, markup equals 20%, and selling price equals 120% (100% + 20%). Example 16.3 shows computations of markup amount and selling price for an item costing $8.50 (base) with a markup rate of 20%.

EXAMPLE

16.3

Problem: The Novelty Shoppe purchased a new toy for $8.50. The store plans a 20% markup prior to selling the product. What are the markup and selling price of each product?

Solution: **Step 1.** Find the markup amount.

Cost × Markup rate = Markup
$8.50 × 0.20 = $1.70

Step 2. Find the selling price.

Cost + Markup = Selling price
$8.50 + $1.70 = $10.20

If the cost and selling price are known, the markup rate can be computed by dividing the markup by the cost of the product, as shown in Example 16.4.

EXAMPLE

16.4

Problem: A product cost $4.80. The selling price is $6.12. The markup is $1.32 ($6.12 − $4.80). What is the markup rate? (Amount / Base = Rate)

Solution: Markup / Cost = Markup rate
$1.32 / $4.80 = 0.275 (27.5%)

● **Complete Assignment 16.1** ●

Computing Markup Based on Selling Price

Most retail stores base the markup rate on the selling price. Using this method, the selling price is the base representing 100%. The markup rate represents the portion of the sales price that is markup. As in previous illustrations, the selling price minus the markup equals cost. Stated in percentage terms, with a markup rate of 25% based on a base selling price, selling price amount equals 100%, markup equals 25%, and cost equals 75% (100% − 25%).

Computing markup amount and cost price   EXAMPLE
16.5

Problem: The Sports Center sells binoculars for $42.00 with a markup rate of 30% based on selling price. What are the markup amount and cost price?

Solution: **Step 1.** Find the markup amount.

(Base) × (Rate) = (Amount)
Selling price × Markup rate = Markup
$42.00 × 0.30 = $12.60

Step 2. Find the cost price.

Selling price − Markup = Cost
$42.00 − $12.60 = $29.40

The rate of markup based on selling price can be computed when both the cost and selling price are known. Markup rate equals the amount of the markup divided by the selling price, as shown in Example 16.6.

Computing markup and markup rate   EXAMPLE
16.6

Problem: A product costing $45.00 sells for $60.00. What are the markup and markup rate (based on selling price)?

Solution: **Step 1.** Find the markup amount.

Selling price − Cost = Markup
$60.00 − $40.00 = $20.00

Step 2. Find the markup rate (based on selling price).

(Amount) / (Base) = (Rate)
Markup / Selling price = Markup rate
$20.00 / $60.00 = 0.25 (25%)

When the cost and markup rate based on selling price are known, the selling price can be computed by dividing the cost by the rate representing cost, as shown in Example 16.7.

EXAMPLE

16.7

Problem: The Urban Department Store purchased a new line of wrist watches costing $120.00 each, and the store desires a markup of 60% based on selling price. What are the rates representing cost and selling price of the watches?

Solution: **Step 1.**   Find the rate representing cost.

100% − Markup rate = Cost rate
100% −   60%   = 40% (0.40)

Step 2.   Find the selling price.

 Cost / Cost rate = Selling price
$120.00 / 0.40 (40%) = $300.00

In Example 16.7, notice that 40% of the selling price represents cost and that 60% of the selling price represents markup. In this example, the selling price represents 100%.

● **Complete Assignment 16.2** ●

● **Complete Assignment 16.3** ●

ASSIGNMENT 16.1   Markup Applications

1. Find the markup for each of the following items. The first item is completed as an example.

Item	Selling Price	Cost	Markup
	$180.00	$160.00	$20.00
1	18.00	12.00	$ _____
2	5.35	4.18	$ _____
3	125.00	97.25	$ _____
4	79.15	42.79	$ _____
5	84.16	76.40	$ _____

2. Compute the selling price for each of the following items. The first item is completed as an example.

Item	Cost	Markup	Selling Price
	$10.00	$ 2.40	$12.40
1	8.60	1.20	$ _____
2	14.28	3.79	$ _____
3	87.30	15.20	$ _____
4	1.88	0.27	$ _____
5	5.48	1.22	$ _____

3. Compute the cost of each of the following items. The first item is completed as an example.

Item	Selling Price	Markup	Cost
	$14.20	$ 2.00	$12.20
1	5.60	1.20	$ _____
2	81.65	16.85	$ _____
3	3.80	0.76	$ _____
4	1.69	0.32	$ _____
5	14.65	3.15	$ _____

4. A sweater cost $35.50 and sold for $48.50. What was the markup on the sweater?

$ _____

5. A radio costing $28.75 was marked to sell for $37.99. What was the markup on the radio?

$ _____

6. A baseball glove costing $32 had a markup of $12.80. What was the selling price of the glove?

$ _____

7. A clothes dryer cost the retail store $250.00. A 30% markup rate was desired. (a) What was the markup? (b) What was the selling price?

(a) $ _____

(b) $ _____

8. A color television cost $325.00 when purchased from the wholesaler. The retail store desired a markup rate of 40%. (a) What was the markup? (b) What was the selling price?

(a) $ _____

(b) $ _____

9. Best Breakfast Foods, Inc. is able to manufacture Good Morning Breakfast Cereal for $5.60 per case. The cereal is sold to retail food stores for $8.12 per case. (a) How much is the markup? (b) What is the markup rate?

(a) $ _____

(b) _____

176

ASSIGNMENT 16.2 Markup Based on Selling Price

1. Compute the cost for each of the following items when markup rate is based on selling price. The first item is completed as an example.

	A B	Item	C	Markup Rate	D	E	Selling Price	F	G	Cost	H
1		Item		Markup Rate			Selling Price			Cost	
2		========		================			===============			========	
3				0.40			20.00			12.00	
4		--------		----------------			---------------			--------	
5		1		0.25			425.80			*319.80*	
6		--------		----------------			---------------			--------	
7		2		0.20			36.50			*29.20*	
8		--------		----------------			---------------			--------	
9		3		0.35			14.80			*9.62*	
10		--------		----------------			---------------			--------	
11		4		0.45			17.80				
12		--------		----------------			---------------			--------	
13		5		0.60			4.50				
14		========		================			===============			========	

2. Compute the markup percent based on selling price for each of the following items. The first item is completed as an example.

	A B	Item	C	Cost	D	E	Selling Price	F	G	Markup Rate	H
1		Item		Cost			Selling Price			Markup Rate	
2		========		======			===============			============	
3				25.00			40.00			37.5	
4		--------		------			---------------			------------	
5		1		180.00			240.00			*25.*	
6		--------		------			---------------			------------	
7		2		4.20			5.00			*16*	
8		--------		------			---------------			------------	
9		3		6.12			8.00			*24*	
10		--------		------			---------------			------------	
11		4		10.22			14.00				
12		--------		------			---------------			------------	
13		5		6.00			8.00				
14		========		======			===============			============	

177

3. Compute the selling price for each of the following items. The markup rate is based on selling price. The first item is completed as an example.

Item	Cost	Markup Rate	Selling Price
	$ 70.00	65%	$200.00
1	45.00	25%	$ _____
2	180.00	40%	$ _____
3	6.30	30%	$ _____
4	20.30	27.5%	$ _____
5	4.00	20%	$ _____

4. The Animal House of Fun sold dog beds for $32.50. This amount included a 20% markup based on selling price. (a) How much was the markup? (b) What was the cost price?

(a) $ _____

(b) $ _____

5. The Ace Hardware Store sold hammers for $18.00 that cost $13.50. (a) How much was the markup? (b) What was the markup rate based on sales price?

(a) $ _____

(b) _____

6. The Allbright Jewelry Store sold bracelets for $16 that cost $9.04. (a) How much was the markup? (b) What was the markup rate based on sales price?

(a) $ _____

(b) _____

7. Cooper Importers bought decorative pictures for $18.00. A 40% markup rate based on selling price is desired. What should the sales price be to provide the desired markup?

$ _____

8. The Sports Center received a new supply of sports warmup jackets costing $37.80 each. A 30% markup rate based on selling price is desired for this product. (a) What should the sales price be to provide the desired markup? (b) How much should the markup be?

(a) $ _____

(b) $ _____

178

ASSIGNMENT 16.3 **Markup Applications**

1. The Old South Shop manufactures fine candles. Chocolate Delight Bars cost $8.00 per box to manufacture. The company desires a markup of $4.00 per box. (a) If markup is based on cost, what will be the markup rate? (b) If markup is based on selling price, what will be the markup rate? (c) Which method results in the higher stated rate?

    (a) _____

    (b) _____

    (c) _____

2. Novelties of Distinction decided that salaries, rent, and other related expenses equaled 20% of sales ($120,000) for last year. This year's sales are also expected to be $120,000, with markup based on 35% of the sales price. Assume the above forecast is accurate. (a) How much of the $120,000 in sales represents markup? (b) How much will the net profit (markup minus expenses) be for this year? (c) What is the cost price of the merchandise?

    (a) $ _____

    (b) $ _____

    (c) $ _____

3. The Bono Card Shop desires a markup of $80,000 for this year's sales. If sales are $200,000 for the year, (a) what markup rate based on cost is needed to obtain the desired markup? (b) What markup rate based on selling price is needed to obtain the desired markup?

    (a) _____

    (b) _____

4. Queen Appliances needs a markup of $100,000 to break even for the year. Sales for the year were $400,000. (a) What markup rate based on sales price is needed to break even? (b) What markup rate based on sales price is needed to make a profit of $50,000 in addition to expenses of $100,000?

    (a) _____

    (b) _____

5. The Fuller Furniture Center uses a markup of 40% based on cost for all furniture items. Compute the sales price for each of the following items:

    (a) Sofa costing $825 $ _____

    (b) Chair costing $375 $ _____

    (c) Love seat costing $750 $ _____

6. Carie's Office Supply Company is considering adding a new line of desk pads to its inventory. The cost prices and suggested retail prices for three products are shown below.

Product A: Cost = $25.00 and Sales Price = $37.50

Product B: Cost = $28.00 and Sales Price = $41.58

Product C: Cost = $20.00 and Sales Price = $32.00

(a) Which product will result in the highest dollar markup? (b) Which product will result in the highest markup rate based on cost? (c) Which product will result in the lowest markup rate based on cost? (d) Which product will result in the lowest dollar markup?

(a) _____ B _____

(b) _____ C _____

(c) _____

(d) _____ C _____

7. The Bush Bedding Supply Company marks up items to sell for 175% of the cost price. Bath towels cost $8 each. (a) What must the selling price be to produce the desired markup rate? (b) How much will the markup be? (c) What is the markup rate based on selling price?

(a) $ _____

(b) $ _____

(c) _____

8. A retail store outlet is considering a markup rate of 40% based on cost or a markup rate of 50% based on selling price. The store purchases an item for $48. (a) Which markup method will result in the higher selling price? (b) What will the selling price be using the method that results in the higher selling price?

(a) _____

(b) $ _____

180

MARKDOWN ON SALE PRICE

Businesses may reduce the selling price of merchandise for special sales promotions or to encourage sales of slow-moving items. This chapter illustrates computations used by businesses to mark down, discount, or reduce the selling price of merchandise.

Overview of Markdown

A *markdown* is a reduction in the listed selling price of merchandise. Markdown is stated as a percent of the selling price, such as a markdown rate of 20%. Businesses mark up the price of merchandise to determine the selling price, then mark down the selling price to indicate that a discount or special price is being offered. When markup and markdown are computed in the same problem, markup is always computed first. While many businesses offer special discounts, other businesses sometimes inflate the selling price prior to the markdown so that buyers will think they are receiving a special price. In fact, the marked-down price may not be lower than the regular price offered by other suppliers for the same merchandise; in some cases, it may even be higher. Buyers should be aware that the original sales price used in some sales promotions may be a suggested list price or other inflated price and not the regular price charged for the product.

Computing the Amount of Markdown

Businesses often provide sales promotional material that shows the price before and after the markdown (usually called discount in sales promotion literature). The amount of the markdown, the difference between the two amounts, is computed as shown in Example 17.1.

EXAMPLE   Computing markdown amount

17.1

Problem: The Vestal Clothing Store normally sells a shirt for $14.30. The shirt is placed on sale for $11.10. What is the markdown amount?

Solution: Regular price − Discount price = Markdown
               $14.30   − $11.10   = $3.20

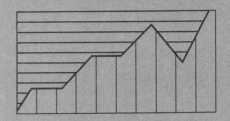

Computing Markdown Stated as a Percent

The markdown is often stated in percent terms as a reduction in the selling price. For example, a product may be promoted as being offered at a 15% discount. The following equations should be used when the markdown is stated as a percent. Once again, the basic formula (Base × Rate = Amount) applies to many examples in this chapter.

EXAMPLE 17.2   Computing sale price based on markdown percent

Problem: The Dinstul Variety Store normally sells a calculator for $15.95. During a special sale, the price is marked down 30%. What is the sale price?

Solution: **Step 1.** Find the markdown amount.

(Base)	×	(Rate)	=	(Amount)
Regular price	×	Markdown rate	=	Markdown
$15.95	×	0.30	=	$4.79 (rounded)

Step 2. Find the sale price.

Regular price − Markdown = Sale price
$15.95   − $4.79   = $11.16

● **Complete Assignment 17.1** ●

Computing Markdown Rate

When the regular selling price and the marked down price are known, the markdown rate can easily be determined. Assume a regular selling price of $15 and a marked down price of $9. The procedures shown in Example 17.3 can be used to compute the markdown rate given these two factors using the formula (Amount / Base = Rate).

EXAMPLE 17.3   Computing markdown rate

Problem: A particular item normally selling for $15 is offered for a marked down price of $9. What is the markdown rate?

Solution: Markdown / Regular price = Markdown rate
$6 ($15 − $9) / $15   =   .40 (40%)

Computing Markup and Markdown

Markup must be computed before computing markdown. The markup rate may be based on either the cost price or the selling price, but the markdown rate is *always* based on the selling price, as shown in Example 17.4.

EXAMPLE

17.4

Problem: Apex wrist watches cost the Baland Discount Store $150. The store has a practice of pricing the watches by adding 40% to the cost price. During a July 4 special sale, the watches are marked down 20% off the regular selling price. What are the regular selling price and sale price of the watches?

Solution: **Step 1.** Find the regular selling price.

Cost price + Markup amount = Regular price
$150   + $60 ($150 × 0.40) = $210

Step 2. Find the sale price.

Regular price − Markdown amount = Sale price
$210   − $42 ($210 × 0.20) = $168

To further illustrate, assume that a special group of table lamps is purchased at a cost of $65 with a markup of $48 per lamp. The lamps are promoted as being offered at a 30% markdown. The sale price is calculated as follows:

Step 1. $65.00 + $48.00 = $113.00 (regular selling price)

Step 2. $113.00 − $33.90 ($113 × .30) = $79.10 (sale price)

Note: The business still makes a gross profit of $14.90 ($79.90 − $65.00) with a gross profit rate of 22.92% ($14.90 ÷ $65.00).

● **Complete Assignment 17.2** ●

ASSIGNMENT 17.1 Markdown and Sale Price Applications

1. The Goonce Department Store decided to reduce each of five glassware items. Since these items had not been selling well, this discount was intended to improve sales of these items and to reduce the inventory level. Compute the sale price for each item. The first item is completed as an example.

A B 1 Item	C Regular Selling Price	D E F Markdown	G H Sale Price
2======	=====================	=========	============
3	37.80	6.15	31.65
4------	---------------------	---------	------------
5 1	42.75	7.30	35.45
6------	---------------------	---------	------------
7 2	40.29	7.30	
8------	---------------------	---------	------------
9 3	38.40	8.35	
10-----	---------------------	---------	------------
11 4	38.55	10.60	
12-----	---------------------	---------	------------
13 5	41.99	10.50	
14======	=====================	=========================

2. The Realprice Specialty Shop has overstocked several items of merchandise. In an effort to reduce the inventory level, the sale prices of these items were reduced. Compute the markdown and sale price for each item. (When computing discounts, round answers to the nearest cent.) The first item is completed as an example.

A B 1 Item	C Regular Selling Price	D E Markdown Rate	F G Markdown	H I J Sale Price
2======	=====================	=============	=========	============
3	35.60	.20	7.12	28.48
4------	---------------------	-------------	---------	------------
5 1	48.50	.10	4.85	43.65
6------	---------------------	-------------	---------	------------
7 2	165.75	.40		
8------	---------------------	-------------	---------	------------
9 3	87.95	.35		
10-----	---------------------	-------------	---------	------------
11 4	156.78	.38		
12-----	---------------------	-------------	---------	------------
13 5	55.75	.25		
14======	=====================	===

3. The All Occasion Gift Shop discounts Christmas cards by 60% during January each year. Style A normally sells for $5.40 per box, and Style B normally sells for $5.75 per box. How much will the sale price be for (a) Style A and (b) Style B?

(a) $ 2.16

(b) $ 2.30

4. The Brea TV Shop offered its 24-inch color television set at a 30% discount during the Easter Sale Days. The set normally sells for $599.60. How much were the (a) markdown and (b) sale price?

(a) $ _179.84_

(b) $ _419.72_

5. East Auto Sales marked down mid-size cars by 12% during the month of October to make space available for newer models. For a car with a list price of $8,875.95, what would be the (a) markdown and (b) sale price?

(a) $ _1,065.11_

(b) $ _7,810.04_

6. The Hartford Department Store purchased a special order of men's suits for their annual Spring Sale. The suits cost the store $80 each and were marked to sell for $150. During the sale, the suits were reduced 20%. (a) How much was the markdown? (b) How much was the sale price? (c) How much gross profit did the store make on each suit?

(a) $ _30.00_

(b) $ _$120.00_

(c) $ _40.00_

7. The Midtown Record Shop discounted top ten records by 10% during a sales promotion campaign. A customer purchased three records with the following regular selling prices: Record 1, $8.50; Record 2, $8.00; and Record 3, $8.80. (a) What was the total discount for the three records? (b) What was the total sale price for the three records?

(a) $ _____

(b) $ _____

8. Rick Brunson decided to buy a new AM/FM radio. Store A offered a radio for $85.50 with a 20% markdown. Store B offered the same quality radio for $92.40 with a 25% markdown. (a) Which store offered the lower price? (b) How much did Rick pay for the lower priced radio?

(a) _____

(b) $ _____

186

ASSIGNMENT 17.2 Markdown and Markdown Rate Applications

1. Compute the markdown percent for each of the following items. (Round percents to two decimal places.) The first item is completed as an example.

	Item	Regular Selling Price	Sale Price	Markdown Rate
		16.00	12.00	25.00%
	1	20.00	13.00	
	2	160.50	128.64	
	3	30.50	28.75	
	4	65.00	59.80	
	5	75.00	37.50	

2. Compute the regular selling price and sale price for each of the following items. (Round amounts to two decimal places.) The first item is completed as an example.

Item	Cost	Markup	Regular Price	Markdown	Sale Price
	40.00	25%	50.00	5%	47.50
1	50.75	40%		20%	
2	4.25	20%		10%	
3	1.26	50%		15%	
4	18.30	30%		18%	
5	2.48	25%		7%	

3. The United Beauty Supply Company provides supplies for hair care centers. The Holly Hills Beauty Salon purchased 10 cases of a new hair spray designed for active persons. The salon purchased the hair spray for $72 per case, which was $6 per can. The suggested retail price was $10 per can. If each can of hair spray was marked down from the list price to show a $2 gross profit, what was the markdown rate?

_20%_

4. The Grisham Corporation manufactures tennis rackets and other sports equipment. Perfect Touch tennis rackets cost $24 to manufacture with a regular selling price to retail stores of $36. During a special sale, the tennis rackets were offered by Grisham Corporation for 1/6 off the regular selling price. (a) What was the price offered to retail stores? (b) What was the profit rate based on cost after the discount?

(a) $ _29.62_

(b) _16%_   — 5.62

5. The Dan Crocker Garden Center purchased rose bushes from a local nursery for $6 per plant. The plants were marked up 100% based on the cost price. During the summer, the plants were offered for sale at a 25% discount. What were the (a) regular selling price, (b) sale price, and (c) gross profit percent based on cost after the markdown?

(a) $ _____

(b) $ _____

(c) _____

6. Randy Rent-A-Car offered cars at a 20% discount from the regular rental price during the July 4 weekend. A compact car normally rents for $38 per day with unlimited mileage. During the holiday weekend, (a) how much discount will be provided, and (b) how much will be saved over the regular rental rate for the three-day weekend?

(a) $ _7.60_

(b) $ _20%_

7. The Village Travel Agency offers a special vacation package for $780 per person. If two persons purchase the package, a 20% discount is given to each person. How much will each person save?

$ _____

8. T-Shirts Unlimited and T-Shirts Now stores each purchased a particular brand of shirt for $8. T-Shirts Unlimited marked up the shirts 25% based on cost, and T-Shirts Now marked up the shirts 50% based on cost. Each store advertised the brand at a 10% markdown. How much was saved by purchasing the shirt from T-Shirts Unlimited?

$ _____

188

COMMISSION ON SALES

People in sales and marketing areas often receive a *commission*, a specified amount of money for making each sale or a *commission rate* based on the sales amount for selling the product or service. In this chapter, you will learn ways to compute the commission for selling products or services.

Overview of Commission

Many salespersons receive a commission as payment for selling products or services. These persons may also receive a basic salary in addition to the commission (called *salary plus commission*), or they may receive only a commission (called *straight commission*) with no additional salary compensation. Real estate and advertising are examples of businesses where compensation is usually based on salary plus commission or straight commission. Many retail clerks also receive a commission on sales. Commission rate is usually stated as a percent of the sales amount.

Persons or businesses may also accept merchandise for resale from another person or business, which is called *consignment*. Persons or businesses, called *principals* or *consignors*, engage another business or person, called *commission merchant* or *consignee*, to act as an agent for selling items such as farm produce, auto parts, cotton, and dairy products. In return for selling the product, a commission is earned by the agent.

A unique feature of the principal/commission merchant arrangement is that title to the goods remains with the principal until sold. Any loss due to spoilage or breakage must be the responsibility of the principal. After selling the product, the commission merchant charges a commission. This commission is based on the total sales price or the *gross proceeds*. The amount, after deducting for advertising, storage, insurance, and similar items necessary to sell the product, is called the *net proceeds*. An *account sales invoice*, a detailed statement of sales and related charges, must be provided to the principal to account for the commission and the sale. The account sales invoice is prepared by the commission merchant and sent to the principal along with a check for the net proceeds.

Computing Salespersons' Commission

Salespersons may receive a commission. Returns are deducted from the amount of sales when computing the commission. The amount of commission is computed by multiplying the sales amount by the commission rate.

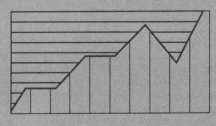

189

EXAMPLE

Computing commission on sales

18.1

Problem: Walter Plough is a salesperson for a company that pays a 6% commission rate. His sales last week were $7,200. What was his commission earned?

Solution: Sales × Commission rate = Commission earned
$7,200 ×   0.06 (6%)   = $432

Marketing representatives for products such as computers, life insurance, office equipment, household furniture, and pharmaceutical supplies often receive a *graduated commission rate* whereby the rate is increased as the sales amount is increased. For example, the commission may be 2% for the first $10,000 in sales and 3% for all sales in excess of $10,000. This serves as an incentive and increases the reward for greater efforts by salespersons.

Frances Cortez receives a 4% commission rate for the first $2,000 in sales, a 5% commission rate for sales from $2,001 to $4,000, and a 6% commission rate for sales above $4,000. During the most recent period, Ms. Cortez had sales of $5,000. Computation of her commission is shown in Example 18.2. Notice that sales times the commission rate equals the commission (Base × Rate = Amount).

EXAMPLE

Computing commission on sales

18.2

Problem: Frances Cortez receives a 4% commission rate for the first $2,000 in sales, a 5% commission rate for sales from $2,001 to $4,000, and a 6% commission rate for sales above $4,000. What will her commission be if sales are $5,000?

Solution: **Step 1.** Find the amount of commission on the first $2,000 in sales at a 4% commission rate.

Sales × Commission rate = Commission
$2,000 ×   0.04   = $80

Step 2. Find the commission on sales from $2,001 to $4,000 at 5%.

Sales × Commission rate = Commission
$2,000 ×   0.05   = $100

Step 3. Find the commission on sales above $4,000 at 6%.

Sales   × Commission rate = Commission
$1,000 ($5,000–$4,000) ×   0.06   = $60

Step 4. Find the sum of commissions from graduated levels to determine total commission earned.

Step 1 + Step 2 + Step 3 = Total commission
$80 + $100 + $60 = $240

● **Complete Assignment 18.1** ●

Computing Commission on Consignment Sales

The commission merchant normally receives a shipment of merchandise (on consignment) for sale. Remember that title to the merchandise remains with the principal until the merchandise is sold or returned by the commission merchant. The customary procedure, at first, sounds complicated, but it is really fairly simple. Simply stated, the commission merchant making the sale receives full payment (gross proceeds) when the goods are sold. The commission merchant deducts a commission based on gross proceeds, deducts amounts for related charges, and sends the remainder (net proceeds) to the principal. An account sales invoice is sent with a check for the net proceeds to show proof of the gross proceeds and related charges.

EXAMPLE

18.3

Problem: Donnelson and Brubaker, commission merchants, receive goods on consignment that are sold for $3,400. Freight ($30) and storage ($65) charges are incurred for the goods. The commission rate is 20%. What is the amount of net proceeds for this transaction?

Solution: **Step 1.** Find the commission amount.

Gross proceeds × Commission rate = Commission
   $3,400   ×   0.20   = $680

Step 2. Find the total of related charges.

Freight + Storage = Related charges
  $30   + $65   = $95

Step 3. Find the net proceeds amount.

Gross   Related   Net
proceeds − Commission − charges = proceeds
 $3,400   − $680   − $95   = $2,625

● **Complete Assignment 18.2** ●

ASSIGNMENT 18.1   Commission on Sales

1. Compute the commission for each of the following salespersons:

Salesperson	Sales	Commission Rate	Commission
John Glaze	$2,800.00	6%	$168.00
Esther Highgate	3,100.00	7%	$ _____
Naomi Jones	2,875.00	4%	$ _____
David Maybry	2,850.00	6 1/2%	$ _____
John Pitts	3,238.00	5 1/2%	$ _____
Charles Rolf	2,637.00	8%	$ _____

Note: Identify the base, rate, and amount before solving each of the following problems.

2. James Davis is an agent for the Carver Real Estate Company and works on his listings for a 2.75% straight commission. Last week he sold a house for $113,500. What was his sales commission?

$ _____

3. Edna Ivey works on a salary plus commission plan. Last week her salary was $250.00 plus a 4½% commission on sales of $7,920. What was her gross pay?

$ _____

4. Arthur Reed sold 13 sets of encyclopedias during the past week. If his commission was $48.50 per set, what was his gross pay?

$ _____

5. Novvel Rector works for a company that pays a commission of 7% on all sales up to $6,000 and 9% on all sales above $6,000. If his sales are $9,500, what is his commission?

$ _____

6. Milton Guthrie worked for Gurley's Furniture Showroom, Inc., with a sales quota of $1,800 per week. He was paid $335 per week plus a commission of 8% on all sales and an additional 2% on sales exceeding the quota. What was his gross pay if his sales for the week were $2,675?

$ _____

7. David Monger works for Dixie Carpet Sales, Inc. They pay a weekly salary of $485.00 plus a commission of 8% for all sales exceeding the quota. His territory carries a sales quota of $2,500 per week. What would his gross pay be on sales of $4,875.00?

$ _____

8. Diggons Auto Sales pays its employees $150.00 for each car sold. During the week, Sarah Dabbs sold 5 cars with total sales of $53,500. (a) What was her commission? (b) What was her commission rate?

(a) $ _____

(b) _____

9. A salesperson for the Greenwich Department Store received a commission of $822.50 for selling items that totalled $23,500. What was the commission rate?

_____

194

ASSIGNMENT 18.2 **Commission on Consignments**

1. A commission merchant sold goods held on consignment for $3,250 with the following related charges: freight, $50.00; storage, $60.00; and handling, $35.00. A commission of 7% was charged. What were the (a) commission and (b) net proceeds?

   (a) $ _____

   (b) $ _____

2. A principal sent goods to Lakefront Auto Parts with a total retail value of $3,875.00. The contract called for a commission of 4.4%. Lakefront charged $61.54 for freight and $11.60 for handling. (a) How much was the commission? (b) What were the net proceeds?

   (a) $ _____

   (b) $ _____

3. Fruit Basket, Inc. received 380 bags of apples with a retail sales price of $6.50 per bag. Related charges were freight, $75.00; spoilage, $53.00; and handling, $53.00. A commission of 8½% was charged. (a) How much was the commission? (b) What amount should Fruit Basket, Inc. send to the principal?

   (a) $ _____

   (b) $ _____

4. Demarco and Associates received 10 microcomputers on consignment with an average retail price of $4,995. Charges were as follows: freight, $120.00; storage, $130.00; and guarantee, 1% of gross proceeds. The commission rate was 15%. Assuming that the microcomputers sold for an average retail price of $4,995, what were the (a) total charges, (b) commission, and (c) net proceeds?

   (a) $ _____

   (b) $ _____

   (c) $ _____

5. Complete the following account sales invoice:

ACCOUNT SALES INVOICE			No. 56382-LM	

SOLD FOR THE ACCOUNT OF: Bates Battery Manufacturers
5100 Poplar Avenue
Memphis, TN 38117

Commission: 15%   Date: September 23, 19—

Model No.	Quantity	Cost Per Unit	Extension	Total
12V-28A	18	$47.20	$ _____	
12V-26A	24	56.44	$ _____	
8V-30A	8	52.75	$ _____	
8V-30B	12	50.48	$ _____	
			GROSS PROCEEDS	$ _____
		CHARGES: Commission	$ _____	
		Freight	$ 88.50	
		Storage	$150.00	
		Handling	$124.00	
		TOTAL CHARGES		$ _____
		NET PROCEEDS		$ _____

● **Complete Unit 4 Spreadsheet Applications** ●

196

UNIT 4   SPREADSHEET APPLICATION 1: Markup and Markup Rates

The following spreadsheet is used to compute the markup, markup rate based on selling price, and markup rate based on cost price. Totals for markup, selling price, and cost price amounts are also computed. The markup is computed by subtracting the cost price from the selling price. The markup rate based on selling price is computed by dividing the amount of markup by the base selling price. The markup rate based on cost price is computed by dividing the markup by the cost price. Enter your answers in the spaces provided on the spreadsheet.

	A	B	C	D	E	F	G	H	I	J	K
1	Beacon Stores				MARKUP AND MARKUP RATES						
2	==										
3									Markup Rate Based on		Markup Rate Based on
4	Item		Selling		Cost		Markup		Selling Price		Cost Price
5	Code		Price		Price		Amount				
6	-------		----------		----------		----------		---------------		-------------
7			200.00		150.00		50.00		25.00%		33.33%
8	A1		180.00		140.00						
9	A2		275.00		220.00						
10	A3		420.00		320.00						
11	A4		320.00		175.00						
12	A5		140.00		90.00						
13	A6		280.00		230.00						
14	A7		185.00		110.00						
15	A8		240.00		190.00						
16	A9		420.00		345.00						
17	A10		450.00		280.00						
18	-------		----------		----------		----------		---------------		-------------
19	Total								XXXXXXXXXXXXXX		XXXXXXXXXXXXX
20	======		==========		==========		==========		===============		=============

Refer to the completed spreadsheet above to answer the following questions:

1. What is the markup amount for Item A3? _____

2. What is the markup amount for Item A8? _____

3. What is the markup rate based on selling price for Item A5? _____

4. What is the markup rate based on cost price for Item A6? _____

5. What is the markup rate based on cost price for Item A10? _____

6. Which item had the highest markup rate based on selling price? _____

7. Which item had the lowest markup rate based on cost price? _____

8. What was the total of the markup amount column? _____

9. How many items had markup rates higher than 26.00% based on selling price? _____

10. How many items had markup rates lower than 50.00% based on cost price? _____

UNIT 4   SPREADSHEET APPLICATION 2: **Sales Commissions**

The following spreadsheet is used to determine commissions earned based on rates of 18%, 22%, 25%, and 30%. This information will let the company know the effect that these various rates will have on the amount of commission earned by the sales force. Totals are also computed for each sales and commission column. Commission is computed by multiplying the base *sales amount* by the commission rate. This rate will be 0.18 for Column E, 0.22 for Column G, and so forth.

```
            A      B      C      D      E      F      G      H      I      J      K
1   Koffman Variety Store              SALES COMMISSIONS
2   ===============================================================================
3                        Sales |Commission |Commission |Commission |Commission
4   Employee            Amount |        18% |        22% |        25% |        30%
5   --------- |--------- |---------- |---------- |---------- |----------
6   Abson         1,480 |           |           |           |
7   Baker         1,735 |           |           |           |
8   Cooke         1,800 |           |           |           |
9   Davis         1,575 |           |           |           |
10  Eisley        1,485 |           |           |           |
11  Getz          1,362 |           |           |           |
12  Houck         1,587 |           |           |           |
13  Jensen        1,438 |           |           |           |
14  Moody         1,372 |           |           |           |
15  Noonan          980 |           |           |           |
16  Poole         2,140 |           |           |           |
17  Wertz         1,900 |           |           |           |
18  --------- |--------- |---------- |---------- |---------- |----------
19  Total     |         |           |           |           |
20  ===============================================================================
```

Refer to the completed spreadsheet above to answer the following questions:

1. What was the commission for Baker based on a commission rate of 0.18?   _____

2. What was the commission for Getz based on a commission rate of 0.18?   _____

3. What was the commission for Jensen based on a commission rate of 0.22?   _____

4. What was the commission for Moody based on a commission rate of 0.25?   _____

5. What was the commission for Wertz based on a commission rate of 0.30?   _____

6. Which salesperson earned the highest amount of commission?   _____

7. Which salesperson earned the lowest amount of commission?   _____

8. What is the amount of difference between the total commission based on a com-   _____
   mission rate of 0.18 and the total commission based on a commission rate of 0.25?

9. What is the total of the sales amount column?   _____

10. How many salespersons had a commission amount greater than $300.00 based on   _____
    a commission rate of 0.18?

• Complete Unit 4 Self-Test •

UNIT 4 SELF-TEST **Marketing Mathematics**

Note: Identify base, rate, and amount before solving each of the following problems.

1. Annette Collins bought merchandise on August 14 with an invoice price of $425.86. Cash discount terms were 2/10, n/30. The invoice was paid on August 20. How much was the (a) cash discount and (b) net amount?

   (a) $ _____

   (b) $ _____

2. Crossnoe Printing Services has cash discount terms of 4/10, 2/20, n/45. On an invoice to Security Alarm Systems dated January 18 for $1,200, how much will be due if the invoice is paid (a) January 23, (b) January 31, and (c) February 18?

   (a) $ _____

   (b) $ _____

   (c) $ _____

3. Analytical Laboratories sells products with cash terms of 4/5, 2/10, n/20 EOM. The invoice amount was $680, and the date was February 5. What was the cash price to be received if the invoice was paid on each of the following dates: (a) February 8, (b) March 8, and (c) April 1?

   (a) $ _____

   (b) $ _____

   (c) $ _____

4. Lorentz Appliances bought merchandise with terms of 3/10, 2/15, n/30. An invoice for $760 was dated March 28. Compute the following items: (a) the last date of payment to receive the 3% discount, (b) the last date to receive the 2% discount, and (c) the last date to pay the full amount due.

   (a) _____

   (b) _____

   (c) _____

5. Compute the net price for an invoice showing a list price of $1,500 and trade discount terms of 5/20/10. Complete the schedule shown below to provide the solutions.

List Price $_____

First Trade Discount $_____

First Net Price $_____

Second Trade Discount $_____

Second Net Price $_____

Third Trade Discount $_____

Third and Final Net Price $_____

6. Quick Business Services offers trade discount terms of 40/20. How much is the net price for a list price of $5,000?

$_____

7. Future Brides Unlimited offers merchandise with trade discount terms of 20/10 and cash discount terms of 1/10, n/30. The list price for Invoice No. 1821, dated August 15, shows merchandise purchases of $500 plus $20 delivery charges. Payment was made on August 21. Compute the (a) amount of the trade discount, (b) amount of the cash discount, and (c) amount needed to pay the bill.

(a) $_____

(b) $_____

(c) $_____

8. A refrigerator cost $720.00 when purchased from the wholesaler. The retailer received a 30% markup based on cost. What were the (a) markup and (b) selling price?

(a) $_____

(b) $_____

9. An electric toaster costing $36.25 was marked to sell for $52.20. What were the (a) markup and (b) markup rate based on cost price?

(a) $_____

(b) _____

202

UNIT 4 SELF-TEST (continued)

10. The Book Depot sold a particular book for $20.80 that cost $16.00. (a) How much was the markup, and (b) what was the markup rate based on cost price?

    (a) $ _____

    (b) _____

11. The Ritz Jewelry Store sells anklets for $32 that cost $18.08. (a) How much is the markup, and (b) what is the markup rate based on sales price?

    (a) $ _____

    (b) _____

12. The House of Lights sells a "touch-on" table lamp for $120 that cost $90. (a) How much is the markup, and (b) what is the markup rate based on sales price?

    (a) $ _____

    (b) _____

13. Clothes of Distinction paid $16.96 for a new line of sweaters. A markup rate of 75% based on cost is desired. What will the sales price of the sweaters be with this markup?

    $ _____

14. A new sports car sold for $20,000, which provided a profit of $8,000. What was the markup rate based on (a) sales price and (b) cost price?

    (a) _____

    (b) _____

15. The Novelty Shoppe discounts Christmas cards by 75% during January each year. If cards normally sell for $6.80 per box, how much will the (a) discount and (b) sales price be?

(a) $ _____

(b) $ _____

16. The Turner Tire Store bought a line of nylon tires for $48 and then added a 50% markup based on cost. If the tires are then reduced 20%, what will the sales price be?

(a) $ _____

17. Nadine Kidd worked for $150 per week plus a commission equal to 8% of sales. If her sales for the week were $2,500, what was her salary for the week?

(a) $ _____

18. Leon Milligan receives a 6% commission rate on sales up to $3,500 and a 9% rate for sales in excess of $3,500. On sales of $5,200, how much commission would he earn?

(a) $ _____

19. William Miner earns $353 per week or a commission rate of 3½% of sales, whichever is greater. On sales of $12,500, how much would he earn for the week?

(a) $ _____

20. Allison Dickerson earns a 5% commission rate on sales up to $2,500 and a 7% rate for sales in excess of $2,500. On sales of $3,600, how much commission would she earn?

(a) $ _____

204

Accounting and Financial Mathematics

Accounting has been called the "heart of business" because much of the activity of a business concern relates directly or indirectly to the accounting area. Common mathematical computations relative to accounting and financial control are included in this unit. Computations relating to the important area of payroll accounting are illustrated here.

Some skills you can achieve in this unit include the following:

- **Determining gross pay for hourly and piece-rate employees.**
- **Determining overtime pay due employees.**
- **Completing a payroll register and worksheet.**
- **Using Internal Revenue Service (IRS) withholding tax tables and percentage methods to compute income tax deductions from gross pay.**
- **Using the percentage methods to compute income tax deductions.**
- **Using the tax table and formula method to compute payroll deductions for Social Security (FICA).**
- **Determining property tax rates and assessed valuation of real property.**
- **Computing property taxes due from business and individual property owners.**
- **Determining valuation of merchandise inventory using the specific identification, average cost, FIFO, LIFO, and lower of cost or market methods.**

(Continued on following page)

UNIT 5

- Computing cost of merchandise available for sale and merchandise turnover ratio.
- Comparing valuation methods for costing merchandise inventory.
- Computing depreciation and book value amounts for plant and equipment using sum-of-the-years' digits, straight-line, declining-balance, and units-of-production methods.
- Comparing methods for computing depreciation of plant and equipment assets.
- Finding depreciation amounts using the Accelerated Cost Recovery System (ACRS) method.
- Making computations needed to utilize information on balance sheets.
- Making computations needed to utilize information on income statements.
- Analyzing comparative data on balance sheets and income statements.
- Completing a check deposit ticket and banking check register.

PAYROLL COMPUTATIONS

Every business, large or small, must compute the payroll and payroll taxes for employees. Some computations are required simply to keep records of wages and salaries paid to employees, while other computations are necessary for reports to state and federal governmental agencies. This chapter presents procedures for computing the payroll and methods for computing payroll taxes. Since many companies have pay periods as often as once each week, accurate payroll computations are essential.

Payroll Terminology Overview

A single company may use several procedures for computing the payroll. For example, some employees may be paid weekly, while others are paid biweekly (once every two weeks) or monthly. Some employees are paid on an *hourly basis plan*, while others are paid on a *piece-rate plan* according to the amount of work produced. Still others are paid on a *straight salary plan*, which is a fixed amount each pay period. Amounts earned on an hourly basis or a piece-rate basis are generally called *wages*, and amounts earned on a straight salary plan are generally called *salaries*. For example, factory workers usually earn wages, and supervisors and office personnel usually earn salaries.

Regardless of the procedure, the first task in computing payroll is to compute *gross wages* (pay before deductions) for individual employees. Computations are then made to determine the various deductions required for Social Security and state and/or federal income taxes, as well as optional deductions requested by employees for items such as savings bonds, retirement fund, credit union, and insurance. Gross pay minus amounts for required and optional deductions equals *net pay*.

Computing Gross Pay for Salaried Employees

Office, executive, supervisory, and similar employees are often paid an annual or monthly salary. These classes of employees are paid a specified salary with no allowance for overtime. For example, a person may be employed at an annual salary of $18,000, which represents a monthly salary of $1,500 ($18,000 ÷ 12), a weekly salary of $346.15 ($18,000 ÷ 52), or a biweekly salary of $692.31 ($18,000 ÷ 26).

Salaries are usually quoted at monthly or annual amounts and can be converted to accommodate various payroll periods mentioned above for preparing periodic payrolls. For a second example, assume that an employee is hired for a monthly salary of $1,600. This equals an annual salary of $19,200 ($1,600 × 12), a weekly salary of $369.23 ($19,200 ÷ 52), or a biweekly salary of $738.46 ($19,200 ÷ 26).

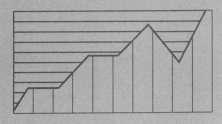

Computing Gross Pay for Hourly Employees

Employees may receive an hourly wage amount based on factors such as experience, type of work performed, and quality of work produced. The normal work week is usually considered to be 40 hours or less. Workers are usually paid a specified hourly rate for the first 40 hours worked and overtime pay for hours worked in excess of 40. Overtime pay is usually at least one and one-half times the regular hourly rate.

EXAMPLE 19.1

Computing gross pay for hours worked

Problem: Hector Cruz earned $9.50 per hour while working 35 hours last week. What was his gross pay?

Solution: Hours worked × Pay rate = Gross pay
                       35   × $9.50   = $332.50

Persons working in excess of 40 hours each week receive the regular rate for the first 40 hours worked. Hours worked in excess of 40 provide a rate that is at least 1½ (1.5) times the regular pay rate.

EXAMPLE 19.2

Computing gross pay for hours worked

Problem: William Speros worked 43 hours last week. His regular pay rate is $10.00 per hour. What were his regular pay, overtime pay, and total gross pay?

Solution: **Step 1.** Compute regular pay.

40 × Pay rate = Regular pay
40 × $10.00   = $400.00

Step 2. Compute overtime pay.

Overtime hours × Pay rate × 1.5 = Overtime pay
   3 (43 − 40)   × $10.00 × 1.5 = $45.00

Step 3. Compute total gross pay.

Regular pay + Overtime pay = Gross pay
  $400.00   + $45.00   = $445.00

Employers are required by the federal government to pay overtime pay equal to at least one and one-half times the regular wage for all hours worked in excess of 40 during a week. This overtime rate is the generally accepted rate for most companies, but some companies may pay a higher overtime rate for special holidays. In addition, some companies pay on an overtime basis for all hours worked in excess of 8 on any particular day even if the total hours worked during the week is not in excess of 40. Unless instructed otherwise, assume that the overtime rate is one and one-half times the regular rate for problems in this chapter.

To compute the hours worked, time is normally computed to the nearest quarter of an hour. For example, an employee who punches in at 8:07 has time computed from 8:00, and an employee who punches in at 8:08 has time computed from 8:15. Time cards and a time clock are often used to record times when employees begin and end their work days.

• Complete Assignment 19.1 •

Computing Gross Pay for Piece-Rate Employees

Some workers, particularly production employees, are paid according to the number of units they make or produce in a period of time. Under the *straight piece-rate plan*, the employee is paid a specific amount for each unit produced to compute gross pay. This plan permits employers to reward employees based on their amount of production. For example, one worker produces 2,320 units during the week at a specific rate of 20¢ per unit. Gross pay is computed as shown in Example 19.3. Employees must be paid a higher rate per item produced as their production increases. Some companies guarantee employees a specific salary amount plus extra compensation for production.

Computing gross pay at piece rate   EXAMPLE
19.3

Problem: Nicole Spencer works in a manufacturing plant. She produced 2,320 units last week. The company paid her $0.20 for each unit. What was her gross pay?

Solution: Units produced × Rate per unit = Gross pay
              2,320   × $0.20   = $464.00

Some employees may earn a specific salary or wage plus extra compensation based on production, as shown in Example 19.4.

EXAMPLE
19.4

Problem: Jane Canty earns an hourly wage of $6.50 plus $0.15 for each unit produced *in excess* of 2,000 units during the 40-hour week. She produced 2,800 units during the week. What was her total gross pay?

(Solution on following page)

Solution: **Step 1.** Find the hourly pay.

Hours worked × Pay rate = Hourly pay
40   × $6.50 = $260.00

Step 2. Find the piece-rate pay.

Units produced
(in excess of 2,000) × Pay rate = Piece-rate pay
800 (2,800 − 2,000) × $0.15 = $120.00

Step 3. Find the total gross pay.

Regular pay + Piece-rate pay = Gross pay
$260.00   + $120.00   = $380.00

Preparing a Payroll Worksheet

The government requires businesses to keep accurate records and to make periodic reports to provide the government with information about each employee's income and deductions.

A record is normally made to show earnings and deductions for employees for each payroll period, which may be weekly, biweekly, or monthly depending on company policy. The record for computing income is called various names, such as *payroll sheet* or *payroll worksheet*. If the record is expanded to include income and deductions, it is usually called a *payroll register*. A typical payroll worksheet is shown in Example 19.5 and includes daily hours worked and weekly earnings.

EXAMPLE **Payroll worksheet**

19.5

PAYROLL WORKSHEET   FOR WEEK ENDING JUNE 15, 19--

Employee	Hours Worked					Total Hours Worked	Hourly Rate	Gross Earnings
	M	T	W	T	F			
Richard Caen	8	7	7	8	7	37	$7.80	$ 288.60
Sue Calhoun	8	8	8	8	8	40	7.20	288.00
Joan Hardin	7	6	8	8	7	36	7.45	268.20
Leslie Herrington	6	0	8	6	6	26	8.55	222.30
Leonard Minarcik	7	8	8	0	8	31	9.58	296.98
Dianne Rossi	7	8	8	8	7	38	7.94	301.72
Pam Rothberg	8	8	8	8	8	40	8.50	340.00
TOTAL EARNINGS								$2,005.80

● **Complete Assignment 19.2** ●

● **Complete Assignment 19.3** ●

ASSIGNMENT 19.1 Computing Payroll: Straight Salary and Hourly Wages

1. Richard Slayer is paid an annual salary of $19,800. What is his (a) monthly, (b) biweekly, and (c) weekly salary amount?

   (a) $ _____

   (b) $ _____

   (c) $ _____

2. Constance Summers is paid a monthly salary of $1,575. What is her (a) annual, (b) biweekly, and (c) weekly salary amount?

   (a) $ _____

   (b) $ _____

   (c) $ _____

3. Max Shiff works the following numbers of hours from Monday to Friday during the week: 8, 8, 7, 7, and 6. What are his gross earnings if his hourly pay rate is $7.30?

   $ _____

4. Clifford Vincent worked 46 hours during the week at an hourly rate of $7.80. How much were his (a) regular earnings, (b) overtime earnings, and (c) gross earnings? (Assume the overtime rate is one and one-half times the regular rate for all hours worked in excess of 40.)

(a) $ _____

(b) $ _____

(c) $ _____

5. Eve Wagner worked the following numbers of hours from Monday to Friday during the week: 8, 10, 9, 8, and 4. Assuming a regular rate of $8.20 per hour and an overtime rate for all hours worked in excess of 8 hours each day, what were her (a) regular earnings, (b) overtime earnings, and (c) gross earnings for the week?

(a) $ _____

(b) $ _____

(c) $ _____

6. Charles Kistler worked the following numbers of hours from Monday to Saturday during the week: 8, 10, 8, 8, 10, and 4. Assume an overtime rate of one and one-half times the regular rate for hours worked in excess of 8 hours each day and an overtime rate of twice the regular rate for hours worked on Saturday. His regular pay rate is $8 per hour. What were his (a) regular earnings, (b) overtime earnings, and (c) gross earnings for the week?

(a) $ _____

(b) $ _____

(c) $ _____

ASSIGNMENT 19.2   Computing Payroll: Piece-Rate and Worksheet

1. Paul Lape produced 825 units during a week. Andrea Lotta produced 837 units during the week. If the piecework rate is 26¢, what were the gross earnings for (a) Lape and (b) Lotta?

   (a) $ _____

   (b) $ _____

2. David Lax produced 918 units during the week, and Larry Kreamer produced 892 units. Company policy is to pay 18¢ for each unit produced up to 750 and to pay 22¢ for units produced in excess of 750. What were the gross earnings for (a) Lax and (b) Kreamer if minimum earnings of $150 are guaranteed?

   (a) $ _____

   (b) $ _____

3. Irene LeBlanc had a weekly output of 429 units, while Kevin Kirshbaum had a weekly output of 385 units. Both worked 40 hours during the week. Company policy is to pay an hourly rate of $6.28 plus 64¢ for each unit produced in excess of 400. What were the gross earnings for (a) LeBlanc and (b) Kirshbaum?

   (a) $ _____

   (b) $ _____

4. Gordon Krag produced 823 units during the week, and Lyn Hamilton produced 761 units. Both worked 40 hours. Company policy is to pay 18¢ for the first 700 units produced and 21¢ for units produced in excess of 700 or $5.38 per hour, whichever is greater. What were the gross earnings for (a) Krag and (b) Hamilton?

   (a) $ _____

   (b) $ _____

5. Complete the following payroll worksheet for the week ending March 7, 19—.

PAYROLL WORKSHEET   FOR WEEK ENDING MARCH 7, 19—

No.	Employee Name	Hours Worked					Total Hours Worked	Hourly Rate	Gross Earnings
		M	T	W	T	F			
1	Jim Crowley	8	7	8	8	5	_____	$7.28	$_____
2	Sam Dean	8	8	5	4	7	_____	7.35	$_____
3	Cory Fry	7	6	8	7	8	_____	7.25	$_____
4	Sue Gore	8	8	8	8	8	_____	8.25	$_____
5	Teri Green	5	8	8	6	6	_____	7.46	$_____
6	Art King	8	8	8	7	7	_____	7.52	$_____
7	June Lee	8	8	7	6	6	_____	7.65	$_____
8	Berdi Nethers	7	7	7	7	7	_____	7.25	$_____
9	Clon Reid	4	4	4	5	7	_____	7.25	$_____
10	Ron Scranton	4	4	4	5	5	_____	7.37	$_____
	TOTAL EARNINGS								$_____

214

ASSIGNMENT 19.3 Computing Payroll: Payroll Register

1. Complete the portion of the following Payroll Register. Hours worked in excess of 40 each week earn an overtime rate of one and one-half times the regular rate.

PAYROLL REGISTER   FOR WEEK ENDING SEPTEMBER 9, 19—

Emp. No.	Status*	**M	T	W	T	F	S	Total Hours	O.T. Hours	Reg. Hours	Pay Rate	Regular Pay	Overtime Pay	Gross Pay
1	M-3	8	8	8	8	8	—				8.50	$	$	$
2	S-1	8	8	8	8	8	4				7.80	$	$	$
3	M-4	6	8	8	8	6	6				8.22	$	$	$
4	S-2	8	10	8	8	10	—				7.96	$	$	$
5	M-3	8	8	8	8	8	8				8.36	$	$	$
6	M-5	10	10	10	10	8	—				7.90	$	$	$
7	M-6	8	8	0	8	8	4				8.18	$	$	$
8	M-3	7	7	7	7	8	—				8.20	$	$	$
9	S-1	4	6	8	8	8	8				8.62	$	$	$
10	M-4	6	6	0	6	6	4				8.10	$	$	$
TOTALS												$	$	$

The "Hours Worked" columns are headed: M, T, W, T, F, S.

*Note: This column indicates marital status and number of withholding allowances.

2. Complete the portion of the following Payroll Register. Hours worked in excess of 8 each day (Monday through Friday) earn one and one-half times the regular rate. All hours worked on Saturday earn twice the regular rate. Do not include the example in your totals. The first item has been completed as an example.

PAYROLL REGISTER   FOR WEEK ENDING APRIL 16, 19—

Emp. No.	Status	Hours Worked						Total Hours	O.T. Hours	Reg. Hours	Pay Rate	Regular Pay	Overtime Pay	Gross Pay
		M	T	W	T	F	S							
	S-1	8	10	8	8	8	4	46	2/4	40	$6.00	$240.00	$ 66.00	$306.00
1	M-2	8	10	8	8	8	4	___	___	___	6.50	$ ___	$ ___	$ ___
2	M-3	8	8	8	8	8	4	___	___	___	6.00	$ ___	$ ___	$ ___
3	M-5	6	6	8	8	6	2	___	___	___	6.50	$ ___	$ ___	$ ___
4	S-1	6	8	0	6	8	0	___	___	___	6.00	$ ___	$ ___	$ ___
5	M-4	8	8	8	8	6	4	___	___	___	6.30	$ ___	$ ___	$ ___
6	M-2	8	6	6	6	6	0	___	___	___	6.35	$ ___	$ ___	$ ___
7	S-2	8	8	10	10	8	3	___	___	___	6.20	$ ___	$ ___	$ ___
8	M-6	8	10	7	8	8	0	___	___	___	6.18	$ ___	$ ___	$ ___
9	S-1	8	8	8	8	8	0	___	___	___	6.23	$ ___	$ ___	$ ___
10	M-3	8	8	8	8	4	0	___	___	___	6.27	$ ___	$ ___	$ ___
TOTALS								___	___	___		$ ___	$ ___	$ ___

3. Donald Spence has an opportunity to be promoted to supervisor at a weekly salary of $380. During the past year he has worked an average of 50 hours per week at a regular hourly rate of $5.80 plus hours worked in excess of 40 at one and one-half times the regular rate. How much will his total weekly pay increase in his new position?

$ _____

PAYROLL WITHHOLDINGS

Many people beginning employment assume that gross pay is the amount of money they will have available for spending. Several item amounts, however, are withheld from the employee's paycheck. The two most common ones are income tax (state and/or federal) and Social Security tax deductions.

Tax Reform Act of 1986

The Tax Reform Act of 1986 overhauled the tax system to make it easier for people to compute the amount of income tax they owe. A dramatic effect of this law was the eventual reduction of the number of tax brackets from 15 to 3—with a series of surtaxes. The new system went into full effect in 1988, with a gradual "blending" during 1987.

Tax Brackets

The Tax Reform Act of 1986, as mentioned above, actually established three tax brackets: 15%, 28%, and 33%. The 33% bracket resulted from the imposition of a 5% *surtax* on top of the "maximum" rate of 28%. The tax laws can change each year to either raise or lower these rates and surtax amounts.

The tables shown in Example 20.1 provide the tax brackets, plus the two surtaxes, in effect beginning in the 1988 tax year. All of these brackets are indexed for inflation, and the intent is to adjust them annually after 1989.

EXAMPLE **Income tax rates (1988)**

20.1

Married Couple Filing Jointly	
Taxable Income	Tax Rate
$0–$29,750	15%
29,751–71,900	28%
71,901–149,250	33% (5% surtax)
149,251–171,090*	33% (second 5% surtax)
over 171,090	28%

Single	
Taxable Income	Tax Rate
$0–$17,850	15%
17,851–43,150	28%
43,151–89,560	33% (5% surtax)
89,561–100,480*	33% (second 5% surtax)
over 100,480	28%

Married Filing Separately

Taxable Income	Tax Rate
$0–14,875	15%
14,876–35,950	28%
35,951–113,300	33% (5% surtax)
113,301–124,220*	33% (second 5% surtax)
over 124,220	28%

Head of Household

Taxable Income	Tax Rate
$0–$23,900	15%
23,901–61,650	28%
61,651–124,790	33% (5% surtax)
124,791–134,710*	33% (second 5% surtax)
over 134,710	28%

*The 33% bracket (surtax bracket) assumes two personal exemptions for a married couple and one for a single person, married person filing separately, or head of household. The bracket is extended upward by an additional $10,920 of income for each additional exemption, including children.

Amounts in the tax table in Example 20.1 are based on *taxable income* for the entire year. Example 20.2 applies the amounts in the tax table to an income tax calculation.

EXAMPLE   Computing income tax liability

20.2

Problem: Lamar Fite is single with a taxable income of $52,000. What is his income tax liability for the year? (Base × Rate = Amount)

Solution: **Step 1.**   Find the tax for the first bracket.

Base income	×	Tax rate	=	Amount of taxes due
$17,850	×	0.15	=	$2,677.50

Step 2.   Find the tax for the second bracket.

Income		× Tax rate	= Taxes due
$26,300 (43,150 − 17,850) ×		0.28	= $7,364.00

Step 3.   Find the tax for the third bracket.

Income		× Tax rate	= Taxes due
$8,850 (52,000 − 43,150) ×		0.33	= $2,920.50

Step 4.   Find the total taxes due.

Bracket 1 + Bracket 2 + Bracket 3 = Total taxes
$2,677.50 + $7,364.00 + $2,920.50 = $12,962.00

(See note on following page.)

Note: The amount multiplied by the tax rate for *each* bracket includes *only* the earned income that is included in that bracket. The sum of the taxes due from the combined brackets then becomes the total taxes due for the annual income, as shown above.

Exemptions from Income

Taxpayers are not required to pay taxes on the entire amount of gross pay or income they received during the year. Each taxpayer is allowed personal exemptions of income from taxes for him/herself, spouse, and each dependent. The Tax Reform Bill of 1986 set this amount at $1,950 for 1988, $2,000 for 1989, and $2,000 for 1990 and after, plus an adjustment for inflation. Example 20.3 illustrates personal exemptions of income in calculating income tax.

Computing income tax exemption   EXAMPLE
20.3

Problem: Bernard and Betty Getty claimed themselves plus two children as personal exemptions when filing their tax return. What is the amount of their personal exemptions, based on 1988 amounts?

Solution: Number of exemptions × $1,950 = Personal exemption
4   × $1,950 = $7,800

Taxpayers also have the option of itemizing certain expenses such as mortgage interest and real estate taxes. These *itemized deductions* are exempt from taxable income. An alternative is to allow a *standard deduction*. Amounts for the standard deduction for 1988 are shown below. The amounts will probably be increased for years beyond 1988, but the method of computation will be similar. The following standard deduction amounts for 1988 will be increased in later years to account for inflation:

STANDARD DEDUCTION AMOUNTS FOR 1988

Single person	$3,000
Married filing jointly	5,000
Married filing separately	2,500
Head of household	4,400

EXAMPLE

20.4

Problem: Bernard and Betty Getty have itemized deductions totaling $3,875. Should they include these deductions or include the standard deduction, based on filing a joint return?

Solution: Based on the table shown above, their standard deduction will be $5,000. Since this amount is greater than their itemized deductions ($3,875), they should take the standard deduction.

The actual tax rates are based on *taxable income,* which is the amount that remains after amounts for personal exemptions and itemized or standard deductions are subtracted from gross income.

EXAMPLE   Computing amount of taxable income

20.5

Problem: Bernard and Betty Getty had combined earned income amounting to $38,750. What is the amount of taxable income? Assume four personal exemptions ($7,800) and a standard deduction ($5,000), as computed in the above examples.

Solution: **Step 1.**   Determine the amount of exempted income.

Personal exemptions	+	Standard deduction	=	Exempted income
$7,800	+	$5,000	=	$12,800

Step 2.   Determine the amount of taxable income.

Gross income	−	Exempted income	=	Taxable income
$38,750	−	$12,800	=	$25,950

The previous tax rate table can then be used to determine the amount of tax liability for the year.

EXAMPLE   Computing amount of income tax

20.6

Problem: Bernard and Betty Getty have taxable income amounting to $25,950. What amount of taxes is due?

Solution: Taxable income × Tax rate = Taxes due
$25,950   ×   0.15   = $3,892.50

Income Tax Withholding

The previous discussion shows how the final taxes due for the year are computed. Most individuals prepare income tax returns once each year. If the calendar year is used as the basis for the return, the return must be filed by April 15 each year. Employers withhold an amount from every paycheck. The tax return is then used to balance the amount withheld during the year with the amount of taxes due that year. If the amount withheld is greater than the amount due, the taxpayer applies for a refund. Otherwise, the taxpayer pays the government the amount of the difference when the tax return is filed with the Internal Revenue Service at the end of the year.

Computing amount of income tax refund　　EXAMPLE

20.7

Problem: John Richardson's employer withheld $4,278 from his gross pay during the year for income taxes. Taxes due for the year totaled $3,725. What is the amount of refund due?

Solution: Amount withheld − Amount due = Refund
　　　　　　　　　$4,278　　　−　　　$3,725　　=　　$553

Withholding Tax Tables

Most employers use tax tables or computer software programs to compute the amount that should be withheld from employee pay for income tax purposes. Some examples of the amount of federal income tax withheld from workers' paychecks are shown in Example 20.8. The amount of allowances claimed varies with the number of dependents and factors such as itemized deductions and whether or not a spouse works.

Selected income tax withholding amounts　　EXAMPLE

20.8

SINGLE TAXPAYER			MARRIED TAXPAYER		
Weekly Wages	Allowances	Amount Withheld	Weekly Wages	Allowances	Amount Withheld
$ 75	0	$ 8	$ 75	0	$ 4
75	1	3	75	1	0
150	0	20	150	0	16
150	1	15	150	2	5
250	0	35	250	0	31
250	1	30	250	2	20

(Continued on following page)

SINGLE TAXPAYER			MARRIED TAXPAYER		
Weekly Wages	Allowances	Amount Withheld	Weekly Wages	Allowances	Amount Withheld
250	2	24	250	4	9
400	0	67	400	0	53
400	1	56	400	2	42
400	2	47	400	4	31
450	0	81	500	0	68
450	1	70	500	2	57
450	2	60	500	5	41
450	3	50	600	0	87
500	0	95	600	2	72
500	1	84	600	4	61
500	2	74	600	6	50
600	0	128	600	8	39
600	1	115	700	0	115
600	2	102	700	2	95
600	3	92	700	4	76
700	0	163	800	0	143
700	1	150	800	2	123
700	2	137	800	4	102
800	0	198	1,000	0	206
800	1	172	1,000	2	181
			1,200	0	275
			1,200	4	223

The amount of tax to be withheld from the employee's paycheck is determined by using the table, as shown in Example 20.9.

EXAMPLE
20.9

Computing weekly income tax withholding

Problem: Ron Steiner is single with 1 allowance. He earns $450 per week. What is the amount of weekly withholding from his paycheck?

Solution: Find the earnings under the Weekly Wages column in the table. Find the amount of withholding under the Withholding column, based on an allowance of 1. The amount located should be $70.

Withholding for FICA Taxes

With only a few exceptions, employees working in the United States must pay FICA (Federal Insurance Contributions Act) tax, which is more commonly called the Social Security tax. This program was enacted in 1937 and was first designed to assist workers who become unable to work, to provide a retirement pension, and to assist family members when a worker dies. Protection against illness was added through the Medicare program in 1966.

The amount of tax to be withheld is determined by multiplying the tax rate by the gross wages (base) up to a specified amount. The original FICA rate was 1% of gross earnings on the first $3,000 earned each year. Congress has increased both the rate and the amount gradually over the years to its 1987 rate of 7.15% of the first $43,800 in gross earnings each year. No FICA taxes are withheld after an employee earns $43,800 in a calendar year.

The tax rate and gross earnings used to compute the tax change periodically by acts of Congress. The method of computing the tax, however, does not change. For low-income wage earners, the amount of FICA tax may be greater than the amount of income tax withheld.

Computing FICA tax withholding   EXAMPLE

20.10

Problem: Ron Steiner earns $450 per week. What amount of FICA taxes will be withheld during the year?

Solution: **Step 1.** Find the annual income amount.

Weekly earnings $\times$ 52 = Annual earnings
$450 $\times$ 52 = $23,400

Step 2. Find the FICA tax withheld.

Annual earnings $\times$ FICA rate = FICA withheld
$23,400 $\times$ 0.0715   = $1,673.10

Remember that the FICA tax is based on a maximum of $43,800 gross earnings.

Computing FICA tax withholding   EXAMPLE

20.11

Problem: Anne Myer earns $62,785 annually. What amount of FICA taxes will be withheld from her earnings during the year?

Solution: Gross earnings
(up to $43,800) $\times$ FICA rate = FICA withheld
$43,800 $\times$ 0.0715   = $3,131.70

Computing Net Pay

Net pay represents the amount of the paycheck. Deductions from gross pay are made for income tax and FICA tax amounts. In addition, deductions for items such as insurance contributions, credit union contributions, and union dues may also be deducted from gross pay to compute the net pay amount, as shown in Example 20.12.

EXAMPLE 20.12   Computing net pay

Problem: Carlton Bowers is single with one allowance. He has $600 weekly earnings. Income tax ($115) and FICA tax ($42.90) deductions are made each week. In addition, $21.75 is deducted for insurance contributions. What is the amount of net pay?

Solution: **Step 1.** Find the total amount deducted.

Income   FICA   Insurance
 tax   +   tax   + premium = Deductions
$115.00 + $42.90 + $21.75   = $179.65

Step 2. Find the net pay amount.

Gross pay − Deductions = Net pay
 $600.00   − $179.65   = $420.35

Payroll applications require accuracy and attention to details. Many bookkeeping, financial, and accounting functions relate directly to this area.

• **Complete Assignment 20.1** •

• **Complete Assignment 20.2** •

ASSIGNMENT 20.1 Computing Income Tax Due

Note: You will use tax tables in the text for several problems in this assignment.

1. John and Rachel Moore are married with 3 children. How many exemptions can they claim on their income tax?

   _____

2. Howard Tucker is divorced. He has custody of his son, who is 13 years old. How many exemptions can he claim on his income tax?

   _____

3. Torrey Dodson is single with a taxable annual income of $16,750. What is his income tax liability for the year?

   $ _____

4. Beverly Ronsiek is single with a taxable annual income of $24,785. What is her income tax liability for the year?

   $ _____

5. Alicia Rosenfield is married. However, she and her husband are filing separate tax returns. Her annual income is $25,875. What is her income tax liability for the year?

   $ _____

6. Emmett and Maxine Greganti are a married couple filing a joint return. Their combined annual income is $48,860. What is their income tax liability for the year?

   $ _____

7. Michael Polk is single with a taxable annual income of $52,750. What is his income tax liability?

   $ _____

8. Patsy and Carl Latimer are a married couple with a combined annual income of $83,985. If they file a joint return, what is their income tax liability?

   $ _____

9. Sue Dempsey has 3 personal tax exemptions. If each exemption equals $1,950, what is the amount of her personal exemptions, based on 1988 amounts?

$ _____

10. Scott and Ethel Petrowski are married and filing a joint tax return. Their itemized deductions total $4,387. They decide to take the larger of the itemized deductions or their standard deduction. Based on 1988 amounts, what amount will they be able to deduct?

$ _____

11. Terry and Thomas Rogers earned income last year amounting to $43,570. Assume 3 personal exemptions and the standard deduction for a joint return. What is the amount of their taxable income?

$ _____

12. Delores Grantham is single. Her only personal exemption is herself. Her income last year was $27,800. Assuming that she takes the standard deduction, what is the amount of her taxable income?

$ _____

13. Kent Halzup is single with 1 allowance. His weekly earnings are $500. What amount should be withheld from his paycheck for income taxes each week?

$ _____

14. Alga Kingsford is a married taxpayer with 4 allowances. Her weekly earnings are $700. What amount should be withheld from her weekly paycheck for income taxes?

$ _____

15. Debra Finley's gross earnings are $476 per week. Based on a FICA rate of 7.15%, what amount should be withheld for FICA taxes from her weekly paycheck?

$ _____

16. John and Betty Dilworth have combined annual salaries of $3,650 each month. Based on a FICA rate of 7.15%, what amount should be withheld for FICA taxes each month?

$ _____

ASSIGNMENT 20.2   Computing Payroll Withholdings

1. Compute the portion of the payroll register shown below using the appropriate withholding tax table shown in the text. (Do not include amounts in the example in your totals.) Round all amounts to the nearest cent. The first item has been completed as an example.

Note: The Status column is coded; for example, S-1 means single with 1 allowance. Assume a 7.15% FICA rate.

PAYROLL REGISTER   FOR WEEK ENDING JULY 8, 19—

No.	Employee Name	Status	Gross Pay	Federal Income Tax	FICA	Other	Total Deductions	Net Pay
		S-1	$400.00	$56.00	$28.60	(insur.) 35.00	$119.60	$280.40
1	Craig, Carmie D.	M-8	800.00	$	$	-0-	$	$
2	Dees, Lucy A.	S-0	400.00	$	$	-0-	$	$
3	Hodgin, Allen C.	S-1	75.00	$	$	-0-	$	$
4	Huff, Millie R.	M-2	250.00	$	$	(cr. un.)* 30.00	$	$
5	Kelsey, Donald A.	M-2	500.00	$	$	-0-	$	$
6	Larson, Felix T.	M-2	400.00	$	$	-0-	$	$
7	Maddox, Tony B.	M-2	800.00	$	$	-0-	$	$
8	Monroe, Linda K.	M-8	600.00	$	$	(insur.) 35.00	$	$
9	Parr, Willie J.	S-0	700.00	$	$	-0-	$	$
10	Piretti, Bernice	S-1	700.00	$	$	-0-	$	$
11	Poynor, Ted P.	M-0	700.00	$	$	-0-	$	$
12	Ryndes, Eddie E.	S-2	700.00	$	$	-0-	$	$
13	Shaul, Percy O.	S-1	800.00	$	$	(cr. un.) 18.00	$	$
14	Wade, Roland A.	M-4	800.00	$	$	-0-	$	$
15	Young, Adam T.	S-1	150.00	$	$	-0-	$	$
	TOTALS		$	$	$	$	$	$

*credit union

2. Janet Ross, a single person with 2 personal allowances, had prior earnings for the year of $36,000. During the current week, she earned $600. Using information in the text, compute the (a) federal income taxes and (b) FICA taxes that should be withheld from her current earnings.

(a) $ _____

(b) $ _____

3. Thomas Curtis, a married person with 4 allowances, had prior earnings for the year of $8,628. During the current week, he earned $700. Using information in the text, compute the (a) federal income taxes and (b) FICA taxes that should be withheld from his current earnings.

(a) $ _____

(b) $ _____

4. Lillian Watkins' earnings for the year totaled $18,675.40 prior to her current month's earnings of $1,418. Assume that the income tax withholding rate is 15% of gross pay with a 7.15% FICA rate. What are her monthly (a) deduction for federal income taxes, (b) deduction for FICA taxes, and (c) net pay?

(a) $ _____

(b) $ _____

(c) $ _____

5. Sandra Swenson's earnings for the year totaled $12,785.83 prior to her current week's earnings of $700. She is single and claims 1 allowance on her W-4 form. Use the tax withholding table and a 7.15% FICA rate to compute withholdings. What are her weekly (a) deduction for federal income taxes, (b) deduction for FICA taxes, and (c) net pay?

(a) $ _____

(b) $ _____

(c) $ _____

PROPERTY AND PROPERTY TAXES

Property taxes are assessed on real property (such as homes, land, and buildings) by counties, cities, states, and school districts as a way to raise money for schools, roads, parks, police and fire protection, and other public services. Property taxes are assessed against individuals and businesses owning real property. Material in this chapter shows you how to compute individual and business property tax assessments.

Determining Property Tax Rate and Assessment

Governmental units that use property taxes as one source of income generally develop a budget to match anticipated operational expenses against anticipated income. This budget is usually completed on an annual basis.

The governmental unit sets the property tax rate and assessment based on the worth of the assessed property in the area. Although rates and bases vary widely, the method for computation is fairly uniform (Amount/Base = Rate).

EXAMPLE   **Computing property tax rate**

21.1

Problem: The assessed valuation of property in Fentress County is $3,500,000,000. In order to collect funds for a $140,000,000 budget, what tax rate will be needed?

Solution:

Revenue amount needed	/	Base of assessed valuation	=	Tax rate
$140,000,000	/	$3,500,000,000	=	0.04 (4%)

Using this same procedure, determine the needed tax rate to raise $150,000,000 (amount) if property has an assessed valuation of $5,000,000,000 (base) by using the following steps:

Step 1. Amount needed equals $150,000,000.

Step 2. (Amount) ÷ (Base) = (Rate)
$150,000,000 ÷ $5,000,000,000 = 0.03 = 3% tax rate

The large amounts used in these examples are realistic. Property tax valuations may amount to billions of dollars.

● **Complete Assignment 21.1** ●

229

Determining Property Tax Amount

To determine the tax assessment for property owners, the assessed valuation of each piece of property must be known.

EXAMPLE	**Computing property tax**
21.2	

Problem: Joseph Burger owns property with an assessed valuation of $54,000. The property tax rate is listed as $2.50 per $100. What is the property tax amount?

Solution: **Step 1.** Find the number of units of $100.

Assessed valuation / Expressed unit = No. of units
$54,000   / $100   =   540

Step 2. Find the property tax amount.

No. of units × Tax per unit = Property tax
540   × $2.50   = $1,350

Property tax bills are usually paid quarterly or semiannually with the entire amount due within a certain period of time (such as 30 days) after the end of the year. A penalty is usually assessed for late payment of taxes.

Some businesses and individuals receive special tax rates. For example, a business may be given a special tax rate to encourage the business to build a plant in an area where employment is low or to encourage a new business to locate in the area. Schools, churches, and non-profit organizations often receive special tax rates or may be exempted from property taxes.

Expressing the Tax Rate in Various Ways

The tax rates in the preceding examples were expressed as decimals (such as 0.04 and 0.03) and as percents (such as 4% and 3%). However, the tax rate can be expressed in other ways. A comparison of how the 0.04 tax rate can be expressed is given in Example 21.3.

Expressing tax rates   EXAMPLE

21.3

Decimal—0.04 times assessed value
Percent—4% of assessed value
Mills   —40 mills per dollar (10 mills equal 1 cent)
Cents   —4 cents per dollar of assessed value
Dollars —$4 per hundred dollars of assessed value
Dollars —$40 per thousand dollars of assessed value

If the tax rate is expressed in mills per dollar of assessed valuation, the computation can be made by moving the decimal place three places to the left. For example, 35 mills equals $0.035 (35 divided by $1,000).

Computing property tax   EXAMPLE

21.4

Problem: Venessa Greenway owns a house with an assessed valuation of $92,500. The property tax rate is 32 mills per dollar of assessed valuation. What is the property tax amount?

Solution: (Base)   (Rate)   (Amount)
Assessed valuation $\times$ (mills/$1,000) = Property tax
         $92,500 $\times$ $0.032   = $2,960
Note: (32/$1,000 = $0.032)

Rates are often expressed as $2.50 per $100 or $25 per $1,000 so that smaller numbers can be used to make computations easier.

The computer can be used to compute property tax amounts as shown by the spreadsheet in Example 21.5.

Property tax spreadsheet   EXAMPLE

21.5

```
    A       B      C      D     E     F     G      H
 1PROPERTY  TAX  COMPUTATIONS
 2===============================================
 3 Property |  Assessed    |   Tax |   Tax
 4 Number   |  Valuation   |  Rate | Amount
 5-----------------------------------------------
 6  X-919   |   74,000     |  4.5% |  3,330
 7  X-920   |  112,000     |  4.5% |  5,040
 8  X-921   |   87,000     |  4.5% |  3,915
 9  X-922   |   76,000     |  4.5% |  3,420
10  X-923   |   89,000     |  4.5% |  4,005
11  X-924   |  124,000     |  4.5% |  5,580
12  X-925   |   56,000     |  4.5% |  2,520
13===============================================
```

● **Complete Assignment 21.2** ●

ASSIGNMENT 21.1 Tax Rate and Assessed Valuation

1. Henderson County assessed property at 40% of its true value. Compute the assessed valuation of each of the properties in Column A and enter the answers in Column E of the following spreadsheet.

	A	B	C	D	E	F
1			PROPERTY TAX VALUATION			
2	===					
3	Property		True Value		Assessed Valuation	
4	======================================		============		=======================	
5	Metts Construction Company		280,000		112,000	
6	--------------------------------------		------------		-----------------------	
7	Malley Beauty Supply		85,500		34200	
8	--------------------------------------		------------		-----------------------	
9	Murphy's Grocery		230,800		92320	
10	--------------------------------------		------------		-----------------------	
11	Murtta Insurance Agency		88,700			
12	--------------------------------------		------------		-----------------------	
13	Nash Salon of Beauty		57,500			
14	--------------------------------------		------------		-----------------------	
15	Dave Rogers Interiors		99,200			
16	--------------------------------------		------------		-----------------------	
17	Pet Grooming Shoppe		62,500			
18	--------------------------------------		------------		-----------------------	
19	Professional Cleaners		119,000			
20	--------------------------------------		------------		-----------------------	
21	Praffer Metals Company		375,000			
22	--------------------------------------		------------		-----------------------	
23	Pyum Deli Shoppe		136,800			
24	--------------------------------------		------------		-----------------------	
25	Assessed valuation rate:		40%			
26	=======================================					

2. Palican City has taxable real property with an assessed valuation of $120,682,000. The city's budget for next year is $8,280,000, with $3,017,050 to be raised from collection of property taxes. In order to collect the needed taxes, what tax rate will be needed?

    .07

3. Whiteville Unified School District has taxable real property of $680,500,000. Under Budget Plan A, $23,817,500 will be needed from property taxes. Under Budget Plan B, $26,539,500 will be needed from property taxes. What tax rate will be needed for adoption of (a) Budget Plan A and (b) Budget Plan B?

    (a)   0.03

    (b)   2.2% - 0.03

233

4. Taxable real property in Apple Valley County is $790,500,000. Under the budget adopted by the city and county governments, $23,458,000 will be needed for the city, and $17,391,000 will be needed by the county from property taxes. City residents must pay the county rate *plus* the city rate, while county residents pay *only* the county rate. What is the rate to be paid by (a) city residents and (b) county residents?

(a) ⎯⎯⎯⎯⎯⎯

(b) ⎯⎯⎯⎯⎯⎯

5. Real property in Brownsville is assessed at 40 percent of true value for residences and at 25% of true value for businesses. Assuming that a house and a business in Brownsville each have a true value of $127,500, what is the assessed valuation of (a) the residential property and (b) the business property?

(a) $ ⎯⎯⎯⎯⎯⎯

(b) $ ⎯⎯⎯⎯⎯⎯

6. Cane County assesses business property at 35% of its true value, and Bruner County assesses business property at 50 percent of its true value. A study shows that the Jones Chair Company can locate in either county with a true value of real property of $350,500. What will be the assessed valuation of property if the company locates in (a) Cane County and (b) Bruner County?

(a) $ ⎯⎯⎯⎯⎯⎯

(b) $ ⎯⎯⎯⎯⎯⎯

7. Property in Howard County has a true value of $88,798,528,000. If property is assessed at 35% of its true value, what is the assessed valuation of property in Howard County?

$ ⎯⎯⎯⎯⎯⎯⎯⎯⎯⎯⎯⎯

ASSIGNMENT 21.2 Property Tax Computations

1. Compute the assessed valuation and annual property tax for each of the following pieces of property. The first property is given as an example.

Property	True Value	Valuation Percent	Assessed Valuation	Tax Rate	Annual Tax
	$ 80,000	40	$32,000	0.03	$960.00
A	60,000	40	$ _____	0.03	$ _____
B	128,500	35	$ _____	0.035	$ _____
C	98,750	24	$ _____	0.042	$ _____
D	176,800	66	$ _____	0.05	$ _____
E	350,000	37	$ _____	0.0317	$ _____

2. Compute the annual tax for each of the following pieces of property:

Property	Assessed Valuation	Tax Rate	Annual Tax
A	$ 60,000	3.5 percent	$ 2100
B	86,900	$4.50 per hundred	$ 3870
C	98,000	$3.17 per hundred	$ 3106.60
D	94,000	46 mills	$ 4,324
E	120,000	38.8 mills	$ 4,656
F	135,000	4.4 percent	$ 5,940

3. The tax assessor uses a 40% assessment. The true value of property is $125,000 with a tax rate of 3.5%. What is the (a) assessed value and (b) annual tax for the property?

(a) $ __50,000__

(b) $ _____ ?

4. Business property with an assessed value of $350,000 is located in a city with a tax rate of 3.289%. The business is granted a special tax rate of 2.5%. How much is saved by receiving the special tax rate?

$ _____

5. Toone County has property with an assessed value of $89,580,700,000 and a tax rate of 0.04. How much will the county receive in property taxes during the year?

$ _____

6. The tax rate for Carter City is $3.50 per $100. For Carter County it is $2.40 per $100. A resident owning a house with an assessed value of $140,000 must pay property taxes to both city and county units. How much will his tax bill be for the (a) city, (b) county, and (c) city and county combined?

(a) $ _____

(b) $ _____

(c) $ _____

7. Wanda Tharpe paid a property tax bill of $1,125 for the year. The tax rate was $2.50 per $100 of assessed value. What is the assessed value of her property?

$ _____

8. Mitch Canty has a house with an assessed value of $40,800. The property is assessed at 34% of its true value. What is the true value of his property?

$ _____

236

MERCHANDISE INVENTORY VALUATION AND TURNOVER

Supermarkets, car parts outlets, department stores, and similar companies maintain a supply of goods for sale to other companies or to consumers. The cost value assigned to the supply of goods available for sale is called *merchandise inventory*. In this chapter you will learn about different methods that companies use to determine or estimate the cost value to be assigned to the merchandise inventory.

Overview of Merchandise Inventory

Companies that sell merchandise or goods periodically determine the value of the supply on hand by counting or computing an estimate of the merchandise inventory available on a given date. The Internal Revenue Service permits companies to select one of several methods to estimate the cost valuation of the merchandise available for sale at the end of the accounting period. Companies with expensive items can actually count the items and determine the cost valuation. However, companies with many small items or with a wide variety of items purchased on various dates may find that a physical count is not possible or practical. This estimate is important because the amount of inventory affects the assets (merchandise available for sale) and the expenses (cost of goods sold) of the company. Four of the most common methods for cost valuation of merchandise inventory are explained in this chapter: (1) specific identification, (2) average cost, (3) first-in, first-out (FIFO), and (4) last-in, first-out (LIFO).

Merchandise inventory is normally priced at the cost of the goods or the market price of the goods, whichever is lower. This amount, determined by the *lower of cost or market* method, will usually result in goods being valued at the cost price, especially in a period of rising prices. Companies like to maintain records to determine how often the inventory is sold during a given period of time, such as a quarter or a year. A *merchandise turnover ratio* can be computed to determine the average number of times the inventory is sold during the period. Gross profit on sales can be determined by subtracting the cost of goods sold from the sales to estimate the profit before operating expenses are deducted. Although the Internal Revenue Service is liberal about permitting companies to choose an appropriate pricing method for its inventory, the method chosen must be used consistently during each accounting period.

Inventory Valuation Methods

Merchandise items are purchased at various times throughout the year at various costs. Periodically, at least once a year, companies

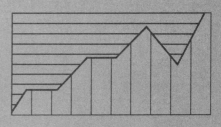

count the number of items on hand and make a cost valuation. Most companies that sell expensive items (such as automobiles) will need to make a specific identification of the cost of items sold and will be able to assign an exact cost value to the merchandise inventory. This method is impractical (maybe even impossible) for a supermarket because of the quantity of items sold each day. Today, however, computer technology enables businesses to identify and record the type and number of merchandise items they sell.

The data presented in Example 22.1 will be used to illustrate four methods for determining the cost valuation of the merchandise inventory. This shows purchases of items during the year. (Assume that a physical count shows that 25 items are on hand at the end of the year.)

EXAMPLE 22.1	**Transactions relating to purchase of inventory item #A-277**			
	January 1	Beginning inventory	15 units @ $18	$ 270.00
	January 14	Purchased	17 units @ $20	340.00
	February 11	Purchased	15 units @ $21	315.00
	July 4	Purchased	18 units @ $22	396.00
	September 9	Purchased	15 units @ $25	375.00
		Total available	80 units	$1,696.00

Specific Identification

Companies that deal in expensive items such as automobiles can use the invoice to determine when an item has been sold. Each car has a specific identification number, and the actual cost of the automobile being sold is indicated. Companies such as department stores and supermarkets use computers to scan identification codes during the checkout process to determine what specific items are being purchased. The increasing use of computers will enable more types of companies to provide accurate and current data about specific items being sold and about items remaining in inventory. Assume that sales invoice codes are used to provide data about the 25 items listed below that remain in inventory.

EXAMPLE 22.2	**Valuation of merchandise inventory: Specific identification method**		
	3 items from the January 1 inventory	@ $18 =	$ 54.00
	8 items from the February 11 purchase	@ $21 =	168.00
	7 items from the July 4 purchase	@ $22 =	154.00
	7 items from the September 9 purchase	@ $25 =	175.00
	25 items	TOTAL COST =	$551.00

Average Cost Method

The *average cost* method, which is also called the *weighted cost* method, for determining the cost valuation of merchandise inventory provides a way to obtain the average cost of units of merchandise on hand during the accounting period. Computation of cost using the average cost method involves the following procedures: (1) Compute the average cost per unit by dividing total cost by the total number of units for each item of merchandise available during the accounting period. (2) Compute the value of merchandise inventory by multiplying the number of units on hand at the end of the period by the average cost.

Using the illustration of Item #A-277, the following calculations are made to compute the value of merchandise inventory using the average cost method.

Valuation of merchandise inventory: Average cost method — EXAMPLE 22.3

Step 1. Total cost ÷ Number of items available = Average cost

$1,696.00 ÷ 80 = $21.20

Step 2. Items on hand × Average cost = Merchandise inventory

25 × $21.20 = $530.00

First-In, First-Out (FIFO) Method

The *first-in, first-out* (FIFO) method is used when stores attempt to sell the oldest items in inventory first. For example, a grocery store will normally rotate merchandise to keep the oldest merchandise in front on the shelves so that it will be sold first. This method assumes that the oldest merchandise will be sold first, so the merchandise purchased most recently will be on hand at the end of the accounting period. Follow the procedure used in Example 22.4 to determine the value of the merchandise inventory for Item #A-277. Determine the cost of the last 25 items purchased by multiplying the number of units by the cost per unit.

Valuation of merchandise inventory: FIFO method — EXAMPLE 22.4

15 units from September 9 purchase @ $25 = $375.00
10 units from July 4 purchase @ $22 = 220.00
25 units   Merchandise inventory value = $595.00

Last-In, First-Out (LIFO) Method

The *last-in, first-out* (LIFO) method is used when the latest purchases are to be sold first. Therefore, merchandise inventory at the end of an accounting period consists of items available at the beginning of the period plus early purchases. Follow the procedure used in Example 22.5 to determine the value of the inventory for Item #A-277. Determine the cost of the first 25 items available or purchased during an accounting period by multiplying the number of units by cost per unit.

EXAMPLE   **Valuation of merchandise inventory: LIFO method**

22.5

15 units in the beginning inventory @ $18	=	$270.00
10 units from January 14 purchase @ $20	=	200.00
25 units Merchandise inventory value	=	$470.00

● **Complete Assignment 22.1** ●

Lower of Cost or Market Pricing

The objective of pricing merchandise inventory is to obtain a logical and practical price for the type of product being evaluated. Previous discussion assumed a *cost* basis for determining the value. Another approach is to value merchandise inventory at original cost per unit or current cost (market price) needed to replace merchandise items. This approach is often practical for items that decrease in value over a period of time. If this method is used, the company records an inventory value of the original cost or market price, whichever is lower, for each type of merchandise on hand. To illustrate this pricing method, assume that 4 items are on hand on the date of the inventory valuation. The item numbers, quantity on hand, original cost price, market price, and cost valuation at the lower of cost or market value are shown in Example 22.6.

EXAMPLE   **Pricing of inventory**
             at the lower of cost or market value

22.6

Item No.	Quantity on Hand	Original Unit Cost	Market Unit Cost	Lower of Cost or Market Value
F-38	30	$2.80	$2.85	$ 84.00
F-43	56	2.73	2.65	148.40
G-78	62	4.99	4.90	303.80
H-17	52	6.70	6.75	348.40
		Merchandise Inventory Value		$884.60

Merchandise Inventory Turnover Ratio

Valuable information can be provided by determining how often the company sells an amount equal to the average supply of goods on hand during the accounting period. A *merchandise inventory turnover ratio* can be computed by dividing the cost of goods sold by the *average merchandise inventory*. This indicates how many times merchandise inventory "turns over" or is sold during a fiscal period. Average merchandise inventory is computed by dividing the sum of the beginning and ending inventories by 2. If an inventory is taken more often than twice a year, the sum of the inventories taken is divided by the number of times the inventory is taken to determine an average inventory amount. A turnover ratio can be computed for the entire merchandise inventory, as well as for individual items, to determine how fast items are selling.

Assuming a beginning inventory of $125,000, an ending inventory of $119,000, and purchases of $360,000 for the period, the merchandise inventory turnover ratio can be determined using the procedures shown in Examples 22.7 and 22.8.

Computing cost of goods available for sale and cost of goods sold

EXAMPLE

22.7

Step 1. Add the purchases to the beginning inventory to compute the cost of goods available for sale.

$125,000 + $360,000 = $485,000 (goods available for sale)

Step 2. Subtract the ending inventory from the cost of goods available obtained in Step 1 to compute the cost of goods sold.

$485,000 − $119,000 = $366,000 (cost of goods sold)

Once the cost of goods sold has been determined, the average merchandise inventory is computed by dividing the sum of the beginning and ending inventories by 2. Then, the average merchandise inventory is divided into the cost of goods sold to compute the merchandise inventory turnover ratio.

Computing merchandise inventory turnover ratio

EXAMPLE

22.8

Step 1.

Beginning inventory	+	Ending inventory	=	Sum of inventories	÷	Number of inventories	=	Average merchandise inventory
$125,000	+	$119,000	=	$244,000	÷	2	=	$122,000

Step 2.

Cost of goods sold	÷	Average merchandise inventory	=	merchandise turnover ratio
$366,000	÷	$122,000	=	3

In this example, a turnover ratio of 3 was computed. This means that sales equaled 3 times the average merchandise inventory for the accounting period. Companies will strive for different turnover ratios depending on the nature of the product being sold. For example, a supermarket must have a much higher turnover ratio than an automobile dealership to be successful.

Comparison of Cost Valuation Methods

The method chosen to determine cost valuation for merchandise inventory affects the cost of goods sold amount and, ultimately, the profit to be reported for income tax purposes. Using the merchandise inventory valuations previously obtained by each of the four methods, the results provide a comparison of values as shown in Example 22.9. For the purpose of this example, assume that for each method, the cost of merchandise available for sale is $1,696. The greater the cost of goods sold, the lower the profit figure for tax purposes. Many companies choose the LIFO method in a period of rising prices for this reason.

EXAMPLE

22.9

Comparison of valuation methods for costing merchandise inventory

Method	Merchandise Valuation	Cost of Goods Sold
Specific Identification	$551.00	$1,145.00
Average Cost	530.00	1,226.00
FIFO	595.00	1,101.00
LIFO	470.00	1,226.00

● **Complete Assignment 22.2** ●

ASSIGNMENT 22.1 Computing Cost of Merchandise Inventory

1. Carter Farm Supply, Inc., compiled the data shown below relative to Item #C-611. A physical count of the inventory item on December 31 indicates that 23 items are *on hand*. Complete the extensions and determine the cost valuation of the ending inventory using each of the following methods: specific identification, average cost, FIFO, and LIFO.

Date	Transaction	Quantity/Unit Cost	Extension
January 1	Beginning Inventory	12 units @ $12	$ *144*
March 23	Purchase	4 units @ $20	$ *80*
May 8	Purchase	15 units @ $14	$ *210*
September 18	Purchase	9 units @ $16	$ *144*
December 3	Purchase	10 units @ $18	$ *180*
TOTAL MERCHANDISE AVAILABLE FOR SALE = *50* units $ *758*			

(a) Cost valuation using the specific identification method. (Records show that 7 units purchased on May 8, 6 units purchased on September 18, and 10 units purchased on December 3 are *on hand*.)

$ *560.⁰⁰*

(b) Cost valuation using the average cost method.

$ *$439.⁰⁰*

(c) Cost valuation using the FIFO method.

$ *$324*

(d) Cost valuation using the LIFO method.

$ *$224*

243

2. Inventory records for Item #X-784 indicate the beginning inventory and purchases during the month of October as shown below. Computer records indicate that 680 units *were sold* during the month. Complete the extensions and determine the cost valuation of the ending inventory on October 31 using each of the four methods discussed in the text.

October	Transaction	Quantity/Unit Cost	Extension
1	Beginning Inventory	110 units @ $2.87	$
7	Purchase	140 units @ $2.91	$
9	Purchase	145 units @ $2.90	$
17	Purchase	145 units @ $2.92	$
20	Purchase	130 units @ $2.92	$
28	Purchase	130 units @ $2.94	$
TOTAL MERCHANDISE AVAILABLE _____ units			$

(a) Cost valuation using the specific identification method. (Computer records show that all of the merchandise has been sold except for 120 items purchased on October 28.) Carry answer to three decimal places.

$ _____

(b) Cost valuation using the average cost method.

$ _____

(c) Cost valuation using the FIFO method.

$ _____

(d) Cost valuation using the LIFO method.

$ _____

244

ASSIGNMENT 22.2 Computing Cost of Goods Sold and Merchandise Turnover Ratio

1. Inventory records for Item #P-18 show the beginning inventory and purchases during the month of March as indicated below. Complete the extensions and determine the cost valuation of the ending inventory at the end of the month using the (a) FIFO method and (b) LIFO method. There are 60 units on hand at the end of the month.

March	Transaction	Quantity/Unit Cost	Extension
1	Beginning Balance	50 units @ $25	$ 1,250
10	Purchase	40 units @ $26	$ 1,040
15	Purchase	50 units @ $26	$ 1,300
25	Purchase	40 units @ $27	$ 1,080
TOTAL MERCHANDISE AVAILABLE 180 units			$ 4,670

(a) $ $2,290

(b) $ _____

2. Answer the following questions using the same information that was used in Problem 1 above for Item #P-18 and the FIFO and LIFO methods for determining cost valuation of merchandise inventory. (a) How much was the value of the beginning inventory? (b) How much were the purchases for the month? (c) How much merchandise was available for sale during the month? (d) What was the value of the ending inventory? (e) How much was the cost of goods sold for the period?

	(FIFO)	(LIFO)
(a)	$ _____	$ _____
(b)	$ _____	$ _____
(c)	$ _____	$ _____
(d)	$ _____	$ _____
(e)	$ _____	$ _____

3. Determine the merchandise inventory turnover ratio for the Webster Store during each month of the quarter. (Round the turnover ratio to two decimal places.)

Month	Beginning Inventory	Ending Inventory	Cost of Goods Sold	Merchandise Turnover Ratio
First	$50,000	$60,000	$165,000	_____
Second	60,000	64,000	120,000	_____
Third	64,000	58,000	215,000	_____

4. The Lincoln Sporting Goods Store had a beginning merchandise inventory of $56,000, purchases of $300,000, and an ending inventory of $64,000 during the last fiscal year. Indicate the amount of (a) merchandise available for sale, (b) cost of goods sold, and (c) the merchandise turnover ratio. (Round to two decimal places.)

(a) $ _____

(b) $ _____

(c) _____

5. The Bolder Parts Shop completes a physical count of merchandise once each quarter. The balance sheet shows a cost of goods sold of $1,800,000 for the year. During the past year, the following amounts were recorded: January 1, beginning inventory, $328,800; March 31, $352,600; June 30, $345,600; September 30, $350,500; and December 31, $360,400. What were the (a) average inventory during the year and (b) merchandise inventory turnover ratio for the year?

(a) $ _____

(b) _____

DEPRECIATION OF PLANT AND EQUIPMENT

Depreciation is the decrease in value of long-term assets. The Internal Revenue Service permits business firms to consider depreciation as an operating expense for tax purposes. In this chapter, you will learn four methods for computing depreciation to extend this expense over the estimated useful life of long-term assets. In addition, you will learn about a system that is based on an allowance for federal income tax purposes instead of the actual useful life of the asset.

Overview of Depreciation

A business firm owns many types of properties called *assets*. Assets are things of value owned by the business and should be put into two broad categories: current assets and long-term assets. Cash and assets that can be converted into cash, sold, or consumed within one year are classified as *current assets*. Examples of current assets are cash, accounts receivable, supplies, and merchandise inventory. *Long-term assets* will not be consumed, sold, or converted into cash within one year. One important group of tangible long-term assets that will be used for a number of years and are not purchased primarily for resale are known as *plant and equipment* or *fixed assets*. Examples of fixed assets include automobiles, buildings, office equipment, delivery equipment, and land.

With the exception of land, all plant and equipment normally decrease in value due to use, obsolescence, and the passage of time. This decrease in value is called *depreciation*. Land is regarded as having an unlimited life and does not depreciate. The Internal Revenue Service permits business firms to charge depreciation as an operating expense for each accounting period in which the asset is used. Using appropriate guidelines, the expense may be deducted as an operating expense from the profits of the firm. If a company does not prepare interim (monthly or quarterly) financial reports, depreciation is calculated on an annual basis.

The Straight-Line Method

If a business firm decides to depreciate the cost of an asset equally over the asset's estimated useful life, the straight-line method should be used. This method is based on the assumption that the asset will depreciate at the same rate each year. It is the easiest to compute and the most commonly used method for computing depreciation for purposes of financial accounting. The following basic factors should be considered when using the straight-line method:

1. *Total cost* of the property. The total cost includes the purchase price of property plus all expenditures necessary to make an asset ready to use, such as freight, sales taxes, insurance charges, and installation costs.

CHAPTER 23

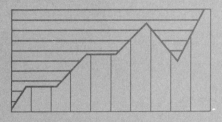

2. *Estimated life* of the asset. This is the number of years that a firm estimates the asset will remain useful. Although this estimate is normally based on past experience with similar assets, it must be determined for each asset involved. The Internal Revenue Service guidelines should be followed in making estimates.

3. *Disposal value* of the property. This is the estimated value that an asset will have at the end of its useful life. (Disposal value is also called *scrap value, salvage value, resale value, residual value, trade-in value,* or *liquidation value.*)

The straight-line method assumes that disposal value will be deducted to determine the total amount that will be depreciated. To determine annual depreciation, the total depreciation is then spread evenly over the useful life of the property by dividing the total depreciation by the number of years in the estimated life. An alternative method is to divide the useful life into the value *1* and then multiply the total depreciation by that quotient. Both procedures are illustrated in Example 23.1.

EXAMPLE   Computing annual depreciation

23.1

Problem: The Carter Delivery Service buys a truck for $14,000. It is estimated that the useful life will be 5 years and the disposal value will be $2,000. What is the annual depreciation?

Solution: **Step 1.** Find the total amount to be depreciated.

  Cost   − Disposal value = Amount depreciated
  $14,000 − $2,000   = $12,000

Step 2. Find the amount of annual depreciation.

Amount depreciated / Years in life = Annual depreciation
      $12,000   /   5   = $2,400

Alternative method:

Step 1. Divide 1 by number of years in useful life.

  1/5 = 0.20

Step 2. Multiply total depreciation by quotient obtained in Step 1.

  $12,000 × 0.20 = $2,400

The *Tax Reform Act of 1986* requires rental property to be depreciated over 27.5 years. Commercial real estate is depreciated over 31.5 years. This act also stipulates that one-half year's depreciation be allowed in the year that personal property is placed into service—regardless of the month—unless over 40% of the property was placed into service during the last quarter. This law also mandates that the straight-line method be used to depreciate real estate.

Computing annual depreciation and depreciation during year of purchase

EXAMPLE

23.2

Problem: The Upper Class Beauty Salon purchased a computer for $1,200 in November. The computer will be depreciated over 5 years, with no disposal value. What are the annual depreciation and the depreciation during the year of purchase?

Solution: **Step 1.** Find the amount of annual depreciation.

Amount depreciated / Years in life = Annual depreciation
$1,200   /   5   = $240

Step 2. Find the depreciation for the year of purchase.

Annual depreciation / 2 = First year's depreciation
$240   / 2 = $120

Note: One-half year's depreciation will be taken the first year.

Book value is the estimated worth of an asset at a certain point in time and is computed by subtracting the *accumulated depreciation* from the total cost of the asset, as shown in Example 23.3.

Computing book value

EXAMPLE

23.3

Problem: The Upper Class Beauty Salon evaluates the book value of the computer after 3 years. Assuming a cost of $1,200, no disposal value, and annual depreciation of $240, what is the book value after 3 years?

Solution: **Step 1.** Find the accumulated depreciation.

Annual depreciation × Years = Accumulated depreciation
$240   ×   3   = $720

Step 2. Find the book value.

Cost − Accumulated depreciation = Book value
$1,200 − $720   = $480

One-half year's depreciation is allowed in the year of purchase. Likewise, one-half year's depreciation is allowed in the year of sale. To keep problems fairly non-technical, assume a full year's depreciation unless otherwise stated in the problem. Also remember that these types of rules are subject to change when new laws are enacted.

> ● **Complete Assignment 23.1** ●

Sum-of-the-Years' Digits Method

The straight-line method computes an equal amount of depreciation for each year of the asset's useful life. However, the value of many assets decreases more rapidly in the early years of life. For example, a new car depreciates most in the first year, less in the second year, and less in each succeeding year. Depreciation methods that compute a large amount of depreciation in the earlier years in the life of the asset are called *accelerated depreciation* methods. The two most popular accelerated depreciation methods are the sum-of-the-years' digits and declining-balance methods. The sum-of-the-years' digits method is discussed in this section.

The value 1 is added to the number of years in the life of the asset. This sum is then divided by the value 2. This answer is then multiplied by the number of years in the life of the asset. This product then becomes the denominator as shown in Step 2 of Example 23.4.

EXAMPLE   **Computing first-year depreciation**

23.4

Problem: An asset is purchased for $10,000 with a disposal value of $400. What is the annual depreciation amount during the first year if the asset is depreciated over a life of 5 years?

Solution: **Step 1.**   Find the amount of total depreciation.

Cost   − Disposal value = Amount depreciated
$10,000 − $400   = $9,600

Step 2.   Find the depreciation rate (fraction).

Sum of digits in asset's life = Denominator
$1 + 2 + 3 + 4 + 5$ =   15

Years of remaining life = Numerator
5 (for the first year)   =   5

Step 3.   Find the amount of annual depreciation.

Amount   Depreciation   Annual
depreciated ×   rate   = depreciation
$9,600   ×   5/15   = $3,200

Note that the denominator remains constant each year, while the numerator changes each year to represent the years remaining (4 the second year, 3 the third year, and so forth).

Example 23.5 shows the depreciation amounts for each year.

Computing annual depreciation   EXAMPLE

23.5

Year	Remaining Life	Depreciation Computation	Annual Depreciation
1	5	5/15 × $9,600	$3,200
2	4	4/15 × $9,600	2,560
3	3	3/15 × $9,600	1,920
4	2	2/15 × $9,600	1,280
5	1	1/15 × $9,600	640
15	(Sum of the years' digits) TOTAL DEPRECIATION		$9,600

The depreciation schedule for the full 5 years is shown in Example 23.6. A *depreciation schedule* is usually prepared at the time an asset is acquired to show the cost, depreciation, accumulated depreciation, and book value of the asset over the years of useful life of the asset. Notice that accumulated depreciation amounts from Example 23.5 are subtracted from asset cost to compute the book value, as shown in Example 23.6.

Depreciation schedule: Sum-of-the-years' digits method   EXAMPLE

23.6

End of Year	Amount of Depreciation	Accumulated Depreciation	Book Value
1	$3,200	$3,200	$6,800
2	2,560	5,760	4,240
3	1,920	7,680	2,320
4	1,280	8,960	1,040
5	640	9,600	400

Notice that the book value after 5 years (the estimated life of the asset) is $400, the estimated disposal value.

The Declining-Balance Method

Declining-balance is an *accelerated depreciation method* because the asset depreciates more in the earlier years than in the later years of the asset's life. This method computes depreciation by applying a constant rate to the book value each year. In addition, disposal value is not considered in this method.

Under the new tax law, personal property, including business automobiles and equipment, is depreciated using the 200-percent-declining-balance method. Remember that real estate has a longer life and is depreciated by the straight-line method discussed earlier.

Under this method, the depreciation is twice as large as under the straight-line method for the first year the asset is placed in service, as shown in Example 23.7.

EXAMPLE   Computing first-year depreciation
23.7

Problem: A delivery truck costs $15,000 with a useful life of 5 years. What is the first year's depreciation?

Solution: **Step 1.** Find the declining-balance depreciation rate.

1 / Life $\times$ 2 = Depreciation rate
1 / 5 $\times$ 2 =   0.40 (40%)

Step 2. Find the first year's depreciation.

Book value $\times$ Depreciation rate = Depreciation
  $15,000 $\times$ 0.40   = $6,000

The depreciation is then deducted from the book value (cost in the first year) to compute the new book value after depreciation. The depreciation rate is then applied to the new book value for the second year. This process continues for subsequent years until the accelerated depreciation amount is less than the straight-line depreciation amount. Then, the straight-line method is used to complete depreciating the asset. This makes the process somewhat complicated and means that both methods must be used to determine when to switch methods.

Comparison of Depreciation Methods

A comparison of the declining-balance and straight-line methods for the full 5 years is shown in Example 23.8.

EXAMPLE   Comparing depreciation methods
23.8

Problem: A delivery truck is purchased for $15,000 with a useful life of 5 years and no disposal value. What are the annual depreciation amounts for each method (declining-balance and straight-line)?

(Solution on following page).

Solution:

Year	Straight-Line	Declining-Balance
1	$3,000	$6,000.00 (0.40 × $15,000)
2	3,000	3,600.00 (0.40 × $9,000)
3	3,000	2,160.00 (0.40 × $5,400)
4	3,000	1,296.00 (0.40 × $3,240)
5	3,000	777.60 (0.40 × $1,944)

Notice that the straight-line method produces larger depreciation than the declining-balance method during the third year. Therefore, the tax reform law requires that if depreciation is computed by the declining-balance method for the first 2 years, the straight-line method is used for later years.

EXAMPLE

23.9

Problem: A delivery truck purchased for $15,000 with a useful life of 5 years and no disposal value will be depreciated as shown below. (Review the amounts from Example 23.8 to find the depreciation for each year).

Solution: **Step 1.** Find the book value after the first 2 years.

Asset cost − Accumulated depreciation = Book value
$15,000 − $9,600 ($6,000 + $3,600) = $5,400

Step 2. Find annual depreciation for remaining years.

Book value / Remaining life = Annual depreciation
$5,400 / 3 = $1,800

Notice that depreciation is greater in the early years in the life of the asset. *Cost recovery* is a term used for depreciation in the tax code.

Accelerated Cost Recovery System

The *Accelerated Cost Recovery System* (ACRS) was a tax regulation system that assigned various assets into categories for tax purposes. ACRS applied to assets placed into service after 1980. For example, automobiles were placed into a category that allowed depreciation over a 3-year period. Real estate was placed into a category that allowed for depreciation over 19 years.

The Tax Reform Act of 1986 that took effect in 1987 maintained the ACRS structure. However, the new structure is based on *Asset Depreciation Range* (ADR), which sets the asset's life more closely to the length of time it is expected to be used in business. For example, under the new law automobiles are to be depreciated over 5 years (as opposed to 3 years under the old law). Typical classes of property are shown in Example 23.10.

EXAMPLE 23.10   Typical ACRS classes of assets

- 3-year class: includes small tools used in the manufacture of certain products.

- 5-year class: includes light trucks, automobiles, computer equipment, assets used in research and development, oil and gas drilling, construction, and the manufacture of certain products such as chemicals and electronic equipment.

- 7-year class: includes office furniture and fixtures and most other machinery and equipment.

- 10-, 15-, and 20-year classes: includes a limited number of other assets, including land improvements.

Note that the 150-percent-declining-balance method is used for the 15- and 20-year classes. The 200-percent-declining-balance method is used for all others. The 150-percent basis is 1.5 times the straight-line rate, while the 200-percent method is 2.0 times the straight-line rate. As outlined above, the accelerated method is used until the straight-line rate produces a larger depreciation. Then, the straight-line rate is applied for the remaining life.

Under the tax reform law, computation of depreciation is much more difficult. Formulas must be used rather than using simple tables. However, businesses have the option of using the straight-line method exclusively for the full life of the asset rather than using the accelerated method. Although this procedure is much simpler, it allows less depreciation during the early years.

• Complete Assignment 23.2 •

ASSIGNMENT 23.1 Computing Depreciation: Straight-Line Method

1. Find the total depreciation and the annual depreciation for each of the following assets using the straight-line method:

Asset	Total Cost	Disposal Value	Estimated Useful Life	Total Depreciation	Annual Depreciation
Tools	$ 5,600	$ 600	10 years	$ _____	$ _____
Automobile	9,700	400	5 years	$ _____	$ _____
Equipment	7,500	700	8 years	$ _____	$ _____
Furniture	7,600	300	10 years	$ _____	$ _____
Machinery	30,200	2,600	30 years	$ _____	$ _____
Building	152,040	30,000	27 years	$ _____	$ _____

2. An automobile costing $12,700 with an expected life of 4 years has an estimated disposal value of $1,000. Use the following form to develop a depreciation schedule for the automobile using the straight-line method:

End of Year	Annual Depreciation	Accumulated Depreciation	Book Value
			$12,700
1	$ _____	$ _____	$ _____
2	$ _____	$ _____	$ _____
3	$ _____	$ _____	$ _____
4	$ _____	$ _____	$ _____
AUTOMOBILE: Total cost = $12,700; Disposal value = $1,000; Life = 4 yrs.			

3. Eastmoreland and Associates purchased office equipment for $750 with an estimated life of 5 years and a disposal value of $50. Assuming a straight-line depreciation method, (a) what is the rate of annual depreciation? (b) What will the book value be at the end of the third year? (c) What will the accumulated depreciation be at the end of the third year?

(a) $ _____

(b) $ _____

(c) $ _____

4. Office furniture costing $6,200 was purchased on April 5. The company estimates that the furniture can be used for 12 years with a disposal value of $800. The fiscal year ends on December 31. Assuming a straight-line depreciation method, (a) what will the depreciation be during the first year? (b) What will the depreciation be during the second year? (c) What will the book value be at the end of the eighth year?

(a) $ _____

(b) $ _____

(c) $ _____

5. Modern office equipment cost $18,000 and had an estimated life of 15 years with an estimated disposal value of 20% of its original cost. Assuming a straight-line depreciation method, (a) what is the disposal value? (b) What is the annual depreciation? (c) What will the book value be at the end of the sixth year?

(a) $ _____

(b) $ _____

(c) $ _____

6. Depreciation on an escalator that cost $76,800 was figured at the rate of 12 1/2% a year and has a disposal value of $4,800. What are the (a) estimated life of the asset, (b) amount of the annual depreciation, and (c) book value at the end of the second year?

(a) _____

(b) $ _____

(c) $ _____

256

ASSIGNMENT 23.2 Computing Depreciation: Accelerated Cost Recovery System

1. Ray's Flower Shop owns a truck costing $14,000 with an estimated life of 5 years and no disposal value. Using the 200-percent-declining-balance method, develop a depreciation schedule using the following form:

End of Year	Rate	Annual Depreciation	Accumulated Depreciation	Book Value
				$14,000
1	____	$ _____	$ _____	$ _____
2	____	$ _____	$ _____	$ _____
3	____	$ _____	$ _____	$ _____
4	____	$ _____	$ _____	$ _____
5	____	$ _____	$ _____	$ _____

2. A truck cost $24,000 with an estimated life of 5 years and no disposal value. Use the following form to prepare a depreciation schedule. Use the 200-percent-declining-balance method.

End of Year	Declining-Balance Rate	Annual Depreciation	Accumulated Depreciation	Book Value
				$24,000
1	____	$ _____	$ _____	$ _____
2	____	$ _____	$ _____	$ _____
3	____	$ _____	$ _____	$ _____
4	____	$ _____	$ _____	$ _____
5	____	$ _____	$ _____	$ _____

3. Joan's Florist Shoppe purchased a delivery truck. Under the tax reform act, in which ADR class will this asset be placed?

_____

4. The Carson Insurance Agency purchased 7 new office desks. Under the tax reform act, in which ADR class will this asset be placed?

_____

5. The Embassy Print Shop purchased a delivery truck for $18,000. Using the 200-percent-declining-balance method, what are the (a) depreciation and (b) book value after 1 year?

(a) $_____

(b) $_____

6. The Dreyfus Company purchased small tools that are in the 3-year class for $800. Using the 200-percent-declining-balance method, what are the (a) depreciation and (b) book value after 1 year?

(a) $_____

(b) $_____

7. The Elliot Sports Center purchased an automobile for business purposes costing $12,000. The asset is in the 5-year class. The automobile was purchased in October. Using the 200-percent-declining-balance method, what is the amount of depreciation at the end of the tax year in December?

$_____

8. Aurillian Jordan purchased rental property for $127,500. Based on the straight-line method and an allowable depreciable life of 27.5 years, what is the amount of annual depreciation?

$_____

258

FINANCIAL STATEMENT ANALYSIS

Accountants prepare various reports to provide management and stockholders with knowledge about how well the business is operating financially. The two most popular reports are the balance sheet that shows the financial condition of the business and the income statement that shows the income, expenses, and profit (or loss) for a period of time. In this chapter, you will learn basic ways to evaluate information included on these financial reports.

Comparing Balance Sheets

The balance sheet shows what is owned (assets), what is owed (liabilities), and the net worth (capital or equity) of the business. In other words, the balance sheet shows the financial condition of the business on the day the balance sheet is prepared. Much valuable information can be obtained by comparing data from one period with data from another period to see if items are increasing or decreasing. These changes are usually shown as a percent of increase or decrease of one period over the previous period. The balance sheet shows this comparison. The comparative balance sheet for XYZ Corporation shown in Example 24.1 will be used to provide data for many of the examples in this chapter. You should review the balance sheet for each example to determine where the values in the examples are located.

Analyzing the Balance Sheet

There are several ways that the balance sheet for XYZ Corporation can be analyzed to provide useful information to help management personnel make decisions. Some of the more typical ways are presented here. (All computations are rounded to one decimal place.)

The *amount of working capital* tells a business how much its current assets exceed current liabilities. Current assets minus current liabilities equals amount of working capital, as shown in Example 24.2.

259

EXAMPLE   Comparative balance sheet
24.1

XYZ CORPORATION
Comparative Balance Sheet
December 31, 19Y1 and 19Y2

	Amounts		Increase or Decrease During 19Y2	
	19Y1	19Y2	Amount	Rate
ASSETS				
Current Assets				
Cash	$ 10,000	$ 12,000	$ 2,000	20.0
Accounts Receivable	12,000	15,000	3,000	25.0
Merchandise Inventory	40,000	35,000	(5,000)	(12.5)
Total Current Assets	62,000	62,000	–0–	–0–
Property-Plant-Equipment				
Land	20,000	20,000	–0–	
Building	80,000	72,000	(8,000)	(10.0)
Equipment	10,000	8,000	(2,000)	(20.0)
Total Property-Plant-Equip.	110,000	100,000	(10,000)	(9.1)
Total Assets	$172,000	$162,000	$(10,000)	(5.8)
LIABILITIES AND OWNERS' EQUITY				
Current Liabilities				
Accounts Payable	$ 8,000	$ 10,000	$ 2,000	25.0
Note Payable	4,000	5,000	1,000	25.0
Total Current Liabilities	12,000	15,000	3,000	25.0
Long-Term Liabilities				
Mortgage Payable	50,000	60,000	10,000	20.0
Total Liabilities	$ 62,000	$ 75,000	$ 13,000	21.0
Owners' Equity				
Capital Stock	60,000	60,000	–0–	–0–
Retained Earnings	50,000	27,000	(23,000)	(46.0)
Total Owners' Equity	$110,000	$ 87,000	$(23,000)	(22.3)
Total Liabilities and Owners' Equity	$172,000	$162,000	$(10,000)	(5.8)

Notes: Amounts in parentheses indicate decreases.
    Percents have been rounded to one decimal place.

EXAMPLE   Computing amount of working capital
24.2

Problem: The XYZ Corporation's current assets were $62,000, and current liabilities were $15,000, as shown in the comparative balance sheet in Example 24.1. What was the amount of working capital?

Solution: Current assets − Current liabilities = Working capital
          $62,000   − $15,000   = $47,000

The *current ratio* provides information about how easily creditors can be paid. For example, a bank will be interested in this information when the business applies for a loan because current assets are the primary source of funds for paying current liabilities. Current assets generally consist of cash and other assets that can be quickly converted to cash. Current liabilities generally consist of debts that are short-term (due within one year or less). To compute the current ratio, total current assets is divided by total current liabilities, as shown in Example 24.3. A general rule is that a ratio of 2 to 1 or higher is good.

Computing current ratio   EXAMPLE

24.3

Problem: The XYZ Corporation's current assets were $62,000, and current liabilities were $15,000. What was the current ratio?

Solution: Current assets / Current liabilities = Current ratio
$62,000   / $15,000   =   4.1

The *acid-test ratio*, or *quick ratio*, is similar in purpose to the current ratio. For the quick ratio, however, only current assets or other assets that can be quickly converted to cash (such as accounts receivable) are included. Merchandise inventory usually takes longer to convert and is not included in the acid-test ratio. As a general rule, this ratio should be 1 to 1 or higher. For the XYZ Corporation, total current assets (minus merchandise inventory) is divided by total current liabilities for the year 19Y2, as shown in Example 24.4.

Computing acid-test (quick) ratio   EXAMPLE

24.4

Problem: The XYZ Corporation had $62,000 current assets (including $35,000 in merchandise inventory) and $15,000 current liabilities. What was the acid-test or quick ratio?

Solution: Current assets   Current   Quick
(less merchandise inventory) / liabilities = ratio
$27,000   / $15,000 = 1.8

($62,000 − $35,000 = $27,000)

The *ratio of owners' equity to total liabilities* provides information about how well the owners' worth in the business can cover the total debts of the business. To compute this ratio, the amount of the owners' equity is divided by total liabilities, as shown in Example 24.5.

EXAMPLE
24.5

Computing ratio of owners' equity to total liabilities

Problem: The XYZ Corporation had $87,000 owners' equity and $75,000 total liabilities. What was the ratio of owners' equity to total liabilities?

Solution:

Owners' equity	/	Total liabilities	=	Ratio of owners' equity to total liabilities
$87,000	/	$75,000	=	1.2

The *ratio of assets to capital* shows the degree that the owners' equity is covered by total assets of the business. This ratio is computed by dividing total assets by owners' equity. In 19Y2, the ratio is computed as shown in Example 24.6.

EXAMPLE
24.6

Computing ratio of assets to capital

Problem: The XYZ Corporation had $162,000 total assets and $87,000 owners' equity. What was the ratio of assets to capital?

Solution:

Total assets	/	Owners' equity	=	Ratio of assets to capital
$162,000	/	$87,000	=	1.9

The *ratio of capital to liabilities* provides information about the total liquidity of the business. It compares the owners' claims on the assets with the claims of outside creditors. Owners' equity is divided by total liabilities for 19Y2's ratio, as shown in Example 24.7.

EXAMPLE
24.7

Computing ratio of capital to liabilities

Problem: The XYZ Corporation had $87,000 owners' equity and $75,000 total liabilities. What was the ratio of capital to liabilities?

Solution:

Owners' equity	/	Total liabilities	=	Ratio of capital to liabilities
$87,000	/	$75,000	=	1.2

● **Complete Assignment 24.1** ●

Comparing Income Statements

The income statement shows how the operation of a business has been affected over a period of time. The income statement shows costs, expenses, income, and net income (or loss) over a given period of time. A comparison of income statements provides information about how the operation is performing during one period as compared with another period. For example, annual sales of $2 million may sound good if annual sales for last year were only $1 million. However, annual sales of $2 million may be disappointing if last year's sales were $4 million.

The comparison of amounts on the income statement to determine increases and decreases is similar to the method used for comparing balance sheets. In addition, items on the income statement are often compared with net sales because net sales often serve as a basis for decisions. Both types of comparisons for the income statement for the ABC Corporation are shown in Example 24.8.

Comparative income statement   EXAMPLE

24.8

ABC CORPORATION
Comparative Income Statement
For the Years Ended December 31, 19Y1 and 19Y2

	Years Ended		Change		Percent of Net Sales	
	19Y1	19Y2	Amount	Percent	19Y1	19Y2
Income:						
Net Sales	$800,000	$880,000	$80,000	10.0	100.0	100.0
Cost of Goods Sold	550,000	594,000	44,000	8.0	68.8	67.5
Gross Profit on Sales	250,000	286,000	36,000	14.4	31.3	32.5
Operating Expenses:						
General Expenses	80,000	72,000	(8,000)	(10.0)	10.0	8.2
Selling Expenses	20,000	15,000	(5,000)	(25.0)	2.5	1.7
Total Operating Expenses	100,000	87,000	(13,000)	(13.0)	12.5	9.9
Net Income from Operations	150,000	199,000	49,000	32.7	18.8	22.6

To find the change from the first year (19Y1) to the second year (19Y2), subtract the amount for 19Y1 from the amount for 19Y2. To find the percent of change, divide the change by the amount of the base (19Y1). These computations for the first item on the income statement (net sales) are shown in Example 24.9.

EXAMPLE

24.9

Problem: The ABC Corporation had $880,000 net sales this year and $800,000 net sales last year. What was the percent of change from last year to this year?

Solution: **Step 1.** Find the amount of change.

This year's net sales	−	Last year's net sales	= Change
$880,000	−	$800,000	= $80,000

Step 2. Find the rate of change.

Amount of change	/	Last year's net sales base	=	Rate of change
$80,000	/	$800,000	=	0.10 (10%)

If the amount for 19Y2 is more than the amount for 19Y1, the change and percent will be positive. Otherwise, the change and percent will be negative.

The percent of net sales is computed by using the net sales for each year as the base. Each individual amount is then divided by the base to compute the rate. For example, *cost of goods sold* represents 68.8% ($550,000 ÷ $800,000) of net sales in 19Y1 and 67.5% ($594,000 ÷ $800,000) of net sales in 19Y2. This type of information allows a business to compare items for one period with the same items for another period or to compare items for one company with similar items for other companies.

• Complete Assignment 24.2 •

ASSIGNMENT 24.1 Financial Statement Analysis: Balance Sheet

1. Make computations to complete the blank spaces in the balance sheet shown below. Round percents to one decimal place.

	Amounts		Increase or Decrease During 19Y2	
	19Y1	19Y2	Amount	Rate
ASSETS				
Current Assets				
Cash	$ 40,000	$ 44,000	$	
Accounts Receivable	18,000	24,000		
Merchandise Inventory	40,000	42,000		
Total Current Assets	98,000	110,000		
Property-Plant-Equipment				
Land	75,000	75,000		
Building	100,000	95,000		
Equipment	50,000	40,000		
Total Property-Plant-Equip.	225,000	210,000		
Total Assets	$323,000	$320,000	$	
LIABILITIES AND OWNERS' EQUITY				
Current Liabilities				
Accounts Payable	$ 24,500	$ 29,400	$	
Long-Term Liabilities				
Mortgage Payable	75,000	73,125		
Total Liabilities	99,500	102,525		
Owners' Equity				
Capital Stock	175,000	175,000		
Retained Earnings	48,500	42,475		
Total Owners' Equity	223,500	217,475		
Total Liabilities and Owners' Equity	$323,000	$320,000	$	

2. Compute the following information for each year (19Y1 and 19Y2) using amounts from the comparative balance sheet in Problem 1 above. Round ratios to one decimal place.

Information to be Determined	19Y1	19Y2
Working Capital	$ _____	$ _____
Current Ratio	___ to ___	___ to ___
Acid-Test Ratio	___ to ___	___ to ___
Owners' Equity Total Liability Ratio	___ to ___	___ to ___
Assets to Capital Ratio	___ to ___	___ to ___
Capital to Liabilities Ratio	___ to ___	___ to ___

3. Current assets for the Byrd Building Supply Company include a counter case ($33,000), accounts receivable ($16,000), and marketable securities ($47,000). Total current liabilities amount to $38,400. What is the acid-test ratio?

_____

4. Enco Services' balance sheet provides the following information: Current Assets, $80,000; Plant-and-Equipment, $280,000; Current Liabilities, $20,000; Long-Term Liabilities, $80,000; and Owners' Equity, $260,000. What are the (a) amount of working capital, (b) current ratio, (c) assets to capital ratio, and (d) capital to liabilities ratio?

(a) $ _____

(b) _____

(c) _____

(d) _____

ASSIGNMENT 24.2   Financial Statement Analysis: Income Statement

1. Make computations to complete the blank spaces in the following comparative income statement. Round percents to one decimal place.

	Years Ended		Change		Percent of Net Sales	
	19Y1	19Y2	Amount	Rate	19Y1	19Y2
Income:						
Net Sales	$480,000	$528,000	$ _____	_____	_____	_____
Cost of Goods Sold	230,000	253,000	_____	_____	_____	_____
Gross Profit on Sales	250,000	275,000	_____	_____	_____	_____
Operating Expenses:						
General Expenses	50,000	52,000	_____	_____	_____	_____
Selling Expenses	60,000	69,000	_____	_____	_____	_____
Total Operating Expenses	110,000	121,000	_____	_____	_____	_____
Net Income from Operations	140,000	154,000	_____	_____	_____	_____
Other Income:						
Interest Income	8,000	8,000	_____	_____	_____	_____
Net Income Before Taxes	$148,000	$162,000	_____	_____	_____	_____

2. A company owned by Henryk Jablonski had net sales for the past year of $240,000. Selling expenses were $58,800. What percent of the net sales is represented by selling expenses?

_____

3. The Turner Office Supply Company had net sales of $640,000 and selling expenses of $224,000. A study predicts that an increase in selling expenses of 20% will result in an increase in net sales of 10% for the next year if all other amounts remain the same. Compute the percent of net sales represented by selling expenses (a) last year and (b) under the predicted conditions.

(a) _____

(b) _____

4. Collins Industries had net sales of $580,500 last year. Net income before taxes represented 25% of net sales. What was the amount of net income before taxes for the year?

$ _____

5. Operating expenses for the current year for Biggest Burger, Inc., were $281,250, which represented a 25% increase over the previous year. What were the operating expenses for the previous year?

$ _____

6. Hartwell Charities, Inc., received donations last year amounting to $32,500. The company's goal for next year is $44,525. What percent of increase will be needed to meet the goal?

_____

7. A university has an enrollment of 3,500 students. The Dean of Admissions is projecting a 7% increase for next year. What is the projected enrollment for next year?

_____

• **Complete Unit 5 Spreadsheet Applications** •

UNIT 5   SPREADSHEET APPLICATION 1: **Payroll Report**

The following spreadsheet is used to compute gross wages, income taxes, FICA taxes, and net pay. It is also used to compute totals for the hours worked, gross wages, income taxes, FICA taxes, total taxes, and net pay columns. The number of hours worked is multiplied by the pay rate to compute gross wages. The gross wages amount is multiplied by 0.15 to compute income taxes and by 0.0715 to compute FICA taxes. The sum of the two tax amounts provides total taxes. Total taxes are deducted from gross wages to compute net pay.

```
        A         B        C        D        E        F        G        H
1   Don's Restaurant         PAYROLL  REPORT
2   ===================================================================
3             Hours     Pay     Gross   Income    FICA    Total           Net
4   Employee  Worked    Rate    Wages   Taxes*    Taxes*  Taxes           Pay
5   -----------------------------------------------------------------
6   Boxley       24     6.50
7   Cansler      30     5.95
8   Curle        20     6.25
9   Draper       22     5.15
10  Granacki     35     5.75
11  Jordan       40     6.45
12  McCoy        24     4.80
13  Pipkin       18     5.15
14  Schelly      26     6.85
15  Tsai         30     7.25
16  Wagley       38     6.20
17  -----------------------------------------------------------------
18    Totals            ******
19  ===================================================================
20  *Income Tax Rate = 15% and FICA Tax Rate = 7.15%
```

Refer to the spreadsheet above to answer the following questions:

1. What is the gross wages amount for Jordan?   _____

2. What is the income taxes amount for Pipkin?   _____

3. What is the FICA taxes amount for Draper?   _____

4. What is the total taxes amount for Boxley?   _____

5. What is the net pay amount for Granacki?   _____

6. How many total hours were worked by all employees?   _____

7. How many employees had net pay greater than $100.00?   _____

8. How many employees had total taxes greater than $40.00?   _____

9. How many employees worked exactly 40 hours?   _____

10. What was the total net pay for all employees?   _____

UNIT 5   SPREADSHEET APPLICATION 2: Depreciation Computation

The following spreadsheet is used to compute the depreciation for several assets. Totals are computed for the cost, straight-line, declining-balance, and difference columns. Straight-line depreciation is computed by dividing the cost amount by the class life of the asset. The 200-percent-declining-balance depreciation amount is computed by multiplying the straight-line rate by the value 2 times the cost amount. The difference is computed by subtracting the straight-line amount from the declining-balance amount.

```
     A         B            C          D          E          F          G
 1  Don's Pizza                                DEPRECIATION COMPUTATION
 2  =================================================================================
 3                                     Class   Straight   Declining
 4   #|  Asset            Cost         Life     Line      Balance    Difference
 5  --|  ------------------------------------------------------------------------
 6   1|Car-Al           14,500          5     2,900.00   5,800.00    2,900.00
 7   2|Car-A2           17,680          5
 8   3|Computer          3,475          5
 9   4|Furniture-Al      4,980          7
10   5|Land Improv.     25,700         15
11   6|Machine-Al        6,450          7
12   7|Small tools         800          3
13   8|Truck-Al         14,800          5
14   9|Truck-A2         15,225          5
15  10|Truck-A3         15,780          5
16  11|Truck-A4         16,200          5
17  12|Truck-A5         16,800          5
18    |  ------------------------------------------------------------------------
19    |   Totals                   *******
20  =================================================================================
```

Refer to the spreadsheet above to answer the following questions:

1. What is the straight-line depreciation amount for Car-A2?   _____

2. What is the straight-line depreciation amount for small tools?   _____

3. What is the straight-line depreciation amount for Truck-A4?   _____

4. What is the declining-balance depreciation amount for Furniture-A1?   _____

5. What is the declining-balance depreciation amount for Truck-A2?   _____

6. What is the declining-balance depreciation amount for Computer?   _____

7. What is the total cost of the assets?   _____

8. What is the total straight-line depreciation for all assets?   _____

9. What is the difference in depreciation amounts for Machine-A1?   _____

10. What is the total difference in depreciation amounts for all assets?   _____

• Complete Unit 5 Self-Test •

UNIT 5 SELF-TEST Payroll and Accounting

1. Marilyn Harrison works the following numbers of hours from Monday to Friday respectively during the week: 9, 8, 10, 10, and 8. Assuming a regular rate of $9.60 and an overtime rate of one and one-half the regular rate for hours in excess of ·40, what are her (a) regular earnings, (b) overtime earnings, and (c) gross earnings for the week?

   (a) $ _____

   (b) $ _____

   (c) $ _____

2. Kim Romero produced 3,000 units during the week. If she is paid $0.08 for each of the first 2,000 units produced and $0.10 for each unit produced in excess of 2,000 units, what were her gross earnings?

   $ _____

3. Odella McKinnon produced 900 units during the week. She is paid $6.25 per hour plus $0.10 per unit produced. What are her gross earnings if she worked 40 hours?

   $ _____

4. Darren Feldman earned $425.50 last week. If the FICA rate is 7.15%, what amount will be withheld from his paycheck for this tax?

   $ _____

5. Felton Greason earned $18,750 last year. Based on an income tax withholding rate of 15%, what was his tax liability?

   $ _____

6. Jan Klodzinski earned $32,425 last year. Based on an income tax withholding rate of 15% on the first $17,850 and a rate of 28% on income in excess of $17,850, what was his tax liability?

   $ _____

7. Assume that a personal exemption of $1,950 is allowed for each dependent and a standard deduction of $5,000 for John and Joan McKinley. They are filing a joint return with a total of 4 personal exemptions. Their gross income is $32,876. What is their taxable income?

$ _____

8. Bill McDonald is single. He earned $600 last week. Assume that $115 was withheld for income taxes, that the FICA rate is 7.15%, and that $8 was withheld for union dues. What was his net pay?

$ _____

9. A crafts store in Dover County has a true value of $269,000. If property is assessed at 25% of its true value, what is the assessed valuation of the property?

$ _____

10. Abbey Curland owns a business with an assessed value of $320,500. If the property tax is set at $2.75 per $100 of assessed value, how much property tax must be paid?

$ _____

11. William Vaught owns a house with an assessed value of $175,500. If the tax rate is 0.056, how much in property taxes must be paid?

$ _____

12. The Briar Store's inventory records provide the following information: Beginning balance on April 1 was 25 units @ $5.20; 10 units purchased on April 10 @ $5.30; and 20 units purchased on April 18 @ $5.40. There were 10 units on hand on April 30. What is the value of the ending inventory under each of the following methods: (a) FIFO, (b) LIFO, and (c) average cost?

(a) $ _____

(b) $ _____

(c) $ _____

274

13. During the last fiscal year, the House of Gifts had a beginning inventory of $36,000, purchases of $200,000, and an ending inventory of $28,000. Indicate the amount of (a) merchandise available for sale, (b) cost of goods sold, and (c) the merchandise turnover ratio. Round answers to two decimal places.

(a) $ _____

(b) $ _____

(c) _____

14. A particular computer cost $48,000 with an estimated useful life of 5 years and no disposal value. What is the depreciation during the first year under the (a) straight-line and (b) 200-percent-declining-balance methods?

(a) $ _____

(b) $ _____

15. A delivery truck cost $17,800 with an estimated life of 5 years and no disposal value. Using the straight-line method, what is the book value at the end of (a) the first year and (b) the second year?

(a) $ _____

(b) $ _____

16. An automobile cost $12,800 with an estimated life of 5 years and no disposal value. Using the 200-percent-declining-balance method, what is the book value at the end of (a) the first year and (b) the second year?

(a) $ _____

(b) $ _____

17. A truck costing $15,500 is purchased on July 1. The asset fits into the 5-year class life. Using the 200-percent-declining-balance method, what will the depreciation be on December 31 of (a) the first year and (b) the second year?

(a) $ _____

(b) $ _____

18. An analysis of the balance sheet of Drake's Catering Service yields the following information. Compute the information requested below.

Current Assets	$120,000
Property-Plant-Equipment	$225,000
Current Liabilities	$ 80,000
Long-Term Liabilities	$150,000
Owner's Equity	$115,000

(a) Working Capital $ _____

(b) Current Ratio   _____

(c) Assets-to-Capital Ratio   _____

(d) Capital-to-Liabilities Ratio   _____

19. Bob Zack Plumbers had income last year of $260,500 and income this year of $325,625. What is the company's (a) percent of increase and (b) amount of increase in income?

(a) _____

(b) $ _____

20. Net sales for Ron Lewton Popcorn Supplies for last year were $350,000. The cost of goods sold was $269,500. What percent of net sales is represented by cost of goods sold?

_____

276

Business Finance

Computations relating to the value of money (now and in the future) and the costs associated with the use of money (interest) are included in this unit. Premiums, loss recovery, and surrender value computations for life and property insurance are presented.

Some skills you can achieve in this unit include the following:

- **Using a formula to compute simple interest on loans and savings accounts.**
- **Computing banker's ordinary interest and exact interest.**
- **Using shortcut methods to compute interest amounts.**
- **Determining discount periods for notes.**
- **Computing bank discount and proceeds for non-interest-bearing and interest-bearing notes.**
- **Using a formula to compute compound interest amounts on notes.**
- **Using a table to determine compound interest amounts on notes.**
- **Using a table to determine the present value of amounts and annuities.**
- **Using a table to determine deposits for sinking fund amounts.**

UNIT 6

COMPUTING SIMPLE INTEREST

Businesses and individuals borrow money for a variety of purposes, such as expanding operations, purchasing additional plant and equipment, and obtaining additional cash to operate the business. The amount borrowed (principal), plus the fee for using the money (simple interest), is paid at the end of a specified period of time. Promissory notes and trade acceptances are the most common commercial paper used as evidence for short-term loans of one year or less. Material in this chapter illustrates how simple interest is computed on money borrowed from individuals, banks, and other lending agencies.

Simple Interest Formula

The formula in Example 25.1 can be used to compute the interest amount charged for the use of borrowed money.

EXAMPLE   **Simple interest formula**

25.1

$$\text{Interest} = \text{Principal} \times \text{Rate} \times \text{Time}$$
$$\text{or}$$
$$I = P \times R \times T$$

The *principal* represents the amount of the loan. The *rate* is always expressed as a percent or as a decimal based on the fee charged for using the money for one year. The *time* is always expressed in years or as a fraction of 1 year. These three factors are illustrated in Example 25.2.

EXAMPLE   **Computing simple interest**

25.2

Problem: Floyd Carter borrowed $400.00 with repayment to be made in 1 year. The interest rate was 8%. What was the interest amount?

Solution: *Principal* ×   *Rate*   × *Time* = *Interest*
$400.00   × 0.08 (8%) ×   1   = $32.00

The interest on this same loan will be $16 for six months ($^6\!/_{12}$ or ½ of a year) or $64 for two years as shown in Example 25.3. If the time of the loan is expressed in months, the number of months should be placed over twelve since 12 months is equivalent to 1 year.

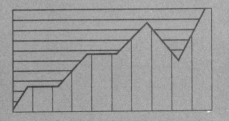

EXAMPLE

Simple interest formula for a period stated in months or years

25.3

$$P \quad \times \quad R \quad \times \quad T = \quad I$$

$$\$400.00 \times 0.08 \times \frac{1}{2} = \$16.00 \text{ (6 months)}$$

$$\$400.00 \times 0.08 \times 2 = \$64.00 \text{ (2 years)}$$

If an electronic calculator is used, the fractional part of a year can be converted to a decimal to obtain the same results. The calculation of interest on this same loan for six months using a decimal value is shown in Example 25.4.

EXAMPLE   **Simple interest formula for period stated as a decimal**

25.4

$$P \quad \times \quad R \quad \times \quad T = \quad I$$

$$\$400.00 \times 0.08 \times 0.5 = \$16.00$$

Example 25.5 presents a summary of the simple interest formula for a loan with a principal of $600, a rate of 9%, and a time (or due date) of 8 months.

EXAMPLE   **Procedure for using the simple interest formula**

25.5

Step 1.   Determine the principal, interest rate, and time of the loan.

Step 2.   Substitute the amounts from Step 1 into the interest formula.

$$I = P \times R \times T \text{ (or } P \times R \times T = I)$$

$$I = \$600.00 \times 0.09 \times \frac{8}{12}$$

Step 3.   Compute the interest.

$$P \quad \times \quad R \quad \times \quad T = \quad I$$

$$\$600.00 \times 0.09 \times \frac{8}{12} = \$144.00/4 = \$36.00$$

To further illustrate, a loan for $620 due in 6 months with a 12% interest rate will earn interest amounting to $37.20, as shown below.

$$P \times R \times T = I$$
$$\$620.00 \times 0.12 \times \frac{6}{12} = \$37.20$$

Computing Ordinary and Exact Interest

Some businesses, banks, and other institutions base the time for loans on a *banker's year* of 360 days if the time of the loan is stated in terms of days. A month is considered to be 30 days or $\frac{1}{12}$ of a year. This method is often referred to as the banker's method because some banks compute interest on the basis of a 360-day year. The interest computed by this method is called *ordinary interest*.

The same basic interest formula ($I = P \times R \times T$) is used to compute ordinary interest. For example, assume that a loan for $450 is due in 45 days with an interest rate of 10%. Using the same steps as in Example 25.5, the interest amount is computed as shown in Example 25.6.

Computing banker's ordinary interest   EXAMPLE

25.6

Step 1. The principal is $450.00, the interest rate is 10%, and the time is 45 days.

Step 2. $I = P \times R \times T$

$I = \$450.00 \times 0.10 \times 45/360$

Step 3. $\$450.00 \times 0.10 \times 45/360 = \$22.50/4 = \$5.625$ (rounded to $5.63)

.125

Note: The final interest amount is rounded to the nearest cent.

In a second example, interest on a 90-day, $1,400 loan with a 12% interest rate is computed as follows:

$$P \times R \times T = I$$
$$\$1,400.00 \times 0.12 \times 90/360 = \$42.00$$

Since the loan bears interest, the borrower will pay the original principal plus interest when the loan is due in 90 days. Therefore, the amount to be repaid is $1,442.00 ($1,400.00 + $42.00).

The procedure for computing *exact interest* is the same as the procedure for computing ordinary interest, except that 365 days are used as the basis for one year. The federal government and Federal Reserve

Banks make interest computations on this basis. Most bank loans are now based on a full 365-day year. The same loan in Example 25.6 earns interest based on a 365-day year as shown in Example 25.7.

EXAMPLE 25.7   Computing exact interest

$$P \times R \times T = I$$
$$\$450.00 \times 0.10 \times 45/365 = \$405/73 = \$5.55 \text{ (rounded)}$$

Using the ordinary-interest method, interest was computed to be $5.63, a difference of 8 cents from the interest computed using the exact-interest method. Interest will always be slightly lower when the exact-interest method is used. Unless otherwise directed, use the ordinary-interest method for problems in this chapter.

● **Complete Assignment 25.1** ●

The 60-Day, 6% Method

A shortcut method for computing ordinary simple interest is called the 60-day, 6% method. The basic principle is that when the time is 60 days and the interest rate is 6%, the interest can be determined simply by moving the decimal two places to the left in the principal amount. Therefore, the interest on a $620.00 loan due in 60 days with a 6% interest rate is $6.20. This can be proven by using the basic interest formula.

$$P \times R \times T = I$$
$$\$620.00 \times 0.06 \times 60/360 = \$6.20$$

Notice that the final computation after cancellation involves multiplying the principal amount by 1% (0.01). This is why moving the decimal point two places to the left in the principal amount provides the correct amount of interest. This method is popular because the solution can often be determined mentally without the aid of a calculator or paper and pencil.

By using logic, the interest amount for interest rates that are multiples of 6% and time periods that are multiples of 60 days can be easily determined. For example, interest on the above loan for 120 days at the same 6% interest rate can be determined by multiplying $6.20 by 2 ($12.40) because the number of days is doubled (60 × 2 = 120). Likewise, an interest rate of 9% is 1½ times 6% (9/6 = 1½). The interest amount is determined by moving the decimal two places to the left ($6.20) and multiplying the resulting amount by 1½ ($6.20 × 1½ = $9.30). Solve the problems in Example 25.8 mentally and test your knowledge of this shortcut method by comparing your answers to the ones provided below the problems.

Sample problems and solutions using the 60-day, 6% method   EXAMPLE

Problems: (a) $300.00 at 9% for 60 days $ _____

          (b) $400.00 at 6% for 30 days $ _____

          (c) $650.00 at 6% for 180 days $ _____

          (d) $1,350 at 8% for 30 days $ _____

          (e) $400.00 at 7½% for 72 days $ _____

Solutions: (a) $4.50, (b) $2.00, (c) $19.50, (d) $9.00, (e) $6.00.

The terms of the loan dictate whether the interest formula or short-cut method is most appropriate. Regardless of the terms, the shortcut method can be used to provide an estimate to indicate whether or not the computed interest amount is a reasonable answer. Because of the possibility of error, two computations are usually made to ensure that the interest amount is correct.

Determining the Due Date

The time when a loan is due is usually stated in terms of days, months, or years. For example, a 30-day loan dated July 15 will be due on August 14. The 16 days remaining in July, plus 14 days in August, account for 30 days. In other words, you must compute the exact due date based on the number of days in each specific month involved.

If the due date is expressed in terms of months, the due date will be the same day of the month as the date of the loan. For example, a one-month loan dated July 15 will be due on August 15. Since some loans contain a provision for penalty if not paid on or before the due date, it is important to accurately determine the due date.

• Complete Assignment 25.2 •

ASSIGNMENT 25.1   Computing Simple Interest

1. Use the formula for computing interest, I = P × R × T, to find the interest for each of the following loans using a 360-day year and a 365-day year. (Round answers to the nearest cent.)

Loan	Ordinary Method 360-Day Year	Exact Method 365-Day Year
$600.00 at 10% for 30 days	$	$
$875.00 at 8% for 75 days	$	$
$850.00 at 12% for 90 days	$	$
$1,250.00 at 12% for 72 days	$	$
$2,400.00 at 9% for 45 days	$	$

2. Use the ordinary-interest method to compute interest on the following loans:

Loan	Ordinary Interest
$840.00 at 9% for 84 days	$ _____
$700.00 at 7 1/2% for 72 days	$ _____
$2,484.00 at 15% for 2 months	$ _____
$600.00 at 10 1/2% for 7 months	$ _____
$24,600.00 at 8% for 5 months	$ _____

3. Examine the following promissory note. Use the interest formula to compute the interest that will be due for the loan. How much interest will be due?

$ _____

PROMISSORY NOTE
Ninety (90) days after current date I promise to pay to the order of Brad Yahonna the sum of Eight hundred fifty and no/100 dollars ($850.00) plus interest at an annual rate of nine (9) percent.
Date: _____
Signed: _____

286

ASSIGNMENT 25.2 Computing Interest and Due Date

1. Use the 60-day, 6% method to compute interest for each of the following loans. Check your answers by using the interest formula.

Loan	60-Day 6% Method	Formula Method
$960.00 at 6% for 60 days	$	$
$620.00 at 6% for 90 days	$	$
$480.00 at 18% for 60 days	$	$
$540.00 at 18% for 30 days	$	$
$850.00 at 12% for 60 days	$	$
$960.00 at 7 1/2% for 60 days	$	$
$540.00 at 6% for 180 days	$	$
$740.00 at 9% for 75 days	$	$
$865.00 at 9% for 120 days	$	$
$1,449.00 at 4 1/2% for 180 days	$	$

2. Evaluate the dates and due dates for the following loans to determine the number of days for each loan. (Assume that February is not included in a leap year.)

Date	Due Date	Number of Days
January 1	February 15	_____
March 4	May 16	_____
July 23	October 12	_____
May 4	July 15	_____
November 7	December 7	_____
January 9	April 15	_____
April 13	July 21	_____
June 3	August 15	_____
February 4	March 28	_____
March 15	May 30	_____

3. Evaluate the date and time to maturity for the following loans to determine the due date. (Assume that February is not included in a leap year.)

Date	Time	Due Date
August 16	75 days	_____
April 3	30 days	_____
July 16	72 days	_____
January 3	90 days	_____
March 13	45 days	_____
April 18	3 months	_____
September 14	45 days	_____
November 21	4 months	_____
February 3	6 months	_____
February 8	120 days	_____

288

DISCOUNTING NOTES

A promissory note is a negotiable instrument, which means that the note can be transferred to a bank or other third party in much the same manner as a check. A major difference is that notes usually bear interest. Interest to be earned between the date the note is passed on to a third party and the maturity date must be accounted for. The bank will deduct a specific interest charge from the maturity value of the note because it will have to wait until the maturity date to receive payment for the loan. In these instances, the deduction for interest is commonly called *discount* or *bank discount*, although it is not a discount in the same sense that a retail store discounts merchandise. Material in this chapter shows you how to compute discounts on notes.

EXAMPLE **A promissory note**

26.1

```
$ _____                                    19 ___
        _____ after date, (without grace) _____ promise
to pay to the order of _____
_____ Dollars
for value received with interest of _____ her cent per
_____ from _____ until paid both
principal and interest payable only in LAWFUL MONEY OF THE UNITED STATES.

Payable at _____
No. _____   Due _____        _____
```

Determining Discount Period

Businesses frequently accept promissory notes, trade acceptances, or installment sales contracts when selling merchandise. The customer agrees to pay the amount at some future time. In order to get money immediately, the business often trades the document to the bank for cash. The bank will charge a fee to reimburse the business for the period of time that the document must be held until the payment due date. This procedure is called *discounting commercial paper* or *notes.*

The due date and discount period must be determined prior to computing the discount amount. Discussion in this chapter relates to discounting of commercial paper by banks. However, other lending agencies and individuals may use the same procedures when discounting notes or other types of commercial paper. Notes will also be used in examples even though other types of commercial paper may be discounted in a similar manner.

The due date will normally be listed as a specific date or as a certain period of time from the date of the note, such as due in 30

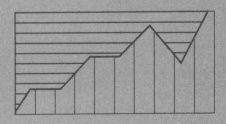

days or due in 5 months. When a due date is stated in months, the due date will be on the same day of the month as the date of the note. For a 2-month loan dated July 8, the due date is September 8.

Assume that a note with a due date of May 18 is discounted on March 13. Computation of the discount period is shown in Example 26.2.

EXAMPLE

26.2

Determining the discount period

Step 1.   Determine the due date.

May 18 (in this example)

Step 2.   Determine the discount date.

March 13 (in this example)

Step 3.   Determine the number of days between the due date and the discount date.

Days in March   = 18
Days in April   = 30
Days in May   = <u>18</u>
Discount period = 66 days

Likewise, a note discounted on September 3 with a due date of October 16 will have a discount period of 43 days as shown below.

Days in September (30 − 3) = 27
Days in October   = 16
Discount period   = 43 days

Discounting a Non-Interest-Bearing Note

The *maturity value* of a note is the total amount of money that will be paid on the due date. *Face value* is the amount of the note without considering interest earned on the note. If the note bears interest, the maturity value equals face value plus interest. In the case of a non-interest-bearing note, the face value and the maturity value are the same and no interest is earned.

Assume that the Perez Office Supply Store has a non-interest-bearing note with a face value of $640.00 and a due date of September 15. In order to obtain cash, the store sells the note to the First National Bank on August 16 (30 days prior to the due date). The bank will not pay the store the full amount ($640.00), but it will charge a fee called the *bank discount*. This fee is usually stated as a percentage of the maturity value. The same formula used to compute simple interest ($I = P \times R \times T$) is used to compute the bank discount. The amount received (called *proceeds*) by the store equals the maturity value less the bank discount.

To further illustrate this example, the steps shown in Example 26.3 are taken to compute bank discount and proceeds. Assume that the bank uses a 12% discount rate.

Computing bank discount and proceeds for a non-interest-bearing note   EXAMPLE

26.3

Step 1. Determine the maturity value.

$640.00 (in this example)

Step 2. Compute the bank discount using the simple interest formula.

			Discount	Bank
Maturity value $\times$	Discount rate $\times$		period =	discount
$640.00	$\times$ 0.12	$\times$	30/360 =	$6.40

Step 3. Compute proceeds by subtracting the discount from the maturity value.

Maturity value $-$ Discount = Proceeds
$640.00 $-$ $6.40   = $633.60

In an additional example, assume that the Perez Office Supply Store has a $300.00 non-interest-bearing note due on April 30 that is discounted at the bank on March 1 at a discount rate of 15%. Using the steps in Example 26.3, proceeds of $292.50 are computed as follows:

Step 1. Maturity value is $300.00.

Step 2. Discount period from March 1 to April 30 is 60 days.

Step 3. $300.00 $\times$ 0.15 $\times$ 60/360 = $7.50 (bank discount)

Step 4. $300.00 $-$ $7.50 = $292.50 (proceeds)

As the above example shows, the Perez Office Supply Store will receive $292.50 from the bank on March 1 in return for the note. On the maturity date (April 30), the bank will collect the maturity value ($300.00). If the person who originally purchased the merchandise does not pay the bank when the note becomes due on April 30, the Perez Office Supply Store must pay the bank the maturity value and attempt to collect from the customer. This provides the bank protection from bad debts.

Remember that the main advantage for a person or business selling a note to the bank is that proceeds are available immediately rather than waiting until the due date to collect the maturity value.

• Complete Assignment 26.1 •

Discounting an Interest-Bearing Note

The face value of a note may bear interest. For this type of note, interest must be computed and added to the face value to compute the maturity value. Except for this computation (Step 1), the procedure for discounting an interest-bearing note is similar to the procedure used to discount a non-interest-bearing note in Example 26.3. To illustrate, assume that McGuire's Dairy accepts a 90-day (due date of July 30) note with a face value of $500 and an interest rate of 12% on May 1. On May 11, the note is sold to the bank with a discount rate of 15%. The bank discount and proceeds on May 11 are computed as shown in Example 26.4.

EXAMPLE	**Computing bank discount and proceeds for an interest-bearing note**
26.4	

Step 1. Determine the maturity value, including interest.

$$P \times R \times T = I$$
$$\$500.00 \times 0.12 \times 90/360 = \$15.00$$
$$P + I = MV$$
$$\$500.00 + \$15.00 = \$515.00 \text{ (maturity value)}$$

Step 2. Determine the discount period.

May 11 to July 30 = 80 days

Step 3. Compute the bank discount by multiplying the maturity value by the discount rate by the time.

$$MV \times R \times T = \text{Bank discount}$$
$$\$515.00 \times 0.15 \times 80/360 = \$17.17 \text{ (rounded)}$$

Step 4. Compute the proceeds by subtracting the bank discount from the maturity value.

$$\text{Maturity value} - \text{Discount} = \text{Proceeds}$$
$$\$515.00 - \$17.17 = \$497.83$$

In Example 26.4, McGuire's Dairy will receive $497.83 from the bank on May 11. On July 30, the bank will collect the maturity value of the note ($515.00). Notice that the proceeds were less than the face value of the note because the discount rate was higher than the interest rate and because McGuire's Dairy held the note for only a short period of time. The proceeds may be higher or lower than the face value depending on how the above factors affect the transaction.

In a second illustration, assume that the Nashika Tool Company accepts a 90-day, $600 note bearing interest at a rate of 4% with a due date of November 30. On October 31, the note is sold to the bank with a discount rate of 12%. The bank discount and proceeds are computed as follows:

Step 1. $600.00 $\times$ 0.04 $\times$ 90/360 = $6.00

$600.00 + $6.00 = $606.00 (maturity value)

Step 2. October 31 to November 30 = 30 days (discount period)

Step 3. $606.00 $\times$ 0.12 $\times$ 30/360 = $6.06 (bank discount)

Step 4. $606.00 − $6.06 = $599.94 (proceeds)

● **Complete Assignment 26.2** ●

Step 1. $600.00 $\times$ 0.04 $\times$ 90/360 = $6.00

$600.00 + $6.00 = $606.00 (maturity value)

ASSIGNMENT 26.1 Computing Discounts on Non-Interest-Bearing Notes

1. Determine the maturity date and discount period for each of the following notes:

Date of Note	Length of Note	Discount Date	Maturity Date	Discount Period
February 11	30 days	February 14	_____	_____
April 18	60 days	May 15	_____	_____
June 3	75 days	July 8	_____	_____
August 8	80 days	October 15	_____	_____
May 7	90 days	July 1	_____	_____

2. Determine the maturity date and discount period for each of the following notes:

Date of Note	Length of Note	Discount Date	Maturity Date	Discount Period
May 16	2 months	May 23	_____	_____
February 3	3 months	March 1	_____	_____
July 16	2 months	July 31	_____	_____
January 28	4 months	February 26	_____	_____
November 18	3 months	January 3	_____	_____

3. Find the (a) bank discount and (b) proceeds for the following non-interest-bearing note. A note with a maturity value of $2,400 is discounted 60 days prior to the due date at a 10% discount rate.

(a) $ _____

(b) $ _____

4. Find the (a) bank discount and (b) proceeds for the following non-interest-bearing note. A note with a maturity value of $3,624.72 is discounted 75 days prior to the due date at a 12% discount rate.

(a) $ _____

(b) $ _____

5. The Pineira Novelty Shoppe accepts a non-interest-bearing note with a date of May 15 and a maturity date of July 29. The face value is $900. The note is discounted on June 14 with a 6% discount rate. What are the (a) length of the note, (b) discount period, (c) discount amount, and (d) amount of proceeds?

(a) _____

(b) _____

(c) $ _____

(d) $ _____

6. Tom Carlton Builders accepts a non-interest-bearing note with a due date of November 15 and a face value of $1,450. The note is sold to the bank on October 16 with a 12% discount rate. What are the (a) discount period, (b) discount amount, and (c) amount of proceeds?

(a) _____

(b) $ _____

(c) $ _____

296

ASSIGNMENT 26.2 Computing Discounts
on Interest-Bearing Notes

1. The Apex Supplies Company holds an 80-day, interest-bearing note with an interest rate of 9%, a face value of $824, and a due date of September 30. On July 21, the note is discounted at the bank for a discount rate of 12%. What are the (a) discount period, (b) discount amount, and (c) proceeds for the note?

(a) _____

(b) $ _____

(c) $ _____

2. Kevin McClain received a 60-day, 6% note from Blanche Madoza for $1,800. The note is dated February 15. He discounted the note at the bank on April 1 at 12%. What are the (a) discount period, (b) discount, and (c) proceeds for the note?

(a) _____

(b) $ _____

(c) $ _____

3. Adam O'Connor receives a 120-day, 10% note from Samuel Dover for $3,600. The note is dated July 31. He discounts the note at the bank on September 29 at 9%. What are the (a) discount period, (b) discount, and (c) proceeds for the note?

(a) _____

(b) $ _____

(c) $ _____

4. Rita Olive purchases farm equipment from the Northside Equipment Center on April 20. She gives an 8% interest-bearing promissory note for $25,000 due in 90 days. On May 20, the Northside Equipment Center discounts the note at the bank with a discount rate of 12%. (a) How much will the Northside Equipment Center receive from the bank on May 20? (b) How much will Rita Olive have to pay the bank when the note comes due? (c) On what date will Rita Olive have to pay the note?

(a) $ _____

(b) $ _____

(c) _____

5. Study the following interest-bearing note to determine (a) what the proceeds will be if the note is discounted on April 20 at 12% and (b) what the maturity value of the note will be on June 4.

(a) $ _____

(b) $ _____

INTEREST-BEARING NOTE		
$8,800.00	Memphis, Tennessee	March 4, 19—

Three months after the above date, I promise to pay to the order of Oren Goldstein the sum of Eighty-eight hundred and no/100 dollars plus interest at the rate of 9 percent.

Signed: _____
Daryl Sparks

COMPUTING COMPOUND INTEREST

Interest is normally expressed as either simple interest (as in Chapter 25) in which the principal does not change over the life of the loan or as *compound interest*. When expressed as compound interest, the principal changes at the end of each time period because the interest for the period is added to the principal amount. Common time periods are daily, monthly, quarterly, semiannually, and annually. Interest on deposit accounts and many other accounts with banks and other financial institutions is often computed using compound interest methods. In this chapter, you will learn how compound interest is computed. An understanding of the theory of compound interest is important as a basis for making an investment or business decision.

Formula Method for Computing Compound Interest

The same basic interest formula used to compute simple interest (I = P × R × T) is used to compute compound interest. The sum of the principal and interest for one period becomes the principal in the formula for the next period. This process is repeated each period with the interest being added to the principal from the previous period each time.

The interest earned is called *compound interest*. The difference between the final sum and the original principal is the compound interest for the loan. A given compound interest rate will yield a greater interest amount than the corresponding simple interest rate because the principal increases each period with compound interest. Likewise, more frequent compounding will yield a greater amount of interest. See Example 27.1.

EXAMPLE | **Computing compounded interest**

27.1

Problem: A deposit of $200 is placed into an account that bears interest, compounded annually, for 2 years at an interest rate of 8%. What is the compounded principal after 2 years?

Solution: **Step 1.** Compute the interest for the first period.

Principal × Rate × Time = Interest
$200 × 0.08 × 1 = $16

Step 2. Find the new principal after 1 year.

Old principal + Interest = New principal
$200 + $16 = $216

(Continued on following page)

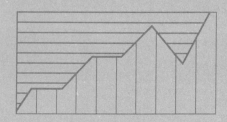

Step 3. Compute the interest for the second period.

New principal × Rate × Time = Interest
$216   × 0.08 ×   1   = $17.28

Step 4. Find the new principal after 2 years.

Old principal + Interest = New principal
$216.00   + $17.28 = $233.28

This process is repeated for additional periods. Remember that the interest is added to the principal from the previous period and that this increased principal is used in computing the interest for the next period. In another example, assume that $1,000 yields interest at a 10% rate compounded annually for 3 years.

Step 1. $1,000.00 × 0.10 × 1 = $100.00 (interest for first year)

Step 2. $1,000.00 + $100.00 = $1,100.00 (principal after first conversion)

Step 3. $1,100.00 × 0.10 = $110.00 (interest for second year)

Step 4. $1,100.00 + $110.00 = $1,210.00 (principal after second conversion)

Step 5. $1,210.00 × 0.10 = $121.00 (interest for third year)

Step 6. $1,210.00 + $121.00 = $1,331.00 (principal after third conversion)

The 3 years' compounded interest computed by subtracting the final sum from the original principal is $331.00 ($1,331.00 − $1,000). This compares to $300.00 computed using simple interest procedures.

EXAMPLE   Computing simple interest
27.2

Problem: Rosie Howard borrowed $300.00 at a 10% simple interest rate for 3 years. What is the interest amount for the 3 years?

Solution: Principal × Rate × Time = Interest
$300.00   × 0.10 ×   3   = $90.00

Here is the reason for the difference in simple and compound interest amounts. In compound interest, the principal plus interest is computed each period, resulting in a larger principal amount each period. Simple interest, however, uses only the original principal amount for the full time. The difference in this example is $31.00 ($331.00 − $300.00). As the time increases, the difference will become even greater.

The frequency of conversion is also an important factor. For example, assume that two investments have interest rates of 12%. However, one investment has a conversion period semiannually (every 6 months), while the second investment has a conversion period quarterly (every 3 months). At the end of 1 year, the principal will be $1,123.60 for the first investment and $1,125.51 for the second investment, as computed in Example 27.3. Both investments begin with an original principal of $1,000.

Computing interest, compounded semiannually   EXAMPLE

27.3

First Investment (Interest Compounded Semiannually for 1 Year)

Step 1. $1,000.00 × 0.12 × 6/12 = $60.00 ⎫
                                                                        ⎬ First 6 months
Step 2. $1,000.00 + $60.00 = $1,060.00 ⎭

Step 3. $1,060.00 × 0.12 × 6/12 = $63.60 ⎫
                                                                        ⎬ Second 6 months
Step 4. $1,060.00 + $63.60 = $1,123.60 ⎭

Computing interest, compounded quarterly   EXAMPLE

27.4

Second Investment (Interest Compounded Quarterly for 1 Year)

Step 1. $1,000.00 × 0.12 × 3/12 = $30.00 ⎫
                                                                        ⎬ First quarter
Step 2. $1,000.00 + $30.00 = $1,030.00 ⎭

Step 3. $1,030.00 × 0.12 × 3/12 = $30.90 ⎫
                                                                        ⎬ Second quarter
Step 4. $1,030.00 + $30.90 = $1,060.90 ⎭

Step 5. $1,060.90 × 0.12 × 3/12 = $31.827 ⎫
                                                                        ⎬ Third quarter
Step 6. $1,060.90 + $31.827 = $1,092.727 ⎭

Step 7. $1,092.727 × 0.12 × 3/12 = $32.78181 ⎫
                                                                        ⎬ Fourth quarter
Step 8. $1,092.727 + $32.78181 = $1,125.50881 ⎭

Notice that the principal sum equals $1,125.51 (rounded) when interest is compounded quarterly and $1,123.60 when interest is compounded semiannually—a difference of $1.91. This illustrates that the more frequently interest is compounded, the higher the compound interest amount will be. Most financial institutions use computers to make the computation, which permits easy determination of interest even if it is compounded on a daily basis. However, individuals need to understand how compound interest is computed even if the computer or compound interest tables (explained in the next section) are used.

● **Complete Assignment 27.1** ●

Table Method for Computing Compound Interest

Computation of compound interest can be simplified by the use of tables. Financial institutions have tables that show the amount that $1.00 will equal at varying rates of interest for extended periods of time up to 100 years or more. The table in Example 27.5 shows how $1.00 will increase for 1 to 30 periods at varying rates of interest from 2% to 10%. Remember that a table used by a financial institution will have smaller increments of interest rates and cover longer periods of time; however, the procedure is similar to the one described here.

EXAMPLE   **Compound interest table**

27.5

GROWTH OF $1 AT COMPOUND INTEREST

Periods	2%	3%	4%	5%	6%	7%	8%	9%	10%	Periods
1	1.020 000	1.030 000	1.040 000	1.050 000	1.060 000	1.070 000	1.080 000	1.090 000	1.100 000	1
2	1.040 400	1.060 900	1.081 600	1.102 500	1.123 600	1.144 900	1.166 400	1.188 100	1.210 000	2
3	1.061 208	1.092 727	1.124 864	1.157 625	1.191 016	1.225 043	1.259 712	1.295 029	1.331 000	3
4	1.082 432	1.125 509	1.169 859	1.215 506	1.262 477	1.310 796	1.360 489	1.411 582	1.464 100	4
5	1.104 081	1.159 274	1.216 653	1.276 282	1.338 226	1.402 552	1.469 328	1.538 624	1.610 510	5
6	1.126 162	1.194 052	1.265 319	1.340 096	1.418 519	1.500 730	1.586 874	1.677 100	1.771 561	6
7	1.148 686	1.229 874	1.315 932	1.407 100	1.503 630	1.605 781	1.713 824	1.828 039	1.948 717	7
8	1.171 659	1.266 770	1.368 569	1.477 455	1.593 848	1.718 186	1.850 930	1.992 563	2.143 589	8
9	1.195 093	1.304 773	1.423 312	1.551 328	1.689 479	1.838 459	1.999 005	2.171 893	2.357 948	9
10	1.218 994	1.343 916	1.480 244	1.628 895	1.790 848	1.967 151	2.158 925	2.367 364	2.593 742	10
11	1.243 374	1.384 234	1.539 454	1.710 339	1.898 299	2.104 852	2.331 639	2.580 426	2.853 117	11
12	1.268 242	1.425 761	1.601 032	1.795 856	2.012 196	2.252 192	2.518 170	2.812 665	3.138 428	12
13	1.293 607	1.468 534	1.665 074	1.885 649	2.132 928	2.409 845	2.719 624	3.065 805	3.452 271	13
14	1.319 479	1.512 590	1.731 676	1.979 932	2.260 904	2.578 534	2.937 194	3.341 727	3.797 498	14
15	1.345 868	1.557 967	1.800 944	2.078 928	2.396 558	2.759 032	3.172 169	3.642 482	4.177 248	15
16	1.372 786	1.604 706	1.872 981	2.182 875	2.540 352	2.952 164	3.425 943	3.970 306	4.594 973	16
17	1.400 241	1.652 848	1.947 901	2.292 018	2.692 773	3.158 815	3.700 018	4.327 633	5.054 470	17
18	1.428 246	1.702 433	2.025 817	2.406 619	2.854 339	3.379 932	3.996 019	4.717 120	5.559 917	18
19	1.456 811	1.753 506	2.106 849	2.526 950	3.025 600	3.616 528	4.315 701	5.141 661	6.115 909	19
20	1.485 947	1.806 111	2.191 123	2.653 298	3.207 135	3.869 684	4.660 957	5.604 411	6.727 500	20
21	1.515 666	1.860 295	2.278 768	2.785 963	3.399 564	4.140 562	5.033 834	6.108 808	7.400 250	21
22	1.545 980	1.916 103	2.369 919	2.925 261	3.603 537	4.430 402	5.436 540	6.658 600	8.140 275	22
23	1.576 899	1.973 587	2.464 716	3.071 524	3.819 750	4.740 530	5.871 464	7.257 874	8.954 302	23
24	1.608 437	2.032 794	2.563 304	3.225 100	4.048 935	5.072 367	6.341 181	7.911 083	9.849 733	24
25	1.640 606	2.093 778	2.665 836	3.386 355	4.291 871	5.427 433	6.848 475	8.623 081	10.834 706	25
26	1.673 418	2.156 591	2.772 470	3.555 673	4.549 383	5.807 353	7.396 353	9.399 158	11.918 177	26
27	1.706 886	2.221 289	2.883 369	3.733 456	4.822 346	6.213 868	7.988 061	10.245 082	13.109 994	27
28	1.741 024	2.287 928	2.998 703	3.920 129	5.111 687	6.648 838	8.627 106	11.167 140	14.420 994	28
29	1.775 845	2.356 566	3.118 651	4.116 136	5.418 388	7.114 257	9.317 275	12.172 182	15.863 093	29
30	1.811 362	2.427 262	3.243 398	4.321 942	5.743 491	7.612 255	10.062 657	13.267 678	17.449 402	30

An examination of the interest table shows that $1.00 will amount to $1.628895 if compounded for 10 periods at an interest rate of 5%. This is found by going vertically to find the period (10), then horizontally to find the amount under the 5% heading. In another example, $1.00 will increase to $4.660957 if left for 20 periods at a compound interest rate of 8%. As before, go to vertical 20 and then horizontally to the figure below the 8% heading to determine the amount ($4.660957).

To compute the amount that a specific figure will increase, simply multiply the figure from the table by the amount. For example, $500 will increase to $814.45 (rounded) if left for 10 periods at a compound interest rate of 5%. The figure for $1.00 ($1.628895) was located. Then, the amount was multiplied by $500 ($500.00 × $1.628895).

To further test your knowledge, compute the amount that $850 will increase to in 12 periods at a compound interest rate of 9%, as shown in Example 27.6.

Computing compounded value and compound interest   EXAMPLE

27.6

Problem: John Wilfong borrowed $850.00. Using the table method, if the amount is computed for 12 periods at 9% interest, what are the compounded value and compound interest for the loan?

Solution: **Step 1.** Find the compounded value at the end of 12 periods.

Table value for   Compounded
9%, 12 periods × Principal =   value
    $2.812665   × $850.00   = $2,390.77 (rounded)

Step 2. Find the amount of compound interest.

Compounded   Original   Compound
    value   − principal =   Interest
  $2,390.77   − $850.00   = $1,540.77

Since interest rates are normally stated as annual rates, adjustments must be made if interest is computed for periods of time other than 1 year. For example, assume that interest is compounded quarterly (four times per year) for 2 years at a 12% rate. The number of periods will be 8 (2 × 4), and the interest rate will be 3% each period (12 ÷ 4). Therefore, $1.00 compounded quarterly with a compound interest rate of 12% will increase to $1.266770. This is determined by going vertically to 8 in the table, then horizontally under the 3% heading.

Likewise, $1.00 will increase to $1.628895 if compounded semiannually at an interest rate of 10% for 5 years. Go vertically to period 10, then horizontally under the 5% heading. Using this same procedure, $350 will increase to $570.11 ($350.00 × $1.628895) under these same terms. Remember to adjust the number of periods and interest rate to fit the situation.

● **Complete Assignment 27.2** ●

ASSIGNMENT 27.1 Computing Compound Interest: Formula Method

1. Compute the compound interest for each of the following loans. (Round final answers to 2 decimal places.)

Loan	Compound Interest
$100.00 for 2 years at 6%, compounded annually	$ _____
$1,400.00 for 2 years at 5%, compounded annually	$ _____
$2,000.00 for 3 years at 10%, compounded annually	$ _____
$1,000.00 for 18 months at 8%, compounded semiannually	$ _____
$875.00 for 1 year at 12%, compounded semiannually	$ _____
$1,000.00 for 9 months at 8%, compounded quarterly	$ _____

2. Carl Gallegos invested $5,000 into an account that pays 8% interest, compounded semiannually. At the end of 18 months, what are the (a) compound interest and (b) compounded amount?

(a) $ _____

(b) $ _____

3. Sue Yoshida can earn $320.00 in interest by loaning $2,000.00 to a friend at 8% interest for 2 years. If the money is invested for 2 years at 8%, compounded semiannually, how much *more* will she earn with this investment than she would earn from the loan to her friend?

$ _____

4. Jean Harlowe invested $4,000 for 2 years at 9% interest, compounded semiannually. What are the (a) compound interest and (b) compounded amount for this investment?

(a) $ _____

(b) $ _____

5. Loretta Spitzer invested $4,750.00 for 18 months at 8% interest, compounded semiannually. What will the compounded amount be after (a) 6 months, (b) 12 months, and (c) 18 months?

(a) $ _____

(b) $ _____

(c) $ _____

306

ASSIGNMENT 27.2 Computing Compound Interest: Table Method

1. Use the compound interest table in Example 27.5 to find the compounded amount and compound interest for each of the following loans. Round answers to two decimal places.

Loan	Compounded Amount	Compound Interest
$785.00 for 5 years at 7%, compounded annually	$ _____	$ _____
$658.00 for 14 years at 9%, compounded annually	$ _____	$ _____
$1,685.00 for 9 years at 10%, compounded semiannually	$ _____	$ _____
$1,260.00 for 10 years at 12%, compounded semiannually	$ _____	$ _____
$1,950.00 for 6 years at 12%, compounded quarterly	$ _____	$ _____
$1,650.00 for 5 years at 8%, compounded quarterly	$ _____	$ _____

2. George Stevens has an opportunity to invest $1,000 at 8% interest, compounded semiannually, or 9%, compounded annually. Both terms are for 15 years. (a) Which investment will yield the most compound interest? (b) How much will the better investment earn in excess of the other investment?

(a) _____

(b) $_____

3. Ronda Andes makes a $1,000 investment at the beginning of each year for 3 years. If interest is compounded semiannually at a 10% rate on each investment, how much will be available at the end of the third year?

$_____

4. The City National Bank pays 8% interest, compounded quarterly, to investors. If Inez Cortesi invests $3,200.00, how much will she have at the end of 5½ years?

$_____

5. Harold Beaty invested $3,000 in a savings certificate when his daughter Rachel was born. If the certificate yields interest at 9%, compounded annually, how much will be available when Rachel is 18 years old?

$_____

PRESENT VALUE AND ANNUITIES

Individuals and businesses use financial information as a basis for planning and making decisions. It helps them to answer questions such as these: Is the value of money likely to go up or down in the future? What amount must be paid periodically to retire a debt? How will periodic deposits accumulate over a period of time? Information such as this is essential for operating and budgeting. This chapter shows how this information is computed and provides specific ways in which it can be used.

Computing Present Value of Money

Inflation, fluctuating interest rates, and other economic conditions make money received in the future worth less than it is today. For example, a dollar buys less today than a dollar bought 30 years ago. Likewise, a dollar will buy less in 30 years than it buys today. This process determines computed present value of money to be received at some future date. For example, $1.00 to be received in 3 years may have a computed present value of only $0.82.

Most financial institutions use computers or tables to determine present value amounts. The table in Example 28.1 shows the present value of $1.00 for 1 to 30 periods with percentages ranging from 2% to 10% in increments of 1%. For example, the present value of $1.00 to be received in 10 periods at a percentage of 5% is $0.613913. In the table, this is found by going vertically to period 10, then horizontally to under the 5% heading.

The present value under the same conditions can be found by multiplying $0.613913 by $500 ($0.613913 × $500.00 = $306.96). This is interpreted to mean that $500 to be received in 15 years with an interest rate of 5%, compounded annually, has a present value of $306.96. Determination of proceeds when compound interest is to be computed in a period less than 1 year requires an adjustment. In this example, semiannual interest computation for 15 years will require 30 periods (every 6 months for 15 years) and an interest rate of 2½% (½ the annual rate since interest is computed at 6-month intervals). Interest compounded quarterly under the same conditions results in using 60 periods and an interest rate of 1¼%.

To prove your answer, consider the following example: Mary Jane Collins will receive $300 in 5 years with a 6% compound interest rate (compounded annually). To determine the present value, multiply $300 by $0.747258 ($300.00 × $0.747258 = $224.1774 rounded to $224.18). To prove this answer, use the value of $1.00 in the compound interest table in Chapter 27. The horizontal value across from 5 periods and under the 6% heading is $1.338226. Multiply this value by $224.18 ($224.18 × $1.338226) to yield a value of $300.00 (rounded). This shows the close relationship between future value and present value. In other words, $224.18 has a future value of $300.00 (5 periods and a compound interest rate of 6%), and $300.00 (due in 5 periods and a compound interest rate of 6%) has a present value of $224.18.

CHAPTER 28

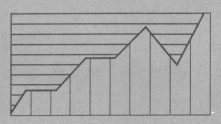

The difference between present and future value is the interest earned, called *compound discount*. In the above example, the compound discount is $75.82 ($300.00 − $224.18 = $75.82).

● Complete Assignment 28.1 ●

EXAMPLE   Present value of $1.00 table

28.1

Periods	2%	3%	4%	5%	6%	7%	8%	9%	10%	Periods
1	0.980 392	0.970 874	0.961 538	0.952 381	0.943 396	0.934 580	0.925 926	0.917 431	0.909 091	1
2	0.961 169	0.942 596	0.924 556	0.907 029	0.889 996	0.873 439	0.857 339	0.841 680	0.826 446	2
3	0.942 322	0.915 142	0.888 996	0.863 838	0.839 619	0.816 298	0.793 832	0.772 183	0.751 315	3
4	0.923 845	0.888 487	0.854 804	0.822 702	0.792 094	0.762 895	0.735 030	0.708 425	0.683 013	4
5	0.905 731	0.862 609	0.821 927	0.783 526	0.747 258	0.712 986	0.680 583	0.649 931	0.620 921	5
6	0.887 971	0.837 484	0.790 315	0.746 215	0.704 961	0.666 342	0.630 170	0.596 267	0.564 474	6
7	0.870 560	0.813 092	0.759 918	0.710 681	0.665 057	0.622 750	0.583 490	0.547 034	0.513 158	7
8	0.853 490	0.789 409	0.730 690	0.676 839	0.627 412	0.582 009	0.540 269	0.501 866	0.466 507	8
9	0.836 755	0.766 417	0.702 587	0.644 609	0.591 898	0.543 934	0.500 249	0.460 428	0.424 098	9
10	0.820 348	0.744 094	0.675 564	0.613 913	0.558 395	0.508 349	0.463 193	0.422 411	0.385 543	10
11	0.804 263	0.722 421	0.649 581	0.584 679	0.526 788	0.475 093	0.428 883	0.387 533	0.350 494	11
12	0.788 493	0.701 380	0.624 597	0.556 837	0.496 969	0.444 012	0.397 114	0.355 535	0.318 631	12
13	0.773 033	0.680 951	0.600 574	0.530 321	0.468 839	0.414 964	0.367 698	0.326 179	0.289 664	13
14	0.757 875	0.661 118	0.577 475	0.505 068	0.442 301	0.387 817	0.340 461	0.299 246	0.263 331	14
15	0.743 015	0.641 862	0.555 265	0.481 017	0.417 265	0.362 446	0.315 242	0.274 538	0.239 392	15
16	0.728 446	0.623 167	0.533 908	0.458 112	0.393 646	0.338 735	0.291 890	0.251 870	0.217 629	16
17	0.714 163	0.605 016	0.513 373	0.436 297	0.371 364	0.316 574	0.270 269	0.231 073	0.197 845	17
18	0.700 159	0.587 395	0.493 628	0.415 521	0.350 344	0.295 864	0.250 249	0.211 994	0.179 859	18
19	0.686 431	0.570 286	0.474 642	0.395 734	0.330 513	0.276 508	0.231 712	0.194 490	0.163 508	19
20	0.672 971	0.553 676	0.456 387	0.376 889	0.311 805	0.258 419	0.214 548	0.178 431	0.148 644	20
21	0.659 776	0.537 549	0.438 834	0.358 942	0.294 155	0.241 513	0.198 656	0.163 698	0.135 131	21
22	0.646 839	0.521 893	0.421 955	0.341 850	0.277 505	0.225 713	0.183 941	0.150 182	0.122 846	22
23	0.634 156	0.506 692	0.405 726	0.325 571	0.261 797	0.210 947	0.170 315	0.137 781	0.111 678	23
24	0.621 721	0.491 934	0.390 121	0.310 068	0.246 979	0.197 147	0.157 699	0.126 405	0.101 526	24
25	0.609 531	0.477 606	0.375 117	0.295 303	0.232 999	0.184 249	0.146 018	0.115 968	0.092 296	25
26	0.597 579	0.463 695	0.360 689	0.281 241	0.219 810	0.172 195	0.135 202	0.106 393	0.083 905	26
27	0.585 862	0.450 189	0.346 817	0.267 848	0.207 368	0.160 930	0.125 187	0.097 608	0.076 278	27
28	0.574 375	0.437 077	0.333 477	0.255 094	0.195 630	0.150 402	0.115 914	0.089 548	0.069 343	28
29	0.563 112	0.424 346	0.320 651	0.242 946	0.184 557	0.140 563	0.107 328	0.082 155	0.063 039	29
30	0.552 071	0.411 987	0.308 319	0.231 377	0.174 110	0.131 367	0.099 377	0.075 371	0.057 309	30

Computing Present Value of an Annuity

Discussion in the previous section related to a single amount that was invested today in order to receive an amount of money at some time in the future. The present value of a future amount was computed. *Annuity* indicates a series of investments made at regular intervals. For example, what single sum must be invested today in order to earn a specified annuity in the future?

Remember that an annuity is a series of regular payments. If $1.00 is to be received in 1 year, what single sum must be invested? If $1.00 is needed at the end of each of the next 2 years, what single sum must be invested? To illustrate this procedure, assume that $1.00 is desired at the end of each of the next 3 years. The Present Value of $1.00 Table can be used to compute the present value assuming a 6% compound interest rate for each of these three $1.00 amounts, as shown in Example 28.2.

Computing present value of an annuity   EXAMPLE

28.2

Present value of $1.00 in 3 periods	$0.839619
Present value of $1.00 in 2 periods	$0.889996
Present value of $1.00 in 1 period	$0.943396
Total needed to receive $1.00 for each of the next 3 periods	$2.673011

Example 28.2 shows that $2.673011 invested today will provide an annuity of $1.00 for each of the next 3 periods. As shown above, the present value of each $1.00 receipt was computed separately using the Present Value of $1.00 Table. A separate table, the Present Value of an Annuity of $1.00, shown in Example 28.3, can provide this figure more easily. Go vertically to period 3, then horizontally to under the 6% heading. This amount ($2.673012) is the same amount shown above in Example 28.2 (with a slight difference due to rounding). Use of this table makes it easier to compute the present value of annuities.

Present value of an annuity of $1.00 table   EXAMPLE

28.3

PRESENT VALUE OF AN ANNUITY OF $1

Periods	2%	3%	4%	5%	6%	8%	10%	Periods
1	0.980392	0.970874	0.961539	0.952381	0.943396	0.925926	0.909091	1
2	1.941561	1.913470	1.886095	1.859410	1.183393	1.783265	1.735537	2
3	2.883883	2.828611	2.775091	2.723248	2.673012	2.577097	2.486852	3
4	3.807729	3.717098	3.629895	3.545951	3.465106	3.312127	3.169865	4
5	4.713460	4.579707	4.451822	4.329477	4.212364	3.992710	3.790787	5
6	5.601431	5.417191	5.242137	5.075692	4.917324	4.622880	4.355261	6
7	6.471991	6.230283	6.002055	5.786373	5.582381	5.206370	4.868419	7
8	7.325481	7.019692	6.732745	6.463213	6.209794	5.746639	5.334926	8
9	8.162237	7.786109	7.435332	7.107822	6.801692	6.246888	5.759024	9
10	8.982585	8.530203	8.110896	7.721735	7.360087	6.710081	6.144567	10
11	9.786848	9.252624	8.760477	8.306414	7.886875	7.138964	6.495061	11
12	10.575341	9.954004	9.385074	8.863252	8.383844	7.536078	6.813692	12
13	11.348374	10.634955	9.985648	9.393573	8.852683	7.903776	7.103356	13
14	12.106249	11.296073	10.563123	9.898641	9.294984	8.244237	7.366687	14
15	12.849264	11.937935	11.118387	10.379658	9.712249	8.559479	7.606080	15
16	13.577709	12.561102	11.652296	10.837770	10.105895	8.851369	7.823709	16
17	14.291872	13.166119	12.165669	11.274066	10.477260	9.121638	8.021553	17
18	14.992031	13.753513	12.659297	11.689587	10.827603	9.371887	8.201412	18
19	15.678462	14.323799	13.133939	12.085321	11.158116	9.603599	8.364920	19
20	16.351433	14.877475	13.590326	12.462210	11.469921	9.818147	8.513564	20

Assume that an annuity of $200 is desired for each of the next 10 periods and that the compound interest rate is 5% per period. An examination of the table yields the figure ($7.721735) needed for an annuity of $1.00. To compute the amount needed for an annuity, multiply this figure by $200 ($200.00 × $7.721735 = $1,544.347). In this example, an investment of $1,544.35 will be sufficient to provide an annuity of $200 if the compound interest rate is 5% per period. As usual, the rates are stated as annual rates. Periods less than 1 year require an adjustment. If $100 per month is desired for 10 years and the interest rate is 12%, the number of periods will be 120 (10 × 12), and the interest rate to be used will be 1% (12% ÷ 12). This will be true for all tables used in this chapter.

For another example, assume that Danny Nash desires to receive $300 per quarter for the next 5 years. If the compound interest rate is 12%, the single sum that must be invested today is $2,975.495 ($200.00 × $14.877475).

• Complete Assignment 28.2 •

Computing Annuity Investments

Investors often place a regular amount into an account. When the amount is deposited, it immediately begins to earn interest and earns compound interest for the duration of the annuity. The table in Example 28.4 shows how periodic deposits will accumulate over a period of time.

EXAMPLE 28.4 Amount of annuity of $1.00 at compound interest table

AMOUNT OF ANNUITY OF $1 AT COMPOUND INTEREST					
Number of Interest Periods	2%	3%	4%	6%	8%
1	1.020000	1.030000	1.040000	1.060000	1.080000
2	2.060400	2.090900	2.121600	2.183600	2.246400
3	3.122608	3.183627	3.246464	3.374616	3.506112
4	4.204040	4.309136	4.416323	4.637093	4.866601
5	5.308121	5.468410	5.632976	5.975319	6.335929
6	6.434283	6.662462	6.898295	7.393838	7.922803
7	7.582969	7.892336	8.214226	8.897468	9.636628
8	8.754628	9.159106	9.582795	10.491316	11.487558
9	9.949721	10.463879	11.006107	12.180795	13.486563
10	11.168715	11.807796	12.486351	13.971643	15.645488
11	12.412090	13.192030	14.025806	15.869941	17.977127
12	13.680331	14.617790	15.626838	17.882138	20.495297
13	14.973938	16.086324	17.291911	20.015066	23.214920
14	16.293417	17.598914	19.913588	22.275970	26.152114
15	17.639285	19.156881	20.824531	24.672528	29.324283
16	19.012071	20.761588	22.697512	27.212880	32.750226
17	20.412312	22.414435	24.645413	29.905653	36.450244
18	21.840559	24.116868	26.671229	32.759992	40.446263

(Continued on following page)

Number of Interest Periods	2%	3%	4%	6%	8%
19	23.297370	25.870375	28.778079	35.785591	44.761964
20	24.783317	27.676486	30.969202	38.992727	49.422921
25	32.670906	37.553042	43.311745	58.156383	78.954415
30	41.379441	49.002678	58.328335	83.801677	122.345868
40	61.610023	77.663298	98.826536	164.047684	279.781040
50	86.270990	116.180773	158.773767	307.756059	619.671768
60	116.332570	167.945040	247.510313	565.115872	1353.470359
70	152.977469	237.511886	379.862077	1026.008100	2937.686480
80	197.647397	331.003909	573.294776	1852.395885	6357.890263
90	252.099789	456.649371	861.102667	3329.539698	13741.853705
100	318.476951	625.506362	1287.128653	5976.670142	29682.276961

As an example, Ramone Ruiz decides to invest $500 per year into an annuity that pays 6% compound interest. To compute the amount in the fund after 10 years, go vertically to period 10 then horizontally to the 6% heading. Multiply the figure at the intersection by $500 to compute the value of the annuity after 10 years, as shown in Example 28.5.

Computing value of annuity   EXAMPLE

28.5

Problem: Ramone Ruiz invests $500 per year into an annuity that pays 6% compounded interest. What is the value of the annuity after 10 years?

Solution: Periodic   Table   Annuity
            investment ×   value   =   value
              $500   × $13.971643 = $6,985.82 (rounded)

In a second example, Brandon Hall decides to deposit $60 per quarter for 15 years in an annuity at 12% compound interest for his son's education. At the end of 15 years, he will have $10,076.70 available in the fund. Go vertically to period 60 (4 × 15), then horizontally to under the 3% (12% ÷ 4%) heading. The figure at the intersection ($167.945040) is multiplied by the periodic deposit ($60.00 × $167.945040 = $10,076.70).

Computing Sinking Fund Amounts

A *sinking fund* involves the systematic accumulation of funds by investing a certain sum of money at the end of each period. A sinking fund differs from an annuity in two ways. First, deposits are made into a sinking fund at the end of each period, whereas deposits are made into an annuity at the beginning of each period. Therefore, interest is earned during the first period for an annuity investment. Secondly, in a sinking fund the accumulated amount is known, but the periodic deposit must be computed. With an annuity the periodic deposit is known, but the final accumulated amount must be computed.

A business may use a sinking fund to determine periodic amounts needed to pay off a bond issue in 15, 20, or 30 years. Other typical uses of a sinking fund are to determine periodic amounts needed to replace a building in 50 years, to replace a piece of equipment in 15 years, or to have a specific pension fund reserve available by a specified date. The sinking fund table in Example 28.6 can be used to make computations for sinking funds in this chapter.

EXAMPLE 28.6   Sinking fund table

ANNUITY THAT AMOUNTS TO $1 AT COMPOUND INTEREST (Sinking Fund Table)					
Number of Periods	2%	3%	4%	6%	8%
1	1.000000	1.000000	1.000000	1.000000	1.000000
2	0.495050	0.492611	0.490196	0.485437	0.480769
3	0.326755	0.323530	0.320349	0.314110	0.308034
4	0.242624	0.239027	0.235490	0.228592	0.221921
5	0.192158	0.188355	0.184627	0.177396	0.170457
6	0.158526	0.154598	0.150762	0.143363	0.136315
7	0.134512	0.130506	0.126610	0.119135	0.112072
8	0.116590	0.112456	0.108528	0.101036	0.094015
9	0.102515	0.098434	0.094493	0.087022	0.080080
10	0.091327	0.087231	0.083291	0.075868	0.069030
11	0.082178	0.078078	0.074149	0.066793	0.060076
12	0.074560	0.070462	0.067552	0.059277	0.052695
13	0.068118	0.067030	0.060144	0.052960	0.046522
14	0.062602	0.058526	0.054670	0.047585	0.041297
15	0.057826	0.053767	0.049941	0.042963	0.036830
16	0.053650	0.049611	0.045820	0.038952	0.032977
17	0.049970	0.045953	0.042199	0.035445	0.029629
18	0.046702	0.042709	0.038993	0.032357	0.026702
19	0.043782	0.039814	0.036139	0.029621	0.024128
20	0.041157	0.037216	0.033582	0.027185	0.021852
25	0.031220	0.027428	0.024012	0.018227	0.013679
30	0.024650	0.021019	0.017830	0.012649	0.008827
40	0.016556	0.013262	0.010524	0.006462	0.003860
50	0.011823	0.008866	0.006550	0.003444	0.001743
60	0.008768	0.006133	0.004202	0.001876	0.000798
70	0.006668	0.004337	0.002745	0.001033	0.000368
80	0.005161	0.003112	0.001814	0.000573	0.000170
90	0.004046	0.002256	0.001208	0.000318	0.000079
100	0.003203	0.001647	0.000808	0.000177	0.000036

The Richards Manufacturing Company purchased a piece of equipment with an estimated life of 10 years and an estimated replacement cost of $18,500. The company decided to make annual deposits into a sinking fund with a compound interest rate of 8%. To compute the amount of periodic deposit needed, go vertically to period 10, then horizontally to under the 8% heading. The figure at the intersection is multiplied by $18,500 to compute the periodic deposits needed, as shown in Example 28.7.

EXAMPLE

28.7

Problem: The Richards Manufacturing Company needs to know the amount that should be deposited annually into a sinking fund for 10 years, at 8% interest, to accumulate $18,500. What amount should be deposited annually?

Solution:

Amount to accumulate	×	Table value	=	Deposit needed
$18,500	×	$0.069030	=	$1,277.06 (rounded)

In a second example, Central Church has a $15,000 bond issue due in 15 years. To compute the semiannual deposits into a 12% compound interest sinking fund needed to pay off the issue, multiply the figure obtained from the sinking fund table by $15,000 ($15,000.00 × $0.012649 = $189.74). Therefore, the church will make a $189.74 deposit at the end of each 6-month period in order to have funds available at the end of 15 years to pay off the bond issue.

Summary of Tables

Typical tables for present value, future value, annuity, and sinking fund investments are presented in this chapter. The appropriate table for each application must be selected. The following general overview of the purpose of each table is given as a reference and review.

1. *Amount of $1.00 at Compound Interest.* This table shows what $1.00 invested today will amount to in the future.
2. *Present Value of $1.00 at Compound Interest.* This table shows what must be invested today to have $1.00 in the future. Stated a different way, the table shows what $1.00 to be received in the future is worth today.
3. *Amount of Annuity of $1.00 at Compound Interest.* This table shows how periodic deposits will accumulate over a period of time.
4. *Annuity that Amounts to $1.00 at Compound Interest.* This table is also called a Sinking Fund Table. This table shows what must be deposited periodically over a specified period of time to amount to $1.00.

● **Complete Assignment 28.3** ●

ASSIGNMENT 28.1 Computing Present Value

1. Waldo Breckheimer can have access to $600 in 10 years. If money is worth 6%, compounded annually, how much is the amount worth today?

   $ _____

2. Cheryl Hawks will receive an inheritance of $8,500.00 in 13 years. If money is worth 5%, compounded annually, how much is the amount worth today?

   $ _____

3. Clyde Holder holds a non-interest-bearing note that will be due in 7 years. If money is worth 9%, compounded annually, how much is the amount worth today if the face value is $750.00?

   $ _____

4. Elizabeth Bottoms is due to receive a bonus of $2,500 in 3 years. If money is worth 10%, compounded semiannually, how much is the bonus worth in today's value?

   $ _____

5. Carol Moduar is scheduled to receive $7,850 in 6 years. If money is worth 8%, compounded quarterly, how much is the amount worth today?

   $ _____

6. Billy Braden's Body Shop did a job for $360 due in 6 months. If money is worth 12%, compounded annually, how much is the bill worth today?

   $ _____

7. Opal Venne is offered $2,800 today or $3,000 in 5 years. If money is worth 8%, compounded annually, (a) which choice should be made and (b) what is the difference in present value of the two amounts?

(a) $ _____

(b) $ _____

8. Stephen Trombley is given an option of paying $6,800 today or $7,300 in 3 years. If money is worth 7%, compounded annually, (a) which choice will result in the lower present value and (b) what is the difference in present value of the two amounts?

(a) $ _____

(b) $ _____

9. Franz Viertbauer will receive $840 in 36 months. If money is worth 6%, compounded annually, how much is (a) the amount today and (b) the amount of compound interest?

(a) $ _____

(b) $ _____

10. Montie Walker loans a friend $600 for 1 year with no interest charge. If money is worth 8%, compounded annually, (a) how much less than the $600 loaned today is the present value of the money to be received in 1 year? (b) Why will Montie receive less in real terms even though the full $600 loan is repaid?

(a) $ _____

(b) _____

318

ASSIGNMENT 28.2   Computing Present Value of Annuities

1. Compute the present value of each of the following annuities. Use the tables in the text of this chapter, as needed, to compute the answers.

Annuity	Present Value
$300.00 every 3 months for 4 years at 8%, compounded quarterly	$
$100.00 every 6 months for 5 years at 12%, compounded every 6 months	$
$680.00 every 3 months for 5 years at 12%, compounded quarterly	$
$3,600.00 each year for 20 years at 6%, compounded annually	$
$3,800.00 every 6 months for 9 years at 8%, compounded semiannually	$
$2,700.00 every 6 months for 7 years at 10%, compounded semiannually	$

2. Lynn Mitchell will enter college next year. Her estimated annual costs are $7,800 per year for 4 years. Lynn works in a department store to pay half of her expenses. How much must her parents invest if Lynn is to receive the remainder in four equal amounts each year and the interest is compounded quarterly at a rate of 8%?

$ _____

3. Andy Hall desires to provide his daughter Sandy an income of $3,500 every 3 months for 4 years. If the prevailing interest rate is 8%, compounded quarterly, what amount must be invested?

$ _____

4. David Guthrie purchased a small business from Linwood Heiberg under an agreement that the seller was to receive $6,500 every 6 months for 8 years. If money is worth 8%, compounded semiannually, what amount must David invest to provide the income for the seller?

$ _____

5. Porter Hart signs a professional football contract. As a signing bonus, he is given an option of $80,000 cash now or a bonus of $7,000 per year for 13 years. If money is worth 8%, compounded annually, (a) which offer is better? (b) How much difference in present value terms is there between the two options?

(a) $ _____

(b) $ _____

320

ASSIGNMENT 28.3 Computing Annuity Investments and Sinking Fund Deposits

1. Robert and Linda Hendrix placed $200 each quarter into an account earning 8% interest, compounded annually, when their son Bryant was born. When Bryant is 5 years old, (a) what amount will be in the account and (b) what amount of interest will have been earned?

(a) $ _____

(b) $ _____

2. The Bellbrook Electric Service placed $6,000 each year into an account earning 8% interest, compounded annually, to provide funds for machinery replacement in 14 years. (a) What amount will be in the fund in 14 years? (b) How much of this amount will represent interest earned?

(a) $ _____

(b) $ _____

3. The Max Line Furniture Center decided to set aside $3,000 every 6 months to provide donation funds for a youth community center scheduled to open in 3 years. If money is worth 12%, compounded semiannually, how much will be available for donation to the youth center in 3 years?

$ _____

4. The Chickasaw Lumber Company invested $6,200 each year for the past 9 years into an account paying 8% interest, compounded annually. The purpose of the account was to have funds available to purchase an adjoining lot. Today, the lot is available for a cash price of $93,250.00. (a) What amount is currently in the fund? (b) What amount of additional money will be needed to purchase the lot?

(a) $ _____

(b) $ _____

5. The Youth Clubs of America issued $80,000 worth of 11-year non-interest-bearing bonds. What amount must be set aside at the end of each year in order to retire the bonds when they become due? Assume that money placed in the sinking fund draws interest at 6%, compounded annually.

$ _____

6. United Teleconferencing Services plans to purchase additional satellite connections that are available for $2,600,000 with 50% due immediately and the balance due in 10 years. A provision is added that a reduction amounting to $100,000 will be provided if the loan is paid within 6 years. (a) If money is worth 6%, compounded annually, how much must be placed in a sinking fund each year to retire the loan in 10 years? (b) If money is worth 8%, compounded annually, how much must be placed in a sinking fund each year to retire the loan in 6 years?

(a) $ _____

(b) $ _____

7. Creative Hair Styles plans to replace all of its equipment in 5 years. The estimated replacement cost is $46,500. If money is worth 8%, compounded quarterly, how much must be placed into a sinking fund each quarter in order to have sufficient funds to replace the equipment?

$ _____

8. The Gossett Custom Auto Shop will need $95,000 in an employees' pension fund in 3½ years. If money is worth 6%, compounded semiannually, how much must be invested each 6 months in order to have the necessary funds available?

$ _____

322

INSURANCE

Unexpected events can cause financial loss to a business or individual. Possibilities of fire, burglaries, car accidents, deaths, health problems, and damage to goods being shipped are typical purposes for which businesses and/or individuals often purchase insurance. *Insurance* provides protection against losses when these or similar events occur. Within legal guidelines, insurance companies set *premiums* to be charged for providing this protection. A *policy* outlines items covered and the amount of coverage provided under certain specified conditions. Typical computations relating to life and property (fire) insurance are presented in this chapter.

Life Insurance

Life insurance is designed to provide financial support for the person designated as beneficiary in the policy when the insured person dies. The beneficiary is often a family member who may be left in a weak financial condition if the policyholder dies unexpectedly. In some instances, companies purchase life insurance to provide protection in the event that a valuable executive dies.

There are several different types of life insurance coverage. The most common types are term, straight life (also called *whole life* or *ordinary life*), limited payment life, and endowment. With all insurance policies, the premium amounts are based on the amount of the face value, age of the insured person, and type of coverage.

Term insurance is in effect for a specified period of time, such as 5 years. Unless the insured person dies within the term of the policy coverage, the beneficiary receives nothing and the protection ends. This type of policy usually pays the greatest benefits for the lowest premiums.

Straight life provides protection throughout the insured person's life, as long as premiums continue to be paid.

Limited payment life policies require that premiums be paid only for a limited number of years or until the insured person reaches a certain age, such as 65 years. Insurance is then provided (often at a reduced face value) for the remainder of the life of the insured.

Endowment life provides protection for a specified number of years. At the end of this time, the insured person can usually have the option of receiving a specified amount of cash or lifetime periodic income payments from the insurance company.

Computing Premiums

The amount charged for premiums varies from company to company and depends on factors such as the age, sex, and health of the insured person. The table in Example 29.1 shows typical annual premiums for persons in various age groups with term, straight life, 20-payment life, and 20-year endowment policies.

CHAPTER 29

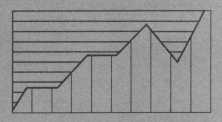

EXAMPLE
29.1

Annual premiums for $1,000 life insurance policy table

Age	Straight Life Premium	20-Payment Life Premium	20-Year Endowment Premium	10-Year Term Premium
21	$13.65	$28.70	$45.13	$4.20
22	13.95	29.20	45.28	4.24
23	14.27	29.72	45.44	4.26
24	14.65	30.27	45.63	4.30
25	15.03	30.83	45.83	4.35

Notes: (a) Multiply the annual rate by 54% for semiannual premiums.
(b) Multiply the annual rate by 28% for quarterly premiums.

To compute the premium due, find the age category for the insured person and then multiply the premium for the type of policy desired by the number of thousands of dollars in coverage needed (Rate × Base = Amount).

EXAMPLE
29.2

Computing insurance premium

Problem: Mark Cammack is 23 years old and desires a straight life policy for $15,000. Using the table in Example 29.1, what is his premium?

Solution:

Premium rate per $1,000 of coverage		Base number of $1,000's		Amount of premium
$14.27	×	15	=	$214.05

If payments are made quarterly, the annual premium ($214.05) is multiplied by 28% ($214.05 × 0.28 = $59.934, rounded to $59.93). For Example 29.2, the premium for $15,000 of straight life coverage is $214.05 if paid annually and $59.93 if paid quarterly.

In a second example, if a 24-year-old student takes out a 10-year term policy with a face value of $30,000, the annual premium is $129.00 ($4.30 × 30 = $129.00).

Cash Surrender Value

To receive cash or for other reasons, persons may surrender (cancel) a policy prior to the end of the period of the policy. With the exception of term policies, many policies provide for a *cash surrender value,* which is the amount the insurance company will pay the insured person on the surrender of the policy. Insured persons can usually borrow up to an amount equal to the surrender value without surrendering the policy. However, this amount must be repaid—usually with interest on the loan. The table in Example 29.3 shows typical surrender values for various lengths of time that policies have been in force.

Typical cash surrender values per $1,000 table   EXAMPLE
29.3

Policy Issued at Age 20			
Policy Life	Straight Life	20-Payment Life	20-Year Endowment
5 years	$ 28.00	$ 72.00	$ 140.00
10 years	76.00	195.00	315.00
15 years	153.00	371.00	520.00
20 years	248.00	502.00	1,000.00
25 years	362.00	672.00	1,000.00
30 years	520.00	795.00	1,000.00

Using the table in Example 29.3, consider the problem in Example 29.4.

Computing cash surrender value   EXAMPLE
29.4

Problem: Brenda Fekula has a $5,000 face value, straight life policy that has been in force for 15 years. Using the above table, what is the cash surrender value of her policy?

Solution:

Cash surrender value per $1,000 in face value	×	Number of $1,000's	=	Cash surrender value
$153.00	×	5	=	$765.00

To further illustrate, a person with a $7,000 face value, 20-payment life policy that has been in force for 25 years can collect a cash surrender value of $4,704.00 ($672.00 × 7).

Remember that premiums and cash surrender values vary depending on the rates set by the insurance company and the background of the insured person. Males typically pay a higher premium than females because the life expectancy of a female is higher than the life expectancy of a male. Persons in dangerous occupations may be required to pay a higher premium also.

● **Complete Assignment 29.1** ●

Property Insurance

Protection against loss or damage of property is called *property insurance*. Coverage includes fire, marine, liability, and casualty insurance. The premiums for property insurance depend on several factors, such as the location of the property, the amount of coverage desired, and the nature of risk related to the coverage. Premium rates are quoted by the number of dollars per $1,000 of insurance coverage. Most owners of real property carry fire insurance coverage. Therefore, fire insurance is discussed in this chapter.

Coverage in case of fire may include a payment for loss up to a certain amount, such as $80,000, or it may include full replacement cost, which means that the property lost to fire will be replaced at current replacement costs.

Coinsurance

Another typical feature is a *coinsurance clause* that distributes the loss between the insured and the insurance company. If a coinsurance clause is in effect, the insured agrees to carry a policy for a stated percentage of the value, such as 80%. Property valued at $100,000 must be insured for $80,000 ($100,000.00 × .80). If the insured carries at least $80,000 worth of insurance, the full amount of losses up to the face value will be recovered. If the property is not insured for the full 80% ($80,000 in this example), only a fraction of coverage will be recovered. Assume that the person in Example 29.5 carries a policy for $60,000. This is 75% ($60,000 ÷ $80,000 = .75) of the 80% coinsurance coverage. Thus a loss of $30,000 will be covered for $22,500, as shown in the example.

EXAMPLE   **Computation of coinsurance recovery amount**

29.5

$$\frac{\text{Insurance}}{\text{carried}} \div \frac{\text{Coinsurance}}{\text{percent}} \times \frac{\text{Property}}{\text{value}} \times \frac{\text{Amount}}{\text{of loss}} = \text{Recovery amount}$$

$$\$60,000 \div (0.80 \times \$100,000.00) \times \$30,000 = \$22,500.00$$

In a second example, a building valued at $80,000 is insured for $32,000 under an 80% coinsurance clause. The recovery amount will be $3,500.00, as shown by the following computation. Assume a loss of $7,000 is incurred.

$$\$32,000.00 \div (0.80 \times \$80,000.00) \times \$7,000.00 = \$3,500.00$$

Computing Premiums

Fire insurance premiums are usually stated as a certain amount per $1,000 of coverage, such as $3.40 per $1,000 of coverage. A building covered for $80,000 will have an annual premium of $272.00, as computed in Example 29.6.

Computing annual premium   EXAMPLE

Problem: An office building is insured for $80,000. What is the annual premium?

Solution:

Numbers of $1,000's		Rate per $1,000		Annual premium
80	×	$3.40	=	$272.00

The usual practice for fire insurance coverage is to round the final annual premium computed to the nearest whole dollar. Location, amount of coverage, and type of coverage determine the rate structure to be used for fire insurance.

In a second example, the Executive Sports Center is located in an area that has a rate structure of $4.25 per $1,000 for buildings and contents. The building is insured for $90,000, and its contents are insured for $45,000. Using the above computation, the premium for this example is determined as follows:

$$\begin{aligned} \text{Building} &= \$90 \times \$4.25 = \$382.50 \\ \text{Contents} &= \$45 \times \$4.25 = \underline{\quad 191.25} \\ \text{Total premium} & \qquad\qquad\quad\, = \$573.75 \text{ (rounded to \$574)} \end{aligned}$$

Rates may be paid annually or at intervals more or less often than once each year. Due to administrative costs, the premium will usually be increased if it is paid more often than once each year (called *short rate*) or be decreased if it is paid several years in advance (called *long rate*).

Assume that the annual premium for a policy is $380. The short rate is 56% of the annual premium for payment at 6-month intervals. The long rate is 181% of the annual premium for payment at 2-year intervals. A 6-month policy will carry a premium of $212.80 rounded to $213.00 ($380.00 × 0.56). If the premium is paid 2 years in advance, the premium for the 2 years of coverage will be $687.80 rounded to $688.00 ($380.00 × 1.81).

A short rate situation may also occur if a policy is canceled prior to its expiration date. In this event, the short rate will be charged. For example, assume that a policy with an annual premium of $278 is cancelled 6 months prior to *expiration date* (the end of the period covered by the policy). The short rate schedule for paying at 6-month intervals will be applied to determine the refund. If this rate is $145.00 for premiums paid at 6-month intervals, the refund will be $133.00 ($278.00 − $145.00).

• Complete Assignment 29.2 •

ASSIGNMENT 29.1 Computations for Life Insurance

(Use the tables in the text of this chapter, as needed, to answer the following questions.)

1. Charlene Bodine purchased a straight life policy at age 22 with a face value of $36,000. What is the amount of her annual premium?

$ _____

2. Harry Maynard purchased a 20-year endowment life insurance policy at age 23 with a face value of $48,000. What is the amount of his annual premium?

$ _____

3. Reginald Moore purchased a 10-year term life insurance policy at age 21 with a face value of $80,000. What is his semiannual premium?

$ _____

4. Geneva Miller purchased a 20-payment life insurance policy at age 25 with a face value of $75,000. What is her quarterly premium?

$ _____

5. Isaac Morris purchased a life insurance policy at age 21 with a face value of $90,000. What is his premium for (a) a straight life policy and (b) a 10-year term policy?

(a) $ _____

(b) $ _____

6. Pauline McQueen, age 23, is undecided about whether to purchase a 20-payment life or a 10-year term policy. She desires $65,000 coverage. If she pays annual premiums for 5 years, how much will be saved in premiums during the 5 years?

$ _____

7. Dalton Frazier, age 21, and Walter Garcia, age 25, each purchased a 20-payment life insurance policy with a face value of $76,000. After 20 years of annual payments, how much will (a) Dalton and (b) Walter pay in total premiums?

(a) $_____

(b) $_____

8. Albert Gandy, age 25, and Edward Regan, age 25, each purchased a life insurance policy with a face value of $85,000. Albert purchased a straight life policy, and Edward purchased a 20-year endowment policy. After 10 years of annual payments, what is the difference in total premiums paid by the two men?

$_____

9. Freda Vaughn has a straight life policy with a face value of $36,000 that was purchased 20 years ago when she was 20 years old. What is the cash surrender value of the policy today?

$_____

10. Claudette Minns has a 20-payment life policy with a face value of $42,000 that was purchased 30 years ago when she was 20 years old. What is the cash surrender value of the policy today?

$_____

11. Phillip Hughes purchased a 20-year endowment life insurance policy at age 23. The policy has a face value of $40,000 and was purchased 20 years ago. What are the (a) total premiums paid and (b) cash surrender value of the policy?

(a) $_____

(b) $_____

12. Linda Rainey purchased a straight life policy at age 24. The policy has a face value of $60,000 and was purchased 15 years ago. What are the (a) total premiums paid and (b) cash surrender value of the policy?

(a) $_____

(b) $_____

330

ASSIGNMENT 29.2   Computations for Property Insurance

1. The McCall Development Corporation has a building valued at $200,000. Under an 80% coinsurance clause, the company carries $120,000 coverage. A fire causes $70,000 in damages. How much of the loss will the company recover?

    $ _____

2. Professional Sporting Goods, Inc., has a building valued at $120,000. Under an 80% coinsurance clause, the company carries $72,000 coverage. A fire causes $18,000 in damages. How much of the loss will the company recover?

    $ _____

3. Cedar Lake Nurseries decided to insure a building valued at $90,000 for $46,800 under an 80% coinsurance clause. Weather damage covered by the policy amounts to $6,000. How much of the loss will the company recover?

    $ _____

4. The Loving Care Pet Shop purchased a building with a value of $75,000 that is insured for up to 80% of its value. A fire caused $16,787 in damages. How much of the loss will the company recover?

    $ _____

5. Sabrina Worley purchased a home with a value of $85,000. Under an 80% coinsurance clause, she insured the house for $68,000. For a covered loss of $18,570, how much will she recover?

    $ _____

6. Travis Johnston acquires a building with a value of $87,000. Its contents are valued at $22,000. He purchased a policy under a 90% coinsurance clause with a face value of $46,980 for the building and $11,880 for the contents. A fire caused $6,000 damages to the building and $7,600 damages to the contents. How much will be recovered for the loss (a) to the building and (b) to the contents?

    (a) $ _____

    (b) $ _____

7. The Hill Hardware Store purchased an insurance policy with a face value of $90,000 on an office building and a second policy with a face value of $120,000 on a warehouse building. If the annual insurance premiums are $3.45 per $1,000 in coverage on the office building and $3.60 per $1,000 in coverage on the warehouse, how much are the annual premiums on the (a) office building and (b) warehouse?

(a) $ _____

(b) $ _____

8. The Portsmouth Family Center purchased a new building with a value of $92,000. They decided to insure the building for the full value. The Ashmore Insurance Company offers coverage on a 3-year policy for an annual premium of $3.50 per $1,000 in coverage, and the Eastland Insurance Company offers coverage for an annual premium of $3.62 per $1,000 in coverage. Over a 3-year period, (a) what will the total premium be for a policy with the Ashmore Insurance Company? (b) What will the total premium be for a policy with the Eastland Insurance Company? (c) What will be saved during the 3 years if the Ashmore Insurance Company is chosen?

(a) $ _____

(b) $ _____

(c) $ _____

9. The Anderson Appliance Center purchased a policy with a face value of $120,000 on its building and $70,000 on the building contents. If insurance premiums are $3.80 per $1,000 in coverage, what will the premium be for (a) the building, (b) the contents, and (c) both the building and its contents?

(a) $ _____

(b) $ _____

(c) $ _____

10. The Shade Shop insured its building and contents for $56,000 and $18,000 respectively. If insurance rates are $4.25 per $1,000 in coverage, what amount will the premium be for (a) the building, (b) the contents, and (c) the building and its contents?

(a) $ _____

(b) $ _____

(c) $ _____

• Complete Unit 6 Spreadsheet Applications •

332

UNIT 6   SPREADSHEET APPLICATION 1: Simple Interest

The following spreadsheet is used to determine the interest due and amount needed to repay various loans. Totals and averages are also computed. The following formula is needed to compute the interest due:

$$Principal \times Interest\ Rate \times Days/365$$

The amount repaid is computed by adding the interest due to the principal for each loan. The total for each column should be computed, except for Columns C and D. The average for each column can be computed by dividing the total of values in the column by 10 (since there are 10 values in each column).

```
          A         B          C          D         E          F         G
 1  Dalton Finance Co.              **SIMPLE INTEREST**           ##########
 2  ====================================================================##########
 3  Loan                Interest  No. of  Interest    Amount ##########
 4  Number    Principal     Rate    Days       Due    Repaid ##########
 5  ---------------------------------------------------------------##########
 6  X-347       800.00    0.080      90                       ##########
 7  X-348     1,250.00    0.100     120                       ^^^^^^^^^^
 8  X-349       650.00    0.090      85                       Compute
 9  X-350     2,500.00    0.085      75                       Exact
10  X-351     3,200.00    0.125      65                       Interest
11  X-352     1,400.00    0.120     195                       ^^^^^^^^^^
12  X-353     3,600.00    0.105     225                       ##########
13  X-354       900.00    0.145     115                       ##########
14  X-355     4,520.00    0.095     480                       ##########
15  X-356     3,750.00    0.120     150                       ##########
16  ---------------------------------------------------------------##########
17  Totals            XXXXXXXXXXXXXXXXXX                       ##########
18  ---------------------------------------------------------------##########
19  Averages                                                   ##########
20  ====================================================================##########
```

Refer to the spreadsheet above to answer the following questions:

1. What was the interest due for Loan X-349? $ _____

2. What was the interest due for Loan X-352? $ _____

3. What was the interest due for Loan X-355? $ _____

4. What was the amount repaid for Loan X-348? $ _____

5. What was the amount repaid for Loan X-354? $ _____

6. What was the amount repaid for Loan X-356? $ _____

7. What was the average length of the loans?   _____

8. What was the average amount repaid? $ _____

9. What was the total amount repaid? $ _____

10. How many loans had interest due amounts greater than $1,000?   _____

UNIT 6   SPREADSHEET APPLICATION 2: Note Proceeds

The following spreadsheet is used to determine the maturity value and proceeds for various loans that are discounted prior to their maturity date. The interest for each loan should be computed and added to the loan amount to compute the maturity value. The discount for each loan should be computed and subtracted from the maturity value to compute the proceeds. Totals for each column, except Columns C and F, should be computed. Averages for each column should be computed. The maturity value and proceeds for the first loan are shown in the spreadsheet. Include these amounts while computing totals and averages.

	A	B	C	D	E	F	G	H
1	Dalton Finance Co.			**NOTE	PROCEEDS**			
2	======	======	======	======	======	======	======	======
3	Loan	Loan		Loan	Maturity	Discount	Discount	
4	Number	Amount	Rate	Time	Value	Rate	Time	Proceeds
5	------							------
6	Y-101	800.00	0.09	150	829.59	0.08	95	812.32
7	Y-102	600.00	0.10	225		0.08	100	
8	Y-103	500.00	0.08	300		0.06	150	
9	Y-104	400.00	0.08	420		0.06	250	
10	Y-105	600.00	0.12	90		0.10	60	
11	Y-106	1,200.00	0.10	100		0.10	30	
12	Y-107	600.00	0.15	200		0.12	75	
13	Y-108	700.00	0.09	325		0.10	90	
14	Y-109	300.00	0.11	400		0.12	280	
15	Y-110	500.00	0.12	600		0.10	150	
16	------							------
17	Totals		xxxxxxxxx			xxxxxxxxx		
18	------							------
19	Averages							
20	======	======	======	======	======	======	======	======

Refer to the spreadsheet above to answer the following questions:

1. What is the maturity value for Loan Y-102? $ _____

2. What is the maturity value for Loan Y-108? $ _____

3. What is the proceeds amount for Loan Y-109? $ _____

4. What is the proceeds amount for Loan Y-110? $ _____

5. What is the total loan amount? $ _____

6. What is the total maturity value? $ _____

7. What is the average maturity value? $ _____

8. What is the average proceeds? $ _____

9. How many loans had maturity values less than $600.00?   _____

10. How many loans had proceeds greater than $600.00?   _____

• **Complete Unit 6 Self-Test** •

UNIT 6 SELF-TEST Business Finance

1. Using the ordinary method, what is the amount of interest for a 9%, 84-day loan for $1,680?

   $ _____

2. Using the ordinary method, what is the amount of interest for an 8%, 75-day loan for $1,750?

   $ _____

3. Using the ordinary method, what is the amount of interest for an 8%, 5-month loan for $12,300?

   $ _____

4. Using the exact method, what is the amount of interest (rounded to 2 decimal places) for a 9%, 72-day loan for $675?

   $ _____

5. A 60-day promissory note is dated June 15. What is the due date for the loan?

   _____

6. A note dated August 13 is paid on November 3. How many days elapsed between the two dates?

   _____

7. A 60-day note dated April 19 is discounted on May 13. How many days are in the discount period for the note?

   _____

8. A 90-day note dated September 28 is discounted on October 11. How many days are in the discount period for the note?

   _____

9. Find the (a) bank discount and (b) proceeds for the following non-interest-bearing note: a note with a maturity value of $1,200 discounted 90 days prior to the due date at a 9% discount rate.

   (a) $ _____

   (b) $ _____

10. June Berkshire discounted a note with a maturity value of $800 at a 6% discount rate 60 days prior to the due date. What are the (a) discount and (b) proceeds for the note?

(a) $ _____

(b) $ _____

11. Arthur Simmons accepts a 120-day, 10% interest-bearing note from Harriet Crowe for $1,800. The note is dated August 31. He discounts the note at the bank on September 30 at 6%. What are the (a) discount period, (b) discount, and (c) proceeds for the note?

(a) _____

(b) $ _____

(c) $ _____

12. Johnny Watkins invested $5,000 into an account that pays 8%, compounded semiannually. At the end of 18 months, what are the (a) compound interest and (b) compounded amount?

(a) $ _____

(b) $ _____

13. The Kirk Driswald Decorating Service loaned $4,000 to a customer at 5% interest for 2 years. If the interest is compounded annually, what are the (a) compound interest and (b) compounded amount after 2 years?

(a) $ _____

(b) $ _____

338

UNIT 6 SELF-TEST (continued)

14. The Good Vision Optical Center borrowed $3,000 at 8% interest, compounded quarterly. At the end of 1 year, what are the (a) compound interest and (b) compounded amount?

(a) $ _____

(b) $ _____

15. Ann Hewlett invested $9,400 for 18 months at 8% interest, compounded semiannually. What is the compounded amount after (a) 6 months, (b) 12 months, and (c) 18 months?

(a) $ _____

(b) $ _____

(c) $ _____

(Refer to the appropriate tables in Chapter 28 to solve Problems 16 through 19 below.)

16. Dutch Schroer is scheduled to receive $9,850 in 6 years. If money is worth 8%, compounded quarterly, how much is the amount worth today?

$ _____

17. The Quince Hardware Company holds a non-interest-bearing note that will be due in 11 years. If money is worth 7%, compounded annually, how much is the amount worth today if the face value is $8,500?

$ _____

18. Florence Brigman is scheduled to receive $1,800 (an annuity) each year for 20 years at 6% interest, compounded annually. What is the present value of the annuity?

$ _____

19. Lisa Dunsworthy will enter college next year. Her estimated annual cost per year is $7,000. If Lisa is to attend college for 4 years, how much must her parents invest today if she is to receive the money in 4 equal payments (1 each year) at the beginning of each year? Assume an interest rate of 6%, compounded annually.

$ _____

20. The annual premium for a 20-payment life insurance policy is $28.70 per $1,000 in coverage if the insured is 20 years old. Mitzi Herrmann purchases this policy with a face value of $48,000 when she is 20 years old. What is the amount of her annual premium?

$ _____

21. The Maxy Advertising Agency has property valued at $200,000. A local insurance company agrees to provide fire protection for $3.40 per $1,000 in value. If full coverage is provided, what is the annual premium for this policy?

$ _____

340

Statistics, Graphs, Stocks, and Bonds

This unit shows how data can be analyzed, grouped, or placed in summary or graphic form to provide useful information. Computations relating to stocks and bonds, two long-term investments, are also included in this unit.

Some skills you can achieve in this unit include the following:

- **Computing simple statistics, including the mean, median, and mode for grouped and ungrouped data.**
- **Arranging a frequency distribution and group data in summary form.**
- **Constructing line graphs, bar graphs, and circle graphs for presenting data in a graphic format.**
- **Reading typical graphs used to represent data in summary form.**
- **Reading a newspaper composite listing showing stock transactions.**
- **Computing cash dividends for common and preferred stock.**
- **Computing discounts and/or premiums on the sale of stock.**
- **Reading a newspaper listing showing bond issues.**
- **Computing accrued interest earned on bonds.**
- **Computing rate of return on sale of stock.**
- **Computing discount and/or premium on sale of bonds.**
- **Computing rate of return on sale of bonds.**
- **Computing bond discount and bond premium amortization.**

UNIT 7

SIMPLE STATISTICS

Data must be analyzed in order to provide useful information for making business decisions. *Business statistics* is the area of business mathematics in which data is collected, tabulated, summarized, and presented numerically in a way that can be easily interpreted and understood. For example, a listing of each individual sale made during the day by a drug store is not nearly as useful as one figure that shows total sales for the day. Basic business statistics are fun and involve fairly simple computations. This chapter shows you several basic statistical techniques that are typically used in business situations.

Statistics can be used to compare one value, such as a business expenditure, with another value. A 20.8 share of the television audience watching a particular program, for example, can affect advertising budgets for that program.

Measures of Central Tendency

The mean, median, and mode are often used to compute one value that is representative of a set or group of values. These three statistics are also known as *measures of central tendency.*

Mean

The *mean*, which is also called the *average*, is computed by finding the sum of a group of values and then dividing the sum by the number of values in the group. The mean is a misleading value when only a small number of values are used or when a few very high or a few very low values can distort the mean value computed. Calculation of the mean is shown in Example 30.1.

EXAMPLE   Computing the mean

30.1

Problem: The Village Hardware Store had the following sales for the past 5 days respectively: $7,000, $9,000, $7,000, $8,000, and $10,000. What is the mean sales for the week?

Solution: **Step 1.** Find the sum of the values.

$7,000 + $9,000 + $7,000 + $8,000 + $10,000 = $41,000

Step 2. Find the mean (or average) sales.

Sum of values / Number of values = Mean
$41,000   /   5   = $8,200

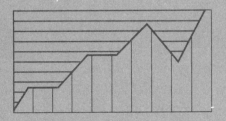

The mean, or average, sales for the week were $8,200. An examination of the sales will show on which days sales were above average and on which days sales were below average. Another use of the mean is to compare one week's average sales with average sales for other weeks in the month or the year.

In a second example, assume that Gary Vickery made the following scores on 4 tests during the term: 89, 88, 92, and 90. His average score for the term (89.75) is computed as follows:

Step 1.   89 + 88 + 92 + 90 = 359

Step 2.   359 ÷ 4 = 89.75 (mean)

Median

The *median* is the middle point in a series of values. To compute the median, the values must be arranged in order from low to high or from high to low. The median value is determined by adding 1 to the number of values in the group and then dividing by 2. Half of the values should fall above the median value, and half of the values should fall below the median value. For example, the median value for a series containing an odd number of values, such as 11 values, is 6. Similarly, the median in a series containing 14 values is 7.5 (halfway between the seventh and eighth values). These computations are shown below.

$$(11 + 1) \div 2 = 6$$
$$(14 + 1) \div 2 = 7.5$$

Consider the steps for calculating the median in Example 30.2.

EXAMPLE   **Computing the median**
30.2

Problem: The Village Hardware Store had the following sales for the past 5 days respectively: $7,000, $9,000, $7,000, $8,000, and $10,000. What is the median sales figure for the week?

Solution: Step 1.   Arrange the values in the group from high to low.

1. $10,000
2.   9,000
3.   8,000
4.   7,000
5.   7,000

Step 2.   Determine the median point.

(No. of values + 1)/2 = Median point
(5   + 1)/2 =   3

Step 3.   Find the corresponding value in the range in Step 1 to locate the median sales value.

The third value is $8,000.

As another example, assume that Gary Vickery took 4 tests on which he received the following scores: 92, 90, 89, and 88. The median of his test scores is determined as follows:

Step 1. Arrange the values in descending order.

1. 92, 2. 90, 3. 89, 4. 88

Step 2. (4 + 1) ÷ 2 = 2.5 (median point)

Step 3. Halfway between the second value (90) and the third value (89) is the median. Take the average of the second and third values.

(90 + 89) ÷ 2 = 89.5 (median score)

The median shows the point in a series of values where half of the values are above the point and half are below the point. As you can see, this is true for each of the medians computed for the examples above ($8,000 and 89.5).

Mode

The *mode* is the specific value that occurs most frequently in a series of values. The usual practice to determine the mode is to arrange the values from highest to lowest and then visually scan the list to determine the single value that occurs most frequently. If there are two values in the same series that occur with equal frequency, the series is bimodal (which means that there are two modes). The mode is the least useful of the statistics discussed in this chapter. Example 30.3 illustrates finding the mode of a series of values.

Computing the mode EXAMPLE

30.3

Problem: The Village Hardware Store had the following sales for the past 5 days respectively: $7,000, $9,000, $7,000, $8,000, and $10,000. What is the mode of this sales distribution?

Solution: Step 1. Arrange the values in order from highest to lowest as in Step 1 of Example 30.2.

Step 2. Scan the range of values to determine the value that occurs most frequently.

Notice that the fourth and fifth values are $7,000 in this group. No other value occurs more than one time. Therefore, the mode in this example is $7,000.

The list of test scores for Gary Vickery does not have a mode since each value occurs only one time. The *range* is the difference between the lowest value and the highest value in the group. After arranging the values in order from highest to lowest, the range is determined by subtracting the lowest value from the highest value. The range for the daily sales used in Example 30.3 is $10,000.00 − $7,000.00 = $3,000.00. This statistic is often used because it shows the difference between values at the two extreme positions in the series.

● Complete Assignment 30.1 ●

Frequency Distributions for Grouped Data

The values in the preceding section were ungrouped with each value listed separately. When working with a large number of values, it often becomes more practical to arrange values into categories or groups.

Frequency Distribution

When a large number of values is used, the values are placed into classes with an interval representing the low point and high point of each category. The ranges of the various class widths are normally equal. To illustrate this statistic, the ages of employees who work for American School Products Company will be used. Ages and method for computing the frequency distribution are shown in Examples 30.4 and 30.5.

EXAMPLE   Ungrouped data

30.4

21	48	32	32
25	24	33	54
35	45	52	37
50	53	64	39
66	51	28	43
44	53	27	31

In this ungrouped data, the lowest age is 21 and the highest age is 66. Therefore, the range is 45 (66 − 21 = 45). Arbitrarily, the number of classes desired for the grouping is 5. This information is useful for arranging a frequency distribution, as shown in Example 30.5.

Arranging a frequency distribution   EXAMPLE

30.5

Step 1.   Determine class width by dividing the range by the number of classes desired. (The range is 45 for this example.)

45 ÷ 5 = 9 (class width)

Step 2.   Arrange the categories into classes beginning with the lowest value (21). The number of values determined in Step 1 should be included in each interval.

Interval	Tally
21–29	/////
30–38	//////
39–47	////
48–56	///////
57–66	//

Step 3.   Look at each value to determine the class category. In the tally column, add 1 to the tally for a class each time a value falls into that class. This tally is shown in Step 2.

Statistics for Grouped Data

After values are grouped into classes, the identity of each individual value is lost. Therefore, the mean, median, and mode for the series must be determined from the grouped data. Results are generally considered to be accurate enough since a large number of values is normally used when data is grouped.

Instead of working with an individual value, the midpoint of each class interval is used. The frequency that values fall into each interval is multiplied by the midpoint of the interval to compute the total for the interval. The mean, median, and mode are then computed using basically the same procedures used for individual values. One exception is that the value 1 is not added to the number of values if the number of values is an even number. Also, the modal class is used to represent the mode. Using the age data from Example 30.4, Example 30.6 shows how to group data before computing the measures of central tendency.

Arranging grouped data   EXAMPLE

30.6

Step 1.   Use the class intervals and tallies (frequencies) determined when the frequency distribution was arranged (Example 30.5).

Interval	Frequency	Midpoint	Class Value
21–29	5	25	125
30–38	6	34	204
39–47	4	43	172
48–56	7	52	364
57–66	2	61	122
TOTALS	24		987

Step 2. Determine the midpoint for each class (these midpoints are shown in Step 1 on the previous page).

Step 3. Multiply the frequency by the midpoint for each class to compute the class value, such as 5 × 25 = 125. (These class values are also shown in Step 1 above.)

Step 4. Totals of the class value and frequency columns should also be computed (987 and 24, as shown in Step 1 above).

The data from Example 30.6 is used to illustrate how the mean, median, and mode are determined from grouped data. Arranging grouped data as shown in Example 30.6 prior to computing these statistics makes computation much easier. Use this example as a basis for the following computations.

The mean is computed by dividing the total of the class value column by the total of the frequency column.

EXAMPLE
30.7

Computation of the mean from grouped data

Total class value ÷ No. of values = Mean
987   ÷   24   = 41.125

The median is computed by dividing the total of the frequency column by 2 (24 ÷ 2 = 12). To determine the interval containing the median, count from the bottom of the frequency column to determine where the twelfth value will appear (39–47 category in this example). Since 1 of the 4 values in this interval is needed to reach the twelfth value, the median falls ¼ of the way into the interval. To compute where this point is, multiply the range of the interval (9) by ¼ and then add this product to the low value in the interval, as shown in Example 30.8.

EXAMPLE
30.8

Computation of the median from grouped data

Step 1. Multiply the portion of the interval needed (¼) by the interval range to determine the interval point for the median.

¼ × 9 = 2.25 (interval point)

Step 2. Add the interval point obtained in Step 1 to the lowest value in the interval to compute the median.

2.25 + 39 = 41.25 (median)

The *modal class* is the interval containing the highest number of values. A visual check indicates that this interval is the fourth interval from the top (48–56), which contains 7 values.

● **Complete Assignment 30.2** ●

ASSIGNMENT 30.1 Ungrouped Data Analysis: Basic Statistics

Round each answer to 2 decimal places.

1. The Middle States Savings and Loan Association evaluates employees once each year. Overall ratings of 1 to 100 are possible. The ratings below are for four different locations. Compute the mean, median, mode, and range for each location.

Location A	Location B	Location C	Location D
89	92	60	65
72	75	76	82
93	89	95	91
76	67	82	67
65	94	77	54
70	73	76	89
72	88	82	97
95	67	91	66
	95	73	91
	79	82	78
		70	88
		76	93
			75
			89
			97

Location	Mean	Median	Mode	Range
A	_____	_____	_____	_____
B	_____	_____	_____	_____
C	_____	_____	_____	_____
D	_____	_____	_____	_____

2. There are 45 employees working for the Middle State Savings and Loan Association included in the above evaluations. Compute the (a) mean, (b) median, (c) mode, and (d) range for all employees combined.

(a) _____

(b) _____

(c) _____

(d) _____

3. The Diebold Mobile Catering Service has several trucks. On Monday of last week, the following miles were recorded by the various trucks in the fleet: 132, 176, 180, 96, 120, 176, and 135. What are the (a) mean, (b) median, and (c) mode mileage for the fleet?

(a) _____

(b) _____

(c) _____

4. Seven employees of the Brewer Photo Center make the following weekly salaries respectively: $278, $275, $264, $278, $286, $290, and $310. What are the (a) mean, (b) median, and (c) mode salary for the employees?

(a) $ _____

(b) $ _____

(c) $ _____

5. La Filipina Jewelry had the following daily sales during six days last week: $4,678, $5,289, $4,672, $4,738, $5,389, and $5,432. What are the (a) mean and (b) median daily sales?

(a) $ _____

(b) $ _____

6. Dyson's Cabinet Shop had the following numbers of employees absent each day during the past 11 working days: 7, 8, 6, 9, 5, 6, 7, 10, 3, 4, and 2. What are the (a) mean and (b) median absentee rates?

(a) _____

(b) _____

352

ASSIGNMENT 30.2   Grouped Data Analysis: Basic Statistics

Round each answer to 2 decimal places.

1. City University gives all applicants for its data processing curriculum a computer aptitude test. Scores for a recent test were as follows:

   88, 92, 76, 68, 83, 75, 68, 76, 66, 78, 67, 76, 89, 91, 90, 78, 73, 84, 93, 82, 77, 85, 71, 66, 76, 85, 92, 78, 67, 68, 82, 90, 68, 81, and 91.

   Group the data into 6 categories with equal intervals beginning with the following category: 65–69. Tally the scores in the categories. What are the (a) mean, (b) median, and (c) modal class?

   (a) _____

   (b) _____

   (c) _____

2. Weekly salaries for employees of the Dallas Health Center are grouped into the categories shown below. What are the (a) mean, (b) median, and (c) modal class salaries for the employees?

(a) $ _____

(b) $ _____

(c) $ _____

Interval	Midpoint	Frequency
$201–$250	226	5
$251–$300	276	10
$301–$350	326	25
$351–$400	376	30
$401–$450	426	40
$451–$500	476	10

3. The Discount Car Care Center has a sales staff of 30 employees. The grouped data below shows the number of cars sold by interval category and the number of salespersons falling into each category. What are the (a) mean, (b) median, and (c) modal class for the sales staff during the month?

(a) _____

(b) _____

(c) _____

Cars Sold	Frequency
0– 4	3
5– 9	5
10–14	5
15–19	10
20–24	5
25–29	2

354

DATA REPRESENTATION: SIMPLE GRAPHS

There is an old adage that a picture is worth a thousand words. This adage is also true for data representation. Presentation of data in graphic form provides a quick picture of data and data relationships to help make numeric data understandable. The three most popular graphic forms for presenting data are the line graph, bar graph, and circle graph. In this chapter, you will learn how to construct these graphs.

Constructing Line Graphs

The *line graph* is the oldest and most widely used form of graph. This graph is very useful for showing how values change over a period of time. A grid with a vertical and a horizontal axis is normally used with the time periods placed on the horizontal axis at the bottom of the grid. Value categories are placed on the vertical axis at the left on the grid. Values for each corresponding time period are plotted on the grid with a dot. The dots are then connected to form the line on the graph. The title of the graph is usually placed either above or below the grid.

Enrollment of students at Meadows Junior College of Business for the past 5 years is shown in Example 31.1.

EXAMPLE 31.1

Meadows Junior College enrollment for the years 19Y1 to 19Y5

Year	Enrollment
19Y1	1,880
19Y2	2,865
19Y3	4,115
19Y4	3,871
19Y5	4,652

This data is plotted on the grid shown in Example 31.2. To reduce the range of values on the graph, the data shown in the example is plotted in hundreds. For example, 1,880 is plotted on the grid slightly below 19. Businesses normally reduce values to hundreds, thousands, millions, and so forth in order to reduce the range for plotting purposes and still show an accurate graphic representation of the data.

CHAPTER 31

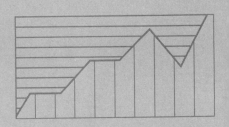

EXAMPLE **Constructing a line graph for student enrollment**

31.2

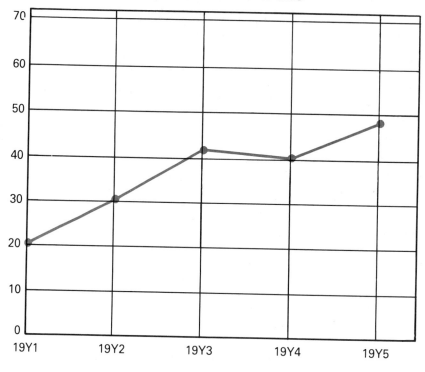

MEADOWS JUNIOR COLLEGE
*Student Enrollment in Hundreds of Students
for the Years 19Y1 to 19Y5*

A glance at this graph shows that enrollment has steadily increased during the past 5 years with a slight decrease during only 1 year (19Y4). In reality, the school may want to make a study to determine reasons that enrollment dropped in 19Y4 while it increased in all other years. The scale (0 to 70) can be adjusted to change the appearance of the graph.

The line graph is often used to make projections. In Example 31.2, the school may project (estimate) enrollment for 19Y6 to be slightly over 5,000 students. Remember that projections are only estimates and are accurate only if a past trend continues into the future.

Two sets of data can be represented on the same graph by separate lines. The graph in Example 30.2 could have included a line for male students, a separate line for female students, and a separate line for total students. A different color (such as red, blue, or green) and a different line pattern (such as ———, -----, or —·—·—) can be used for each different item included in the line graph.

● **Complete Assignment 31.1** ●

Constructing Bar Graphs

The *bar graph* is used to show the relationship and comparison between items of the same kind. The width of each bar should be equal, with the space between the bars about 1/2 to 1 times the width of the bar. The length or height of the bar is used to represent the value.

A grid similar to the one used for depicting the line graph can be used to depict a bar graph with a vertical and horizontal axis. The bars in the graph can run vertically or horizontally depending on the way the graph is arranged. When different bars are used to show different values, color or shading should be used to represent each type of value. When time is a factor in the graph, the periods should be on the horizontal axis.

The same enrollment data pertaining to the Meadows Junior College of Business will be used for the bar graph in Example 31.3, except that in this example the data will be divided by sex of students.

Constructing a bar graph for student enrollment   EXAMPLE

31.3

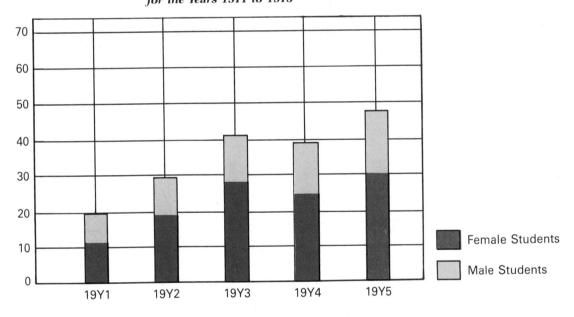

MEADOWS JUNIOR COLLEGE
Student Enrollment in Hundreds of Students
for the Years 19Y1 to 19Y5

Each bar represents total enrollment for a specific year. The bar is divided to show the portion of females and the portion of males included in the total enrollment. Two bars, side by side, could have been used to show enrollment by sex: one bar for female students and one bar for male students. The shading or color used should be designated for each category included in the graph. This is called the *legend* for the graph.

Two bars are used in Example 31.4 to show the relationship between income and expenses at the American Research Center.

EXAMPLE   **Constructing a bar graph for income and expenses**

31.4

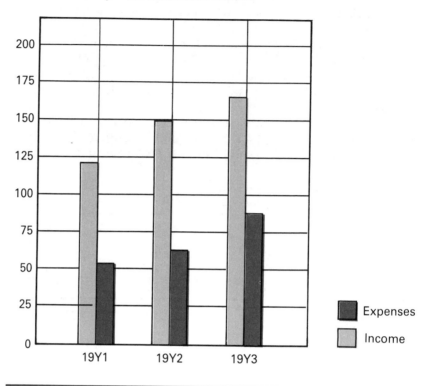

AMERICAN RESEARCH CENTER
*Income and Expenses in Thousands of Dollars
for the Years 19Y1 to 19Y3*

Constructing a Circle Graph

A *circle graph* (often called a *pie chart* because of its design) is used to show how segments relate to the whole. The entire circle (360° of the circumference) represents the whole (100%). The value of each segment is usually converted to a percent of the whole, with the total of all segments equaling 100%. The circle is then divided into segments (slices) depending on how the percentage or the degrees of the segment relate to the whole. For example, a segment representing 25% will take one fourth of the circle, as shown in the circle graph in Example 31.6.

A protractor is often used to draw the circle graph. Since the entire circle represents 360°, each percent equals 3.6°. Therefore, an item that accounts for 21% of the total will require 75.6° (3.6° × 21) on the protractor scale. If you think of the circle as a clock, the first segment should begin at 12 o'clock. If there is no reason for a particular order, the largest segment should be shown first, followed (clockwise) by successively smaller segments until the last segment (the smallest) is shown. A miscellaneous item, regardless of size, should always be shown last. The size of the circle should be large enough to show the items. Therefore, a larger number of items normally requires a larger circle. If the item name will not fit into the segment, the name can be indicated beside the segment with a line drawn to identify the segment.

The table in Example 31.5 presents the sources of income for Midland State College. This table is represented by a circle graph in Example 31.6 that depicts the income by segment. Notice that the amount for each item is converted to a percent (rounded to 2 decimal places).

Midland State College sources of income for the year 19Y1 (in millions of dollars)

EXAMPLE 31.5

Source	Amount	Percentage
Fees	$33	33.67
State	25	25.51
Sports	16	16.33
Grants	12	12.24
Donations	6	6.12
Miscellaneous	6	6.12
TOTALS	98	99.99

Notice that the final percent does not equal 100 due to rounding. The final percent is often *adjusted* so that the total will equal 100.

Constructing a circle graph for sources of income

EXAMPLE 31.6

MIDLAND STATE COLLEGE
Sources of Income for the Year 19Y1

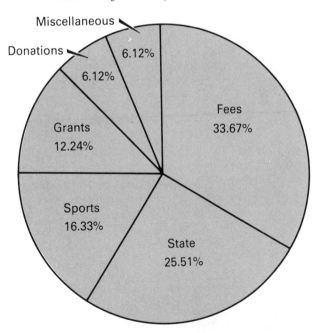

Miscellaneous 6.12%
Donations 6.12%
Grants 12.24%
Fees 33.67%
Sports 16.33%
State 25.51%

• **Complete Assignment 31.2** •

ASSIGNMENT 31.1   Line Graphs

1. (a) Revenues from television advertising for the past 6 years in a large southern city are given below in millions of dollars. Use the graph below to construct a line graph to show this information. Let each bar represent $1 million in revenue. Use a solid line (—) to connect the plotted points.

19Y1	$18.8		19Y3	$24.2		19Y5	$28.6
19Y2	$19.9		19Y4	$30.3		19Y6	$40.1

TV ADVERTISING REVENUE AND PROFIT
in Millions of Dollars
For the Years 19Y1 to 19Y6

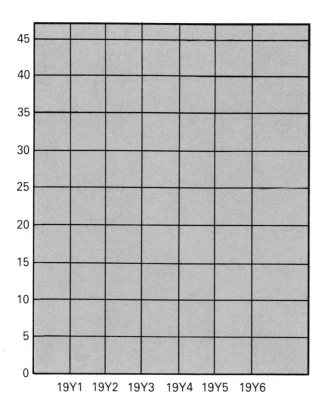

(b) Use this same line graph to show the following profits for the same time periods. Use a broken line (--) to connect the plotted points. Supply an appropriate heading and include a legend.

Profits: 19Y1	$7.5		19Y3	$8.9		19Y5	$5.2
19Y2	$7.5		19Y4	$7.5		19Y6	$4.1

2. The following table presents monthly sales figures for the past 6 months for the Motlow Department Store. Compute the total sales for each month. Use the following line graph to show totals for each month in thousands of dollars. Let each block represent $1,000.

MOTLOW DEPARTMENT STORE
Sales in Thousands of Dollars

	Month 1	Month 2	Month 3	Month 4	Month 5	Month 6
Furniture	$23.8	$18.2	$20.6	$23.2	$24.5	$30.6
Clothing	4.2	3.8	4.1	3.9	4.8	4.7
Radio/TV	2.1	2.6	2.3	2.2	2.8	2.3
Accessories	1.0	1.0	1.0	1.0	1.0	1.0
Other	1.3	2.0	3.0	1.8	2.3	2.2

MOTLOW DEPARTMENT STORE
Monthly Sales
in Thousands of Dollars

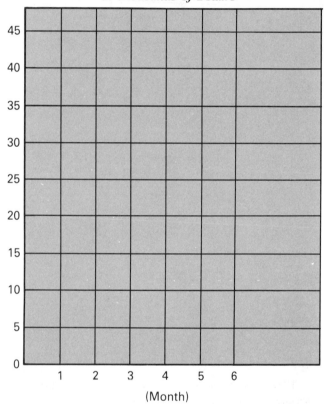

(Month)

ASSIGNMENT 31.2   Bar and Circle Graphs

1. The age-adjustment death rates per 100,000 population for 19Y1 for selected causes of death are listed in the following table. Use the following bar graph to prepare a comparative bar graph to compare Indian and Alaskan death rates (white bar) with death rates of all races (dark bar). Include a legend.

DEATH RATES PER 100,000 POPULATION
Indian/Alaskan Natives vs. All Races
For 19Y1

Cause of Death	Indian and Alaskan Natives	All Races
Vehicle Accidents	79.3	23.7
Other Accidents	61.4	20.0
Homicide	25.5	10.4
Diabetes	22.8	10.0
Suicide	21.8	11.9
Pneumonia	23.1	11.4

DEATH RATES PER 100,000 POPULATION
Indian/Alaskan Natives vs. All Races
For 19Y1

```
  |-------|-------|-------|-------|---|
  |       |       |       |       |   |
  |-------|-------|-------|-------|---|
  |       |       |       |       |   |
  |       |       |       |       |   |
  |-------|-------|-------|-------|---|
  |       |       |       |       |   |
  |       |       |       |       |   |
  |-------|-------|-------|-------|---|
  |       |       |       |       |   |
  |       |       |       |       |   |
  |-------|-------|-------|-------|---|
  |       |       |       |       |   |
  |       |       |       |       |   |
  |-------|-------|-------|-------|---|
  |       |       |       |       |   |
  |       |       |       |       |   |
  |-------|-------|-------|-------|---|
  0      20      40      60      80
```

2. Data in the following table indicates a hypothetical breakdown of families in the United States by income level. Display this data in a circle graph.

FAMILY INCOME
Percentages by Income Levels

Income	Percentage
Less than $5,000	5.6
$5,000 to $9,999	11.9
$10,000 to $19,999	29.7
$20,000 to $34,999	35.2
$35,000 or more	17.6

FAMILY INCOME
Percentages by Income Levels

364

STOCKS

Ownership in a corporation is represented by *certificates of stock* (shares) held by individuals who have invested in the corporation. A typical stock certificate is shown in Example 32.1. A fairly small number of persons may hold stock in some corporations, while several thousand persons may hold stock in other corporations. When a company is incorporated, ownership is evidenced by shares of stock that are issued or sold to people who invest in the business. The Board of Directors may decide to pay *dividends* to stockholders or retain earnings from profitable operation of the business. Shares of stock in many larger corporations can be bought and sold on the New York or American Stock Exchange (NYSE or AMEX), which are listed in most newspapers. Material in this chapter shows computations relating to ownership in corporations.

CHAPTER 32

EXAMPLE   **A stock certificate**

32.1

Buying Corporation Stock at Market Price

The most widely used method for investors to buy stock is to go to a stock broker who will discuss the purchases and provide information

EXAMPLE 32.2 New York Stock Exchange composite listing of transactions

NYSE-Composite Transactions

Quotations include trades on the Midwest, Pacific, Philadelphia, Boston and Cincinnati stock exchanges and reported by the National Association of Securities Dealers and Instinet

52 Weeks High	52 Weeks Low	Stock	Div.	Yld %	P-E Ratio	Sales 100s	High	low	Close	Net Chg.
9¾	5⅞	Craig		..	..	103	9	9	9	−⅛
34⅝	17¾	Crane	1.60b	5.4	..	103	30⅛	29¼	29⅞	+⅞
49½	20	CrayRs		..	33	377	47⅝	46⅛	46⅛	−1⅜
33¼	20¾	CrockN	2.40	7.4	9	71	32½	32⅛	32½	+⅜
25½	16½	CrckN pf	2.18	9.3	..	3	23½	23½	23½	+¼
28⅞	12⅛	CrmpKn	1.04	4.1	16	18	25½	25	25¼	−½
36¾	22¾	CrwnCk		..	11	112	33⅞	33⅝	33⅞	+⅛
33⅞	15¼	CrwZel	1	3.1	..	539	32¾	32⅜	32¾	+⅜
49½	31	CrZel pf	4.63	9.6	..	182	48¼	48	48¼	+⅛
44¼	23⅝	Culbro	1	2.3	14	4	43⅞	43⅝	43⅞	+⅛
45½	12	Cullin s		..	68	334	45½	44¾	45⅛	+⅜
64¼	26	CumEn	2	3.6	..	93	55¾	54¼	54⅞	−⅜
9⅞	7½	CurrInc	1.10	12.	..	20	9⅜	9⅛	9⅜	+⅛
52	32⅝	CurtW	1.20	2.5	11	18	47½	47	47¼	−¼
34	13⅝	Cyclops	1.10	3.8	..	54	29⅜	28¾	29	+⅛
		– D–D–D –								
4⅛	2⅛	DMG		..	..	330	4	3⅞	4	+⅛
39⅞	5¾	Damon	.20	.5	..	142	38¼	37¾	38	.....
39½	21⅞	DanaCp	1.60	4.3	28	903	38½	36¾	37⅝	+⅝
14⅞	8⅝	Daniel	.18b	1.5	9	322	11⅞	11½	11¾	.....
77¼	50½	DartKr	3.84	5.4	11	701	72¼	71	71¼	−¾
73¼	20¼	DataGn		..	56	1156	61¼	59	59	−2⅛
10⅝	4½	DatTer		..	..	5	7⅛	7⅛	7⅛	.....
25⅝	10⅞	Datpnt		..	61	1447	22⅜	21⅜	21½	−¾
13⅛	6¼	Dayco	.16	1.2	167	311	u13⅜	12⅝	13⅜	+⅝
74¾	33½	DayHud	1.20	1.7	17	704	72	71⅜	71½	−¼
19	14⅜	DaytPL	2	11.	7	307	17¾	17½	17⅝	.....
61¼	46⅝	DPL pf	7.37	12.	..	z30	61	61	61	+1
37⅞	14½	DeanF s	.60	1.7	17	119	35⅞	35⅜	35¾	−½
39½	22	Deere	1	2.6	..	1034	38	37½	37¾	.....
17	13¼	DelmP	1.64	9.9	8	1640	16⅞	16⅝	16⅝	−¼
51	25⅜	DeltaAr	1	2.3	..	3771	45½	43⅜	43⅜	−¾
13⅜	4¾	Deltona		..	..	116	12½	12	12⅜	+⅜
47¾	22½	DixChk	1.12	2.5	15	200	45	44¼	44¾	+⅛
35¼	16¼	DenMfg	1.44	4.3	15	114	33½	33	33½	+⅜
36⅞	22⅜	Dennys	.64	1.9	13	448	34⅜	32¾	34⅜	+1⅜
37¼	13⅜	DeSoto	1.24	3.7	18	80	33¾	32¾	33½	+1
15¼	11	DetEd	1.68	11.	8	2237	15⅛	14⅞	15	.....
81½	59	DetE pf	5.50	6.9	..	8	80	80	80	.....
74	57	DetE pf	9.32	13.	..	z150	71½	71½	71½	−¾
61	46½	DetE pf	7.68	13.	..	z90	60	60	60	+⅜
60	44¾	DetE pf	7.45	13.	..	z200	58½	58½	58½	−½
61	44½	DetE pf	7.36	12.	..	z1190	59	58⅜	59	+¾
23¼	17½	DE pfF	2.75	12.	..	11	u23⅜	23¼	23⅜	+¼
25⅞	24½	DE pfQ	3.13	12.	..	43	25⅞	25	25½	+¼
27	23½	DE pfP	3.12	13.	..	8	25	24½	24½	−½
23½	18⅜	DE pfB	2.75	12.	..	2	23	23	23	−⅛
27½	23⅞	DE pfO	3.40	13.	..	37	27⅜	27⅛	27⅛	+⅛
27⅞	24	DE pfM	3.42	12.	..	201	27⅜	27⅛	27⅜	.....
32¼	24⅜	DE prL	4	13.	..	34	31⅜	31	31¼	+⅛
33	24¾	DE pfK	4.12	13.	..	40	32⅜	32	32⅜	−⅛
19	14	DetE pr	2.28	13.	..	3	18⅛	18⅛	18⅛	−⅛
48⅝	21⅜	Dexter	1.10	2.3	18	63	47¾	46⅞	47½	+⅞
15¾	8⅜	DiGior	.64	4.4	17	442	14¾	14½	14⅝	−⅛
29¾	19¾	DiGio pf	2.25	8.0	..	21	28⅞	27⅜	28¼	−¼
26⅜	16½	DiamS	1.76	7.6	12	1990	23½	23¼	23¼	−¼
102	42½	Diebld	1	1.1	20	298	93⅞	92	92¾	+⅛
132⅛	61¾	Digital		..	19	4514	113¼	109¾	110½	−2⅞
84¾	49⅜	Disney	1.20	1.6	24	1303	77¾	75¾	76¾	+1¼
28	19½	DEI	2.28	8.6	7	16	26¾	26⅜	26⅜	−½
4⅞	1⅞	Divrsln		..	..	320	4⅝	4½	4⅝	+⅛
16⅝	11⅝	DrPepp	.84	5.1	40	4021	16⅝	14⅞	16⅝	+1⅞
22¼	5	Dome g	.10	..	..	1565	21½	21	21	−⅜
23¾	18	DomRs	2.40	11.	8	895	22¼	22	22⅛	.....
23½	12¾	Donald	.66	3.0	..	71	22⅜	21½	22¼	+¾
24⅞	8⅜	DonLJ	.24	1.2	14	501	20¾	20¼	20⅝	.....
84	38½	Donnly	1.60	1.9	16	131	83	82½	82½	−¼
44⅜	20	Dorsey	1.10	3.5	..	51	31⅜	31½	31½	−⅛
37	17¾	Dover	.70	2.0	15	752	35¼	34½	35¼	+1
34½	19⅝	DowCh	1.80	5.3	22	4013	34½	34	34	−⅛
53½	17⅞	DowJn s	.60	1.1	37	582	u54½	53¼	53⅞	+⅜

52 Weeks High	52 Weeks Low	Stock	Div.	Yld %	P-E Ratio	Sales 100s	High	low	Close	Net Chg.
38¾	19	GCinm s	.52	1.4	16	404	u38⅞	38½	38½	−⅛
37	25½	GCinm pf	.64	1.8	..	86	36¾	36¼	36½	+¼
25¾	6⅜	GnData		..	..	262	24¾	24	24½	+½
52⅞	24¼	GnDyn	1	1.9	18	4005	52¾	50½	52¾	+2¾
117	60	GDyn pf	4.25	3.6	..	23	u117½	113	117½	+4⅝
112¾	60	GenEl	3.40	3.2	13	2212	106¼	105¼	105¾	−⅜
56¾	30	GenEl wi		..	..	126	53⅜	53	53¼	.....
47¾	33	GnFds	2.40	5.6	7	1898	43¾	42½	42⅞	−⅝
21¼	12¼	GGth	.40	2.0	30	4	20⅛	20⅛	20⅛	.....
19⅜	11	GHost s	.44	2.4	12	212	19	18¼	18⅜	−¼
27¾	7⅜	GnHous	.20	.8	14	50	25	24⅜	24⅜	−½
66⅞	26⅝	GnInst	.50	1.0	16	5153	52¾	51¾	52⅛	+½
57½	38⅝	GnMills	1.84	3.3	13	2463	u57¾	56¼	56⅜	−1⅛
71⅜	39⅝	GMot	2.40e	3.6	14	5751	68¾	67½	67½	−1⅜
40	28½	GMot pf	3.75	9.9	..	5	38	37¾	37¾	−½
52⅛	38¼	GMot pf	5	10.	..	5	50¼	50⅛	50⅛	−⅜
29⅝	5	GNC s	.12	.4	35	49	29	28⅛	28⅜	−⅝
9⅝	4⅜	GPU		..	15	1805	8⅝	8⅛	8½	+⅜
73	33⅞	GenRe	1.28	2.1	13	814	62⅛	61	61⅛	−⅞
6¾	2¾	GnRefr		..	..	87	6½	6¼	6⅜	+⅛
48½	28	GnSignl	1.68	3.7	13	501	45⅜	44¼	44⅞	+⅜
12½	9¼	GTFI pf	1.30	11.	..	z20	11½	11½	11½	−¼
37½	19½	GTire	1.50b	4.0	17	104	37⅜	37⅛	37¼	+⅛
8⅞	3⅝	Gensco		..	..	1229	8½	8⅛	8¼	.....
39⅜	11	GnRad s	.08	.2	55	711	37¼	37	37	−⅜
25⅜	7⅛	Genst g	.60	..	..	x399	u25¾	25½	25½	+⅛
25¾	11½	Gst pf	1.68	6.8	..	x25	25¼	24¾	24¾	+½
47⅜	29¾	GenuPt	1.38	3.3	15	995	42¼	41½	41¾	−½
31⅞	13¼	GaPac	.60	1.9	..	1361	31⅞	31	31¼	−⅝
37	25¾	GaPc pf	2.24	6.1	..	4	37	37	37	+1
29½	25⅜	GaPw pf	3.44	12.	..	39	28⅞	28⅜	28⅜	.....
31¾	24	GaPw pf	3.76	12.	..	21	31¼	31	31	−¼
22¼	16⅛	GaPw pf	2.56	12.	..	12	21¼	21⅛	21¼	.....
22	15½	GaPw pf	2.52	12.	..	6	21½	21⅜	21½	−½
25¼	19¼	GaPw pf	2.75	11.	..	31	24¾	24¾	24¾	−¼
65	49	GaPw pf	7.72	12.	..	z130	63½	62½	63½	+1
31½	19⅜	GerbPd	s1.48	5.0	10	359	29¾	29½	29¾	.....
25⅝	6½	GerbSc	.12	.5	48	194	u26¼	25⅜	26⅛	+1⅛
72½	43	Getty	2.60e	3.8	8	867	68⅛	67⅛	67⅞	−⅛
9½	4½	GiantP		..	..	35	9⅛	9	9	+⅛
16	2¾	GibrFn		..	..	152	15	14½	14⅝	−⅜
22¼	10	GiffHill	.52	2.5	..	948	20½	19½	20½	+¾
51⅜	30¾	Gillette	2.30	5.2	10	913	45½	44⅛	44⅜	−¾
15⅛	8⅛	GleasW		..	..	94	14⅜	13½	14⅜	+⅝
13	7¼	GlobIM	.24	2.3	4	1385	10¾	10½	10⅝	−⅛
60½	22¼	GldNug		..	14	468	60	58	59¼	+1¾
30½	4½	GldWF		..	38	1358	26¾	26¼	26¼	.....
43⅞	16⅜	Gdrich	1.56	3.7	..	965	42½	41¾	42	+⅛
38¼	21⅝	Gdrch pf	3.12	9.1	..	598	35	34½	34½	−⅛
36⅞	21⅜	Goodyr	1.40	4.1	10	4877	34	33⅜	33⅞	+¼
29¾	13⅛	GordnJ	.56	2.1	11	13	27⅛	27	27⅛	+⅛
41⅜	20	Gould	1.72	4.2	20	4042	40⅞	40⅛	40⅝	+⅛
39¾	20½	Gould pf	1.35	3.4	..	1	39¾	39¾	39¾	.....
49⅝	28½	Grace	2.80	5.7	11	319	49½	49	49⅛	−½
56	33⅞	Graingr	1.20	2.2	17	113	55⅜	55	55	−⅜
16¾	8½	Granitv		..	..	2301	16¾	16⅜	16⅝	+⅞
12½	5⅝	GtAtPc		..	20	408	12	11⅜	11½	−¼
38⅝	17⅛	GtLkIn	.80a	2.3	13	18	36	35⅜	35½	−½
27¾	15¾	GNIrn	1.50e	6.8	12	21	22	21	22	+1¼
49	29	GtNoNk	2	4.1	11	328	48¼	47	48¼	+1½
31½	10½	GtWFin	.40	1.5	31	5673	26⅜	25¾	25⅞	−¾
17⅜	7	GWHsp		..	44	1018	u18⅞	16⅜	18⅛	+1⅝
15	11⅞	GMP	1.56	11.	12	9	13⅞	13⅝	13⅞	+⅛
25⅜	12⅝	Greyh	1.20	5.2	9	1408	23⅛	22½	23	−⅛
47	35½	Greyh pf	4.75	11.	..	z90	43½	43½	43½	+1½
7¾	1⅞	Groler n		..	18	449	7⅛	6¾	7	+⅛
15	7	GrowG	.36b	2.9	16	198	12⅞	12⅝	12⅝	.....
5	2¼	GthRty		..	..	18	4⅞	4⅝	4⅝	−¼
11½	3	GrubEl		..	49	71	9⅜	9⅛	9¼	−⅛
62¾	26¾	Grumm	1.60	2.9	16	1980	55¾	54½	55½	+¾
25¼	19⅛	Grum pf	2.80	11.	..	805	24⅜	24¼	24⅜	.....

about various stocks. After a stock is chosen, the broker will issue an order for the agent at the stock exchange to purchase shares of stock at a specified rate when it is available at that price or to purchase the stock at the current rate. Stock is auctioned at the exchange, so the price fluctuates depending on the demand for the stock. Most transactions relate to stocks in companies that are members of the New York Stock Exchange or the American Stock Exchange. A section of the daily rates listing from the New York Stock Exchange is shown in Example 32.2. In addition, about 12% of the stock sold in the two exchanges is sold over the counter. As many as 80 to 100 million shares of stock may be sold daily.

The listing will often give the open price, highest and lowest prices, and the last price for the daily sales of the various stocks. In Example 32.2, the names of the companies are abbreviated. Other headings are P-E Ratio (the last sales price divided by earnings for the past 12 months), Sales (shown in hundreds of shares sold during the day), Close (the price per share at the end of the day), and Net Change (change from the day before). Dividends paid are listed at an annual rate next to the name of the stock.

Notice that the price quotation for stock is always given in eighths, halves, or fourths of a dollar. For example, 50 1/2 is equal to $50.50, and 19 3/8 is equal to $19.375 per share. If the closing price for Heinz Corporation stock is 46 3/4, the cost for purchasing 20 shares will be $935.00 ($46.75 × 20 = $935.00). Similarly, the cost for purchasing 30 shares of Kimberley Clark stock listed at 89 3/8 will be $2,681.25 ($89.375 × 30 = $2,681.25).

Many of the stocks listed do not represent companies that are well known to the general public, but a listing of the 15 most active stocks in the New York Stock Exchange corporate trading for a recent date shows listings for several widely known companies (see Example 32.3).

New York Stock Exchange 15 most active stocks EXAMPLE 32.3

NYSE Most Active

NEW YORK (UPI) — The 15 most active stocks in New York Stock Exchange composite trading Monday.

	Sales	Close	Chg
AmTel&Tel	1,118,800	66 1/2	− 1
RCA Corp	1,102,000	29	+ 7/8
Chrysler	925,400	27 1/8	− [illegible]
PenneyJ.C.	856,400	59 7/8	− 1
DukePwr (x)	724,600	22 3/4	− 1/8
AmerHome	701,100	45 3/8	− 3/4
Catpl Tract	685,600	46 1/4	− 7/8
Schlumberger	683,700	46	− 3/8
IBM Corp	668,900	115 1/4	− 1 1/4
BaldwinUtd	660,800	12 1/2	+ 1 1/4
PanAmAir	631,600	6 3/8	− 3/8
EastmKodak	618,100	74 1/8	Unch
Exxon Corp	586,100	34 1/8	Unch
ChurFriedChick	574,100	28 1/2	+ 5/8
Natomas Co	573,000	17 1/4	+ 3/8

(x)-ExDiv

Sales Net
P-E (hds) Close Chg

On this particular day, American Telephone and Telegraph was the most active stock on the exchange, with 1,118,800 shares of stock being sold. These rates indicate exchanges of stock from previous owners to new owners. The price represents market value with little or no relationship to the original price paid for the stock.

Selling Stock

The certificate of incorporation shows the maximum number of shares, called *authorized capital stock,* that the corporation has authority to issue to investors. As shares of stock are originally issued, the total number issued is the *outstanding capital stock.* Two broad classifications of capital stock are *common stock* and *preferred stock.* Common stock represents the major portion of shares with no guarantee of dividends from profits of the corporation. Preferred stock usually has some provision for preference of distribution of dividends and money from liquidation of the corporation in case it is dissolved. Dividends may be paid in cash (cash dividend) or in additional stock (stock dividend).

The value of the stock as stated on the original stock certificate is the *par value* or *face value* of the stock. Remember from the preceding section that the amount necessary to purchase stock will be determined by market conditions and not by the original par value. Stock originally issued for more than its par value is sold for a *premium,* while stock issued for less than its par value is sold at a *discount.* Calculation of a premium is shown in Example 32.4.

EXAMPLE 32.4

Computing stock premium

Problem: The XYZ Corporation issues 5,000 shares of its stock with a par value of $60 for $70 per share. What is the premium?

Solution: **Step 1.** Compute the par value for the stock.

5,000 × $60 = $300,000

Step 2. Compute the issue price for the stock.

5,000 × $70 = $350,000

Step 3. Compute the total premium.

Issue price − Par value = Premium
$350,000 − $300,000 = $50,000

Likewise, stock issued for less than its par value will show a discount equal to the par value minus the issue price, as shown in Example 32.5. Some stock is issued without a par value, which is called *no-par-value stock.* In this case, no premium or discount is recognized when the stock is issued.

Problem: The Ditney Corporation issued 3,000 shares of stock with a par value of $40 for $30 per share. What is the discount?

Solution: **Step 1.** Compute the par value for the stock.

3,000 × $40 = $120,000

Step 2. Compute the issue price for the stock.

3,000 × $30 = $90,000

Step 3. Compute the total discount.

Par value − Issue price = Discount
$120,000 − $90,000 = $30,000

• Complete Assignment 32.1 •

Computing Dividends on Stock

Dividends on common stock are declared periodically by the corporation's Board of Directors. This amount is usually stated as a percent of the par value of the outstanding stock or as a certain amount for each share of outstanding stock. Example 32.6 illustrates computation of a dividend.

Problem: William Dodd has 50 shares of common stock in the Artex Corporation. What are his dividends if the corporation declares a dividend of $2.40 per share?

Solution: Dividend per share × Shares = Dividend
$2.40 × 50 = $120.00

If the Artex Corporation has 100,000 shares of common stock outstanding, total dividends to be paid will be $240,000.00 ($2.40 × 100,000 = $240,000).

EXAMPLE

32.7

Computing dividends on stock

Problem: The Caltron Corporation declares a dividend of 8% of the par value of each share of outstanding stock. If 5,000 shares of stock with a par value of $10 per share are outstanding, what are the total dividends to be paid?

Solution: **Step 1.** Compute the total par value.

No. of shares × Par value = Total par value
5,000   × $10   = $50,000

Step 2. Compute the total dividends.

Total par value × Dividend rate = Dividends
$50,000   ×   0.08 (8%)   = $4,000

A corporation may allocate a specific amount of funds for dividend distribution. The dividends per share are then computed by dividing the dividend distribution by the number of shares of stock outstanding, as shown in Example 32.8.

EXAMPLE

32.8

Computing dividend per share of stock

Problem: The Stanway Corporation decides to declare dividends in the amount of $50,000. If there are 40,000 shares of stock outstanding, what is the amount of dividend per share?

Solution: Dividends / Outstanding shares = Dividends per share
$50,000   /   40,000   = $1.25

Preferred stockholders receive dividends first; then common stockholders receive their dividends if funds are available. Example 32.9 illustrates computation of dividends for preferred and common stockholders.

EXAMPLE

32.9

Computing dividends for preferred and common stock

Problem: The Rhodes Corporation has 1,000 shares of preferred stock and 1,000 shares of common stock outstanding. Each share has a par value of $10. A dividend of 5% is declared. However, there is only $750 available for dividends. How much will be distributed to preferred and common stockholders?

Solution: **Step 1.**   Compute the dividends for preferred stock.

$$
\begin{array}{ccc}
 & & \text{Preferred} \\
\text{Par value} & \times \text{ Dividend rate } = & \text{dividends} \\
\$10{,}000 \ (\$10 \times 1{,}000) \ \times & 0.05 \ (5\%) & = \$500
\end{array}
$$

Step 2.   Compute the amount left for common stock.

$$
\begin{array}{ccc}
\text{Dividends} & \text{Preferred} & \text{Amount for} \\
\text{available} \ - & \text{dividends} = & \text{common stock} \\
\$750 \quad - & \$500 \quad = & \$250
\end{array}
$$

Computing Rate of Return on Stocks

People who buy and sell stock intend to make a profit on their transactions. They plan for the sales price plus dividends to be high enough to cover brokerage fees, cost of the stock, and a fair rate of return on their investment. The *rate of return* is determined by dividing the amount of the gain by the cost of the transaction. This percent represents the overall rate of return relative to profit on the stock transaction. It does not correspond to an annual rate. For example, in this chapter brokerage fees and taxes are not considered, so the computations are simpler. In reality, they would be additions to the cost of the stock. Example 32.10 illustrates computation of rate of return.

Computing rate of return on stocks   EXAMPLE

32.10

Problem: James Dunavent purchased 100 shares of stock at 62½ and kept the stock for 2 years. Dividends of $4.25 per share were paid each year. He sold the stock for 72¼. What is his rate of return?

Solution: **Step 1.**   Multiply the annual dividend per share by the number of years to compute the gain from dividends per share.

$4.25 \times 2 = \$8.50$ (gain per share from dividends)

Step 2.   Subtract the purchase price from the selling price to compute the loss or gain from sale of stock.

$72.25 - \$62.50 = \$9.75$ (gain on sale of stock)

Step 3.   Add the gain from dividends to the gain (or loss) from sale of stock to compute the total gain (or loss).*

$8.50 + \$9.75 = \$18.25$ (total gain per share)

(Continued on following page)

Step 4.   Divide the total gain (or loss) by the purchase price to compute the rate of return.**

$18.25 ÷ $62.50 = 29.2% (rate of return)

*If a loss on sale of stock is incurred, the loss will be deducted from the dividends (computed in Step 1) in Step 3.
**If a total loss is incurred, the rate will represent a negative return in Step 4.

To illustrate further, assume that Rita Duff purchased 20 shares of stock at 18 1/4 and kept the stock for 3 years. Dividends of $2.10 per share were paid each year. She sold the stock for 15 1/2. Her rate of return is computed as follows:

Step 1. $2.10 × 3 = $6.30 (gain per share from dividends)

Step 2. $15.50 − $18.25 = −$2.75 (loss on sale of stock)

Step 3. $6.30 − $2.75 = $3.65 (total gain per share)

Step 4. $3.65 ÷ $18.25 = 20% (rate of return)

● **Complete Assignment 32.2** ●

ASSIGNMENT 32.1   Buying and Selling Stock

1. Examine the composite prices for stock listed on the New York Stock Exchange shown below. Answer each of the questions about stocks on this listing.

   (a) What is the closing price of Bell and Howell stock?

       $ _____

   (b) What is the closing price of Bay Financial stock?

       $ _____

   (c) Based on the closing price, how much will 100 shares of Conrac stock cost?

       $ _____

   (d) If an investor owns 100 shares of Comb E stock, how much was received in dividends this year?

       $ _____

   (e) Was the Price/Earnings Ratio higher for Bay Financial or Basic Research Company?

       _____

   (f) How many full shares of Bank of New York stock can be purchased for $21,000?

       _____

	P-E	Sales (hds)	Close	Net Chg		P-E	Sales (hds)	Close	Net Chg
BnkARI 1.80	9	93	23⅞	— ⅜	Comb E 1.84	8	459	36¼	+ ⅛
BkBost 2.12	5	304	40⅞	— ⅛	Comdsco .16	27	176	36⅜	— ⅜
Bnk NY 3.40	5	48	59⅜	+ ⅛	ComMetl .44	27	194	40	+ ⅛
Bnk Va 1.32	6	56	29	+ ⅜	Comdor Intl	22	1610	52⅜	—1
BankTr 2.25	5	2110	42⅜	— ⅜	Comwl Ed 3	7	2065	25¼	— ⅛
BkTr pf2.50	...	40	22¾	+ ⅜	CE pfG2.87	...	12	24¾	+ ⅛
Banner	...	159	11¾	+1	CE pfI8.38	...	z50	65	+1½
Bard CR .38	21	279	41¼	—1	CE pfD2	...	3	16	
BarnesG .60	...	35	22½	+1½	CE pfC1.90	...	3	15⅜	+ ¼
Barnt B 1.20	9	189	34¾	— ¼	Com ES 1.96	6	x12	p20¼	
BnB pfA2.38	...	12	37⅞	...	Cm Satellite	16	853	43⅞	—1⅛
BarryWr .40	23	167	b29¾	+ ¼	Com Psy .28	32	201	40	—1⅛
Basic Rs .10	17	83	13	— ¼	Compugrh	19	78	21⅛	
BaushL 1.56	24	105	p52¾	— ¾	Computr Sci	15	1998	p19½	— ½
BaxterTI .56	21	1405	c58¾	—1⅜	Computvis	44	1695	u47¼	—1⅜
Bay Financl	20	36	14⅜	— ⅛	Conagra 1	11	64	29⅛	— ⅜
BaySIG 2.48	15	9	21½	— ⅛	ConeMJ 1.60	18	5	40⅜	+ ⅛
Bearings .1	27	32	38¾	+ ¼	ConnEn 2.80	7	13	24½	
Beat Fd 1.60	8	2879	25⅞	— ⅛	Conn NI 2.20	8	33	19	
BeFpfA 3.38	...	55	48½	— ¼	Conrac .40	13	292	23⅛	— ⅜
Becton 1.15	14	516	45⅞	— ¼	ConsEd 1.88	6	629	22	— ⅜
Beker Inds	...	84	8¼	— ⅛	ConE pf 5	...	8	41½	
BelcoPet .80	9	48	37½	+ ¼	ConsFd 2.32	7	241	42	—1⅛
BeldngH .40	16	99	15¾	— ¼	ConFrg 1.80	12	68	50⅜	— ¾
BellCda 2.08	...	1265	21½	— ⅛	Cons NtGs 2	9	127	p30	— ½
BellHowl .96	...	100	48⅜	—1¼	ConsuP 2.44	7	887	20⅛	
Bell .24	26	59	36⅞	— ⅜	ConP pf 4.50	...	z510	33½	+ ¼

2. Clark Electronics issued 6,000 shares of its stock, which has a par value of $8.00, for $9.00 per share. What was the total (a) par value, (b) issue price, and (c) premium for the stock?

(a) $ _____

(b) $ _____

(c) $ _____

3. Mercury Telecommunications Corporation issued 8,500 shares of its stock, which has a par value of $10.00, for $14.00 per share. What was the total (a) par value, (b) issue price, and (c) premium for the stock?

(a) $ _____

(b) $ _____

(c) $ _____

4. Boone Trucks issued 7,500 shares of its stock, which has a par value of $7.00, for $6.00 per share. What was the total (a) par value, (b) issue price, and (c) discount for the stock?

(a) $ _____

(b) $ _____

(c) $ _____

5. What is the total cost of the following stock purchases: 20 shares @ 14 1/2, 40 shares @ 30 3/8, and 30 shares @ 12 1/4?

$ _____

374

ASSIGNMENT 32.2   Computing Dividends and Rate of Return

Unless otherwise specified, preferred stock will not earn dividends above the stated rate.

1. Determine the amount of dividends that will be paid for each of the following stocks:

Shares	Par Value	Rate of Dividend	Total Dividend
200	20	5%	$ _____
400	100	7%	$ _____
700	30	4%	$ _____
1,500	8	8%	$ _____
2,000	50	6%	$ _____

2. Equidor Parts, Inc., issued dividends of $1.75 per share on its 4,000 shares of outstanding stock. What amount was paid in dividends?

$ _____

3. The Marshall Micro Concepts Corporation had earnings of $62,000 during the past year. If 20,000 shares of stock are outstanding, what were the earnings per share?

$ _____

4. The Miller Appliances Company has 800 shares of preferred stock, par value $10, and 500 shares of common stock, par value $12. A dividend of 5% is declared based on availability of dividends. A total of $600 is available for dividends. How much will be received by (a) preferred stockholders and (b) common stockholders?

(a) $ _____

(b) $ _____

5. Safety Hospital Management, Inc., has 2,000 shares of 6% preferred stock, par value $100 per share, and 1,000 shares of common stock, par value $80. During the year, profits were $20,000. If a 6% dividend is declared for both types of stock, how much will (a) be paid to preferred stockholders, (b) be paid to common stockholders, and (c) remain in retained earnings?

(a) $ _____

(b) $ _____

(c) $ _____

6. Glynda Wilfong purchased 75 shares of common stock 4 years ago at 60 1/2. Annual dividends have averaged $2.50 per share. If she sells the stock today for 75 3/4, what is her rate of return?

_____

7. Lea Ann Goss purchased 50 shares of common stock 2 years ago at 30 1/4. Dividends during the first year were $2.80 per share, and second year dividends were $3.20 per share. If she sells the stock for 42 1/2, what is her rate of return?

_____

8. What is the rate of return on stock purchased 5 years ago at 25 1/4 and selling today for 35 1/2 with annual dividends of $2.20 during the past 5 years?

_____

9. What is the rate of return on stock purchased 1 year ago at 40 1/2 and selling today for 36 1/4 with annual dividends of $1.75 during the past year?

_____

376

BONDS

As shown in Chapter 32, corporations may issue stock to persons who then become part owners. However, a way to raise large amounts of capital without expanding ownership is to borrow money by issuing bonds. A *bond* is a written agreement to pay an amount *(face value)* at some time in the future *(maturity date)*. In addition, the corporation or governmental agency issuing the bond normally pays a stated rate of interest based on the face value of the bond. Like stocks, bonds are often bought and sold on the major security exchanges. In this chapter, you learn about computations needed for corporate borrowing of money by issuing bonds. Example 33.1 illustrates a typical bond.

Issuing Bonds

Bonds are used for long-term borrowing of money. Maturity dates are the dates when the bonds will be paid by the issuer and usually extend to 10 years or longer. In addition to corporate bonds, many local and state governmental agencies issue *municipal bonds*. The federal government also issues *treasury bonds* to borrow money. Interest earned on some governmental bonds is tax exempt from federal income taxes, which helps to make them an attractive investment.

Many bonds are bought and sold on security exchanges for a commission. While the face value is usually in multiples of $1,000, the actual *market price* or *quoted price* of the bond may be higher (sold at a *premium*) or lower (sold at a *discount*) than the face value.

The basic reason for issuing bonds is to borrow money. Investors then buy the bonds and hold them until their maturity or until they are redeemed by the issuer. During this period of time, interest is usually earned by the investor.

Reading Bond Quotations

Bonds may be auctioned or sold to investors on the local level. For example, a church may announce a bond issue and make the bonds available to local investors. However, many large bond issues available to general investors are sold on a national exchange.

A typical listing from the New York Exchange is shown in Example 33.2. The first column shows the name of the corporation issuing the bonds, the original rate of interest, and the maturity date. For example, the first listing (InldStl) shows that the bond pays 9.5% interest and matures in the year 2000.

Current yield shows the actual interest rate if the bond is purchased at the current price. *Volume* shows current sales in units of $1,000. *High* and *Low* show the highest and lowest prices, as percentages of face value, paid for the bond issue during the day. *Close* shows the price at the end of the day as a percentage of face value. *Net Change* shows the difference (plus or minus) between the closing price for the current day and the closing price for the preceding day.

CHAPTER 33

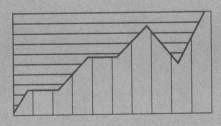

EXAMPLE 33.1 A bond

UNITED STATES OF AMERICA
STATE OF MISSISSIPPI

BEARER

SPECIMEN

YAZOO COUNTY

GENERAL OBLIGATION ROAD AND BRIDGE BOND

SERIES 1983

DOLLARS **5000**

RATE	MATURITY	DATE OF ORIGINAL ISSUE	CUSIP
8.70%	**DUE JUNE 1, 1998**	**JUNE 1, 1983**	**985369 HW 0**

Yazoo County, in the State of Mississippi (hereinafter referred to as the "County"), a body politic existing under the Constitution and Laws of the State of Mississippi, acknowledges itself indebted and, for value received, hereby promises to pay to bearer the principal sum of

FIVE THOUSAND DOLLARS

on the date specified above, upon the presentation and surrender hereof, and to pay interest thereon from the date hereof at the rate per annum specified above. Such interest shall be payable on June 1, 1984 and semiannually thereafter on June 1 and December 1 in each year, until the principal hereof shall have been paid, upon presentation and surrender of the interest coupons appertaining hereto as they severally become due. Both principal of and interest on this bond are payable in lawful money of the United States of America at Bank of Morton, Morton, Mississippi.

Bonds maturing in the years 1994 through 2003, inclusive, are subject to redemption prior to their respective maturities at the election of the County on June 1, 1993, or any interest payment date thereafter, either as a whole or in part (in inverse order of maturity and by lot if less than all of the maturity is to be redeemed), upon not less than thirty (30) days prior notice, at the principal amount thereof plus accrued interest to date of redemption.

This bond is one of a series of three hundred forty (340) bonds of like date, tenor and effect except as to number, rate of interest and date of maturity, numbered consecutively from one (1) through three hundred forty (340), inclusive, aggregating the authorized sum of One Million Seven Hundred Thousand Dollars ($1,700,000) (the "Bonds"), issued to raise money for the purpose of constructing, reconstructing, and repairing roads, highways and bridges, and acquiring the necessary land, including land for road building materials, and rights-of-way therefor.

This bond is issued under the authority of the Constitution and statutes of the State of Mississippi, including Sections 19-9-1 through 19-9-31, Mississippi Code of 1972, and by the further authority of proceedings duly had by the Board of Supervisors of the County, including a Bond Resolution adopted May 2, 1983.

The Bonds are and will continue to be payable as to principal and interest out of and secured by an irrevocable pledge of the avails of a direct and continuing tax to be levied annually without limitation as to time, rate or amount upon all the taxable property within the geographical limits of the County. The County covenants and agrees that it will apply the proceeds of the Bonds to the purpose above set forth, and that so long as any of the Bonds or any of the interest coupons appertaining thereto is outstanding and unpaid, it will levy annually a special tax upon all taxable property within the geographical limits of the County adequate and sufficient to provide for the payment of the principal of and the interest on the Bonds as the same falls due.

IT IS HEREBY CERTIFIED, RECITED AND REPRESENTED that all conditions, acts and things required by law to exist, to have happened and to have been performed precedent to and in the issuance of the Bonds, in order to make the same legal and binding general obligations of Yazoo County, Mississippi, according to the terms thereof, do exist, have happened, and have been performed in regular and due time, form and manner as required by law. For the performance in apt time and manner of every official act herein required and for the prompt payment of this bond, both principal and interest, the full faith and credit of Yazoo County, Mississippi, are hereby irrevocably pledged.

IN WITNESS WHEREOF, Yazoo County, Mississippi, has caused this bond to be executed in its name by the facsimile signature of the President of its Board of Supervisors and countersigned by the manual signature of the Clerk of its Board of Supervisors, thereunto duly authorized, and the Seal of the County to be affixed hereto, and has caused the interest coupons hereto attached to be executed by the facsimile signatures of said officers, all as of the first day of June, 1983.

COUNTERSIGNED:

YAZOO COUNTY, MISSISSIPPI

Clerk of the Board of Supervisors
of Yazoo County, Mississippi

BY: 

President of the Board of Supervisors
of Yazoo County, Mississippi

EXAMPLE 33.2 New York Exchange listing for bonds

Bonds	Cur Yld	Vol	High	Low	Close	Net Chg
InldStl 9½00	12.	65	79⅛	79	79	– ⅜
Intrfst 9¾99	11.	2	85	85	85	.....
Intrfst 7¾05	cv	46	96	95	96	–1
IBM 9½86	9.8	265	98¼	97¼	97⅜	– ⅞
IBM 9⅜04	11.	455	88⅞	87¾	88	– ⅜
IntHrv 4.8s91	9.0	2	53⅛	53⅛	53⅛	....
IntHrv 8⅝95	15.	173	56½	55½	56½	+ ⅝
IntHrv 9s04	16.	143	56	55¼	55½	+ ½
IntHrv 18s02	19.	194	94⅝	93½	93½	–1⅛
InHvC 8⅝91	13.	17	64½	63	64½	+1½
InHvC 7½94	14.	13	52⅞	52¾	52¾	+ ⅛
InHvC 9s84	9.9	23	91⅜	90½	91⅛	– ¼
InHvC 8.35s86	11.	99	73⅝	73¼	73¼	– ¾
InHvC 13½88	16.	60	84½	84⅛	84½	– ¼
IPap 8.85s95	10.	5	85½	85½	85½	.....
IPap 4¼96	cv	6	160	160	160	+4
IntTT 8.9s95	11.	10	84¾	84¾	84¾	– ¼
IntTT 8⅝00	cv	1	156	156	156	.....
Intnr 10¾90	11.	12	98½	98½	98½	–1⅛
Intnr 17½91	14.	10	123	123	123	+1
IntrBk 5½87	cv	50	73¾	73¾	73¾	+ ½
JnM 7.85s04f	..	41	68⅛	67½	67½	.....
JnM 9.7s85f	..	12	84	84	84	– ¾
JonsLI 6¾94	11.	20	63	62⅛	62½	+ ⅜
JoneL 6¾94	11.	4	62⅜	62⅜	62⅜	– ⅝
JoneL 9⅞95	13.	4	80	79	79	–3¼
K mart 6s99	cv	43	101½	100½	101	+ ¼
K Mart 9⅞85	9.9	5	99¼	99¼	99¼	– ¼
Kane 9½90	11.	10	84	83	83	.....
Kellog 8⅝85	8.8	3	98⅛	98⅛	98⅛	.....
KimCl 5⅞91	8.0	1	73⅜	73⅜	73⅜	+ ¼
I TV 5s88	6.8	99	74⅛	74	74	– ⅛

In the first listing (InldStl), the current yield is 12% with $65,000 in bonds being sold during the day. The High, Low, and Closing prices are 79.125, 79, and 79% respectively of the face value of the bond. This shows that the price of the bond ranged from $790.00 to $791.25 during the day, with a closing price of $790.00 (0.79 × $1,000) for each $1,000 bond issue purchased. The current closing price is 0.375% lower than the closing price from the preceding day.

The name of the company issuing bonds is abbreviated in the newspaper listing. Some of the abbreviations, such as IBM, are generally recognized. A security broker provides information about companies to help investors choose bonds for maximum security. For a commission, the broker provides advice and handles the transaction to purchase the bond issue. Broker fees vary on bond sales, but a set fee (such as $5.00 per $1,000 bond) for each bond purchased or sold is typical.

Purchasing Bonds

A fixed rate of interest is specified for each bond. If the bond is purchased between interest dates, the purchaser ordinarily pays the accrued interest since the last payment date. For purposes of computing accrued bond interest, all 12 months are counted as having 30 days, and the year is counted as having 360 days. Example 33.3 illustrates calculation of the accrued interest period, and Example 33.4 illustrates calculation of the accrued interest amount.

Computing accrued interest period   EXAMPLE

33.3

Problem: A bond with a semiannual interest payment date of June 30 is sold on September 15. What is the accrued interest period?

Solution:
June 30 to August 31   = 60 days
August 31 to September 15   = 15 days
Total days of accrued interest = 75 days

Computing accrued interest   EXAMPLE

33.4

Problem: The Belz Corporation issued 20 $1,000 bonds bearing interest at 12%. If the accrued interest period is 75 days, what is the accrued interest to be paid by the purchaser?

Solution: Face value × Interest × Accrued interest = Accrued
                         rate   period   interest
          $20,000.00 ×   0.12   ×   75/360   = $500.00

Remember that each full month counts as having 30 days regardless of the actual number of days in the month.

Other costs of the bond purchase include the market value and broker's commission. These costs are considered in Examples 33.5 and 33.6.

EXAMPLE
33.5

Computing full bond purchase price

Problem: Suzanne Morrison purchased 4 $1,000 bonds at 102, plus accrued interest from January 15 to March 30 at 9%. The broker's commission is $5.00 per $1,000 bond issue. What is the full bond purchase price?

Solution: **Step 1.** Compute the accrued interest period.

January 15 to March 15 is 60 days, and March 15 to March 30 is 15 days.

60 + 15 = 75 days (accrued interest period)

Step 2. Multiply the face value by the interest rate by the time to compute the accrued interest.

$4,000.00 × 0.09 × 75/360 = $75.00 (accrued interest)

Step 3. Multiply the face value by the price quotation to compute the market price.

$4,000.00 × $1.02 = $4,080.00 (market price)

Step 4. Multiply the number of issues by the rate per $1,000 to compute the broker's commission.

4 × $5.00 = $20.00 (broker's commission)

Step 5. Add the accrued interest, market price, and commission to compute the bond purchase price.

$75.00 + $4,080.00 + $20.00 = $4,175.00 (bond purchase price)

In Example 33.5, Ms. Morrison will pay $4,175.00 to purchase the bonds on March 30. Since she will receive interest for the full period on the next interest payment date, the accrued interest ($75.00) will be received back on that date. After deducting the commission, the broker will submit the remainder to the seller. Therefore, the *proceeds to the seller* will be $4,155.00 ($4,175.00 − $20.00).

Some bonds are purchased at a discount. In Example 33.6, Beverley Cafer purchased 2 $1,000 bonds at 88, plus accrued interest from April 2 to July 2 at 12%. The broker's commission is $5.00 per $1,000 bond issue.

Purchasing bonds at a discount   EXAMPLE

Step 1. Accrued interest period is 90 days.

Step 2. $2,000 × 0.12 × 90/360 = $60.00 (accrued interest)

Step 3. $2,000 × 0.88 = $1,760.00 (market price)

Step 4. 2 × $5.00 = $10.00 (broker's commission)

Step 5. $60.00 + $1,760.00 + $10.00 = $1,830.00 (bond purchase price)

The proceeds to the seller will be $1,820.00 ($1,830.00 − $10.00).

> ● **Complete Assignment 33.1** ●

Computing Rate of Return on Bonds

Computation of interest is based on the face value (also called *par value*) of the bonds. Therefore, a bond purchased at 100 will show a rate of return equal to the annual rate of interest. However, bonds are sold at market value, which seldom equals the face value. Bonds sold at a premium will show a rate of return that is less than the stated rate of interest, while bonds sold at a discount will show a rate of return that is higher than the stated rate of interest. The rate of return on the investment is called the *yield* of the bond issue.

Annual Rate of Return

The rate of return is expressed as a percentage, such as a 7.8% annual rate. The rate of return is computed by dividing annual interest by total cost for the bond issue, as shown in Example 33.7.

Computing rate of return   EXAMPLE

Problem: LaVon Finiello purchased 2 $1,000 bonds at 90. The bonds pay an 8% interest rate. A total commission of $10 is charged. What is the rate of return?

Solution: Step 1. Compute the market value.

Face value × Price quotation = Market value
$2,000   × $0.90   = $1,800.00

(Continued on following page)

Step 2.   Compute the total cost.

Market value + Commission = Total cost
    $1,800.00   + $10.00   = $1,810.00

Step 3.   Compute the interest earned.

Face value × Interest rate = Interest earned
    $2,000.00 ×   0.08   = $160.00

Step 4.   Compute the rate of return.

Interest earned / Total cost =   Rate of return
    $160.00   / $1,810.00 = 0.0883977 or 8.84%

Notice that the rate of return is higher than the stated interest because the bonds were purchased at a discount. In Example 33.8, Arlene Alexander purchased 3 $1,000 bonds at 105. The bonds pay an 8% interest rate. A commission of $15 is charged by the broker. The rate of return is computed as shown in Example 33.8.

EXAMPLE

33.8

Computation of rate of return on bonds purchased at a premium

Step 1. $3,000.00 × $1.05 = $3,150.00 (market value)

Step 2. $3,150.00 + $15.00 = $3,165.00 (total cost)

Step 3. $3,000.00 × 0.08 = $240.00 (interest earned)

Step 4. $240.00 ÷ $3,165.00 = 0.0758 or 7.58% (rate of return, rounded)

Since the rate of return is lower than the stated interest rate, the bonds were purchased at a premium.

Discount or Premium Amortization

The discount or premium for bonds with long-term maturity dates is often amortized (spread) over the remaining life of the bond. A premium will reduce the interest rate, while a discount will increase the interest rate. In its simplest form, an equal portion of the discount or premium is accounted for each year with amortization. For example, bonds purchased at a $530.00 premium with a maturity date 10 years in the future will show $53.00 ($530.00 ÷ 10) being deducted from the interest each year. The principal used is based on the average of the market value and face value of the note. Commission and other minor expenses are usually omitted from this computation. This rate is often called the *yield-to-maturity rate.* Amortization of bond premium and rate of return are calculated in Examples 33.9 and 33.10.

Amortization of bond premium and rate of return   EXAMPLE

33.9

Problem: Kurt VanCleave purchased 2 $1,000 bonds bearing 9% interest at 108 with a maturity date 10 years in the future. The premium amount is $160.00 ($2,000.00 × 0.08). What are the amortization of bond premium and rate of return?

Solution: **Step 1.** Multiply the face value by the interest rate to compute the annual interest.

$2,000.00 × 0.09 = $180.00 (annual interest)

Step 2. Divide the amount of the premium by the number of years to compute the annual amortization.

$160.00 ÷ 10 = $16.00 (annual amortization)

Step 3. Subtract the annual amortization from the annual interest to compute the actual annual interest.

$180.00 − $16.00 = $164.00 (actual annual interest)

Step 4. Add the face value to the market value and divide by 2 to compute the average principal invested.

($2,000.00 + $2,160.00) ÷ 2 = $2,080.00 (average principal)

Step 5. Divide the actual annual interest by the average principal invested to compute the amortized rate of return.

$164.00 ÷ $2,080.00 = 0.0788 or 7.88% (amortized rate of return, rounded)

In Example 33.10, Tom Curry purchased 3 $1,000 bonds with a 7% interest rate at 95 with a maturity date 5 years in the future. Using the steps shown in Example 33.9, the discount is amortized over 5 years as shown in Example 33.10. The rate has been rounded to 2 decimal places.

EXAMPLE   **Amortization of bond discount and rate of return**

33.10

> **Step 1.** $3,000.00 \times 0.07 = 210.00$ (annual interest)
>
> **Step 2.** $150.00 \div 5 = 30.00$ (annual amortization)
>
> **Step 3.** $210.00 + 30.00 = 240.00$ (actual annual interest)
>
> **Step 4.** $(3,000.00 + 2,850.00) \div 2 = 2,925.00$ (average principal)
>
> **Step 5.** $240.00 \div 2,925.00 = 0.0821$ or 8.21% (rate of return)

The face value of the bonds will be received on the maturity date. For the bond purchased at a $160.00 premium, amortization is a way to spread the amount above face value over the remaining life of the bond. Likewise, the discount amount paid minus the face value is spread over the remaining life of the bond, which increases the rate of return each year.

Sale of Bonds

The examples and illustrations in this chapter relate to how bond transactions affect the investor. Similar methods are used by the company or agency that issues bonds to determine interest rates and bond yields. Brokers and exchanges usually charge the seller of bonds a fee. These fees must be considered when determining actual expenses and bond yields relating to the bond issued.

● **Complete Assignment 33.2** ●

ASSIGNMENT 33.1   Bond Quotations and Purchase Price

1. Answer the following questions based on the following newspaper listing of bonds sold on the American Exchange:

Bonds	Cur Yld	Vol	High	Low	Close	Net Chg
Altec 6¾s88	10.	12	67	66	67	+1
Altec 15s95	cv	19	118	113	118	+5
AMaiz 11¾00	cv	13	108¼	108¼	108¼	+¼
Anglo 11⅞98	16.	16	75	75	75	.....
Anth 11¼00	cv	32	100	99¼	100	+2¾
BeefC 13s97	cv	132	148	148	148	.....
Bowmr 13½s95	cv	6	110	109	110	+1
CmpC 7¾98	cv	36	116	115	115	+1
ConOG 11½93	15.	10	79	79	79	−⅛
CustE 15s97	cv	41	144	138	138	−4
DamsO 13.2s00	15.	4	90	90	90	+2
Delmed 10½02	cv	22	113	113	113	+½
Digicn 10½01	13.	25	81	81	81	.....
Docu 11½98	13.	15	90	90	90	−1½
DorchG 8½05	cv	47	79	78½	78½	−½
DuroT 5¾92	cv	2	112	112	112	+3
EnMgmt 12s96	cv	24	71	70½	71	+1
Engv 9s95	cv	37	82½	80½	80½	−2
FrntAir 6s92	cv	2	135	135	135	.....
FrntHld 10s07	cv	10	96	96	96	.....

(a) What rate of interest do bonds offered by AMaiz pay?

_____

(b) What is the maturity date for bonds offered by Anth?

_____

(c) What is the current yield being paid for bonds offered by Docu?

_____

(d) How many issues of bonds were sold by CustE?

_____

(e) What was the highest quote during the day for bonds offered by ConOG?

_____

(f) At the close of the day, what was the quote for bonds offered by Engv?

_____

(g) How much did bonds offered by DamsO change from the close of the previous day?

_____

(h) At the close of the day, how much money will be required to purchase $10,000 in bonds from Frontier Airlines?

$ _____

(i) Which company sold the highest volume of bonds during the day?

_____

(j) Based on the closing quote for the day, how much money will be required to purchase $8,000 in bonds from Bowmr?

$ _____

2. On April 25, Randy Vataha purchased 4 $1,000 bonds with an annual interest payment date of February 10. The interest rate is 10%. What is the (a) accrued interest period and (b) accrued interest amount for the bond issue?

(a) _____

(b) $ _____

3. On September 30, Darlene Dempsey purchased 6 $1,000 bonds with an annual interest payment date of June 30. The interest rate is 9 3/4%. What is the (a) accrued interest period and (b) accrued interest amount for the bond issue?

(a) _____

(b) $ _____

4. Assume that Randy Vataha in Problem 2 above purchased the bonds at 105 with a commission of $5 per $1,000. What is the purchase price for the bonds?

$ _____

5. Assume that Darlene Dempsey in Problem 3 above purchased the bonds at 108 with a commission of $5 per $1,000. What is the purchase price of the bonds?

$ _____

6. Charlotte LaCosta purchased 10 $1,000 bonds on November 17, which was 30 days after the interest payment date. The bonds were purchased at 96 with an interest rate of 9% and a commission of $42. What is the (a) amount of accrued interest and (b) purchase price of the bonds?

(a) $ _____

(b) $ _____

7. Gretchen Lee purchased 9 $1,000 bonds on January 23, which was 60 days after the interest payment date. The bonds were purchased at 84 with an interest rate of 8% and a commission of $48. What is the (a) amount of accrued interest and (b) purchase price for the bonds?

(a) $ _____

(b) $ _____

386

ASSIGNMENT 33.2 Computing Rate of Return and Discount or Premium Amortization for Bonds

1. Eight bonds from a recent newspaper listing are shown in the following table. Complete the table to show the annual rate of return for the purchase of the $1,000 bonds. Assume a commission of $5.00 per $1,000 for each bond. (Round rate of return to 2 decimal places.) The discount or premium is not amortized.

Bond	Number Purchased	Price	Interest Rate	Market Value	Total Cost	Annual Interest	Rate of Return
1	4	88	6%	$ _____	$ _____	$ _____	_____
2	6	92	8 1/2%	$ _____	$ _____	$ _____	_____
3	5	94	8%	$ _____	$ _____	$ _____	_____
4	3	104	10%	$ _____	$ _____	$ _____	_____
5	2	102	5%	$ _____	$ _____	$ _____	_____
6	8	106	12%	$ _____	$ _____	$ _____	_____
7	1	96	9%	$ _____	$ _____	$ _____	_____
8	7	101	4%	$ _____	$ _____	$ _____	_____

2. Fred Bassett purchased 21 $1,000 bonds in 1983. He chose IBM, 9 1/2 04 at 88. (a) If interest is computed and paid semiannually, what interest amount will he earn every 6 months? (b) What amount of discount should be amortized each year? (c) Taking the interest and discount into account, what is the amount of actual annual interest? (d) What is the average principal invested? (e) What is the amortized rate of return? (Round to 2 decimal places.)

(a) $ _____

(b) $ _____

(c) $ _____

(d) $ _____

(e) _____

3. Anita Marmino purchased 15 $1,000 bonds in 1984. She chose K-Mart, 6s99 at 101. (a) What amount will she pay for the bonds at this price? (b) What amount is the annual interest? (c) What portion of the premium should be amortized each year? (d) Taking the premium amortization into account, what is the actual annual interest? (e) What is the average principal involved? (f) What is the amortized rate of return? (Round to 2 decimal places.)

(a) $ _____

(b) $ _____

(c) $ _____

(d) $ _____

(e) $ _____

(f) _____

4. Jim Anderson purchased 10 $1,000 Shell Oil 8 1/2 00 bonds at 80 in 1980. What is the amortized rate of return (rounded to 2 decimal places)?

_____

5. Martin Marietta purchased 10 $1,000 American Medical 8s08 bonds at 105 in 1983. What is the amortized rate of return (rounded to 2 decimal places)?

_____

● **Complete Unit 7 Spreadsheet Applications** ●

UNIT 7   SPREADSHEET APPLICATION 1: Sales Analysis

The following spreadsheet is used to compute an analysis of sales for a 5-day period. Compute the average sales amount, highest sales amount, and total sales amount for each day and enter those amounts on Rows 15, 17, and 19.

	A	B	C	D	E	F
1	Bellot's Shoe Store			**SALES ANALYSIS**		
2	==					
3	Salesperson	Monday	Tuesday	Wednesday	Thursday	Friday
4	--					
5	Fitten, D.	246.89	213.54	241.74	275.29	289.52
6	Hilger, A.	205.67	289.32	238.51	271.18	243.56
7	Niesen, E.	190.00	208.00	237.65	255.43	275.22
8	Piraino, H	205.34	213.45	205.35	276.47	253.48
9	Streuli, B.	305.20	204.21	198.11	209.99	224.53
10	Walker, F.	257.98	238.45	253.45	264.35	253.91
11	Warf, J.	235.18	235.43	205.35	305.31	302.25
12	Wintker, F.	305.20	205.16	209.99	345.37	306.21
13	Zetchi, D.	189.00	175.33	201.13	215.73	235.42
14	--					
15	Average					
16	--					
17	High					
18	--					
19	Total					
20	==					

Refer to the spreadsheet shown above to answer the following questions:

1. What is the average sales amount for Monday?　　　　　　　$ _____

2. What is the average sales amount for Wednesday?　　　　　$ _____

3. Which day of the week had the highest average sales amount?　　_____

4. Which salesperson had the highest sales amount on Monday?　　_____

5. Which salesperson had the highest sales amount on Thursday?　　_____

6. Which day of the week had the highest total sales amount?　　_____

7. Which day of the week had the lowest total sales amount?　　_____

8. How many salespersons had sales amounts greater than the average sales amount on Friday?　　_____

9. What was the total sales amount on Thursday?　　　　　　$ _____

10. What was the total sales amount on Friday?　　　　　　　$ _____

UNIT 7 SPREADSHEET APPLICATION 2: Bond Cost

The following spreadsheet is used to compute the market value, commission, and total cost for a series of bond issues. The face value is multiplied by the price quotation to compute the market value. The commission equals $10 per $1,000 of face value. Total cost equals the market value plus the commission. To check your computations, total cost for the first bond (ID Number 1782Q) should be $4,360.

	A	B	C	D	E	F	G
1	Teek State Bank			**BOND COST**			$$
2	==						$$
3	ID	Face	Price	Market	Commission	Total	$$
4	Number	Value	Quotation	Value	($10 per 1,000)	Cost	$$
5	---						$$
6	1782Q	4,000	108				$$
7	1436Q	3,000	105				$$
8	2431Q	5,000	96				$$
9	3254Q	5,000	102				$$
10	7832Q	2,000	95				$$
11	1087R	12,000	97				$$
12	2142R	8,000	92				$$
13	4356R	7,000	112				$$
14	5632R	13,000	94				$$
15	7831R	6,000	91				$$
16	2048Y	5,000	112				$$
17	3154Y	3,000	106				$$
18	4127Y	7,000	96				$$
19	8010Y	10,000	94				$$
20	==						$$

Refer to the spreadsheet above to answer the following questions:

1. What is the market value for ID Number 3254Q? $ _____

2. What is the market value for ID Number 7831R? $ _____

3. What is the market value for ID Number 4127Y? $ _____

4. What is the commission for ID Number 4356R? $ _____

5. What is the total cost for ID Number 2431Q? $ _____

6. What is the total cost for ID Number 2048Y? $ _____

7. What is the ID Number of the bond with the highest total cost?   _____

8. How many bonds were sold for a premium?   _____

9. How many bonds were sold for a discount?   _____

10. How many bonds had a market value greater than $10,000?   _____

● **Complete Unit 7 Self-Test** ●

391

UNIT 7 SELF-TEST Statistics, Graphs, Stocks, and Bonds

1. Employees who work for Copeland's Photo Shop earned the following salaries last week: $303, $310, $320, $308, $310, $314, and $340. What are the (a) mean, (b) median, and (c) mode salaries for the employees?

(a) $ _____

(b) $ _____

(c) $ _____

2. The 5 cabs in the Urban Cab Company's fleet were driven the following numbers of miles last week: 162.6, 150.5, 148.3, 139.4, and 154.7. What are the (a) mean and (b) median miles driven for the fleet?

(a) _____

(b) _____

3. Scores made on the final exam by advanced accounting students at Waverly Junior College are shown below grouped by interval category. What are the (a) mean, (b) median, and (c) modal class for the test?

(a) _____

(b) _____

(c) _____

Scores	Frequency
73– 79	4
80– 86	5
87– 93	7
94–100	4

4. Furniture and appliance sales (in millions of dollars) for the past 12 months in a large city were as follows: January, 6.5; February, 10.2; March, 10.4; April, 10.1; May, 11.3; June, 11.5; July, 12.2; August, 11.4; September, 10.1; October, 11.3; November, 11.5; and December, 12.5. Use the following chart to prepare a line graph to show sales for each month. Let each block on the graph represent $1,000,000.

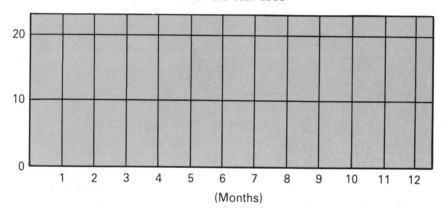

5. Use the same furniture and appliance sales data provided in Problem 4 above to construct a bar graph. Let each block on the graph represent $1,000,000. Use the following chart to prepare the bar graph.

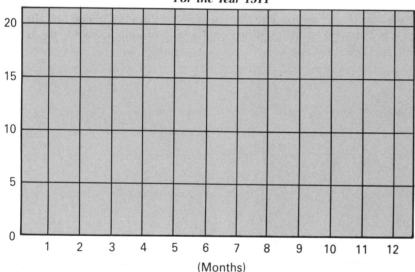

UNIT 7 SELF TEST (continued)

6. The Kraft Equipment Company issues 4,600 shares of its stock, which has a par value of $5.00. The stock is issued for $6.00 per share. What is the total (a) par value, (b) issue price, and (c) premium for the stock?

   (a) $_____

   (b) $_____

   (c) $_____

7. What is the total cost of the following stock purchases: 30 shares @ 15 1/2, 80 shares @ 20 7/8, and 20 shares @ 10 1/4?

   $_____

8. Michelle Goldstein owns 200 shares of stock with a par value of $15. The Board of Directors declared a 7% cash dividend. What amount did she receive in dividends?

   $_____

9. Marjorie Lowell purchased 20 shares of common stock 2 years ago for 40 1/4. Dividends were $3.50 per share each year. If she sells the stock for 45 1/2, what is the rate of return (rounded to 2 decimal places)?

   _____

10. Marshall Electronics, Inc. has 20,000 shares of 5% preferred stock outstanding with a par value of $30 and 20,000 shares of common stock outstanding with a par value of $10. If $40,000 is available for dividends, what amount will be paid to holders of common stock?

    $_____

11. On January 16, Lamar O'Toole purchased 6 $1,000 bonds with an annual interest payment date of January 1. The interest rate is 12%. What are the (a) accrued interest period and (b) accrued interest amount for the bond issue?

(a) _____

(b) $ _____

12. Kristen Cohen purchased 4 $1,000 bonds at 104 with a commission of $5.00 per $1,000. What is the purchase price of the bonds?

$ _____

13. Theodore Ashe purchased 12 $1,000 United Steel 8s08 bonds at 105 in 1983. What is the amortized rate of return (rounded to 2 decimal places)?

_____

14. Caroline Bisno purchased 8 $1,000 bonds in 1984. She chose Kane 9 1/2 00 at 89. (a) What total amount will she pay for the bonds? (b) How much of the discount should be amortized each year? (c) Taking the discount into account, what is the actual annual interest rate?

(a) $ _____

(b) $ _____

(c) _____

396

Computer Information Processing (Spreadsheets)

This unit shows how typical business applications can be arranged for completion using an electronic spreadsheet format.

Some skills you can achieve in this unit include the following:

- **Examining spreadsheet format and layout.**
- **Making computations using a spreadsheet.**
- **Determining information that can be provided by spreadsheet analysis.**
- **Analyzing data comparisons.**
- **Utilizing spreadsheet-generated output.**
- **Learning common business spreadsheet applications.**
- **Recognizing the utility of data presented in spreadsheet format.**
- **Manipulating data shown in spreadsheet format.**

UNIT 8

UNIT 8   SPREADSHEET APPLICATION 1: Mortgage Payment Schedule

The following mortgage loan payment spreadsheet shows various loan amounts, time periods, and interest rates. Formulas are included in the spreadsheet to calculate the monthly principal and interest payments and the total payments over the life of the loan.

	A	B	C	D	E	F
1		FINANCIAL AMERICAN MORTGAGE COMPANY				
2		PAYMENT SCHEDULE				
3	--------	--------	--------	--------	--------	--------
4	Mortgage	Length of	Interest	Monthly	Total	
5	Amount	Loan (Years)	Rate	Pr.&Int.	Payments	
6						
7	$15,000	15	12.00%	$183.53	$33,035.45	
8	$16,000	15	12.00%	$195.77	$35,237.82	
9	$17,000	15	11.75%	$205.23	$36,941.67	
10	$18,000	15	11.75%	$217.30	$39,114.70	
11	$19,000	15	11.50%	$226.30	$40,733.44	
12	$20,000	20	11.50%	$216.17	$51,881.91	
13	$25,000	20	11.50%	$270.22	$64,852.39	
14	$30,000	20	11.50%	$324.26	$77,822.87	
15	$35,000	30	11.00%	$335.49	$120,775.83	
16	$40,000	30	11.00%	$383.42	$138,029.52	
17	$45,000	30	10.75%	$422.89	$152,240.72	
18	$50,000	30	10.75%	$469.88	$169,156.35	
19	$55,000	30	10.50%	$506.59	$182,371.99	
20	$60,000	30	10.50%	$552.64	$198,951.27	

Answer the following questions based on the mortgage loan spreadsheet:

1. What was the highest mortgage amount in the schedule? $ _____

2. What was the lowest mortgage interest rate?   _____

3. What was the maximum number of years allowed for a loan?   _____

4. What was the highest mortgage interest rate?   _____

5. If the mortgage amount was $35,000, what was the interest rate?   _____

6. If the borrower's total payments were $198,951.27, what was the length of the loan?   _____

7. What were the total payments on a 30-year, $50,000 loan? $ _____

8. What was the monthly principal and interest on a 20-year, $20,000 loan? $ _____

9. How much total interest would be charged on a 30-year, $40,000 loan? $ _____

10. How much total interest would be charged on a 30-year, $60,000 loan? $ _____

UNIT 8   SPREADSHEET APPLICATION 2: Accelerated Depreciation

The following accelerated depreciation spreadsheet shows a comparison of the straight-line, sum-of-the-years' digits, and declining-balance methods. Formulas are included to calculate the annual depreciation and total depreciation.

	A	B	C	D	E
1		ACCELERATED ANNUAL DEPRECIATION SCHEDULE			
2					
3	Cost of Asset:		$7,500.00		
4	Disposal Value:		$500.00		
5	Expected Life:		5 years		
6	--				
7	Year Straight-Line||Sum-of-the-Years' Digits||Declining-Balance				
8					
9	1	$1,500.00	$2,500.00	$3,000.00	
10	2	$1,500.00	$2,000.00	$1,800.00	
11	3	$1,500.00	$1,500.00	$1,080.00	
12	4	$1,500.00	$1,000.00	$648.00	
13	5	$1,500.00	$500.00	$388.80	
14					
15	TOTAL	$7,500.00	$7,500.00	$6,916.80	

Answer the following questions based on the accelerated depreciation spreadsheet shown above:

1. What was the cost of the asset being depreciated? $_____

2. What was the disposal value of the asset? $_____

3. What was the expected life of the asset?   _____

4. How much was the annual straight-line depreciation? $_____

5. What was the total depreciation using the straight-line method? $_____

6. What was the annual sum-of-the-years' digits depreciation for Year 3? $_____

7. What was the annual sum-of-the-years' digits depreciation for Year 5? $_____

8. What was the annual declining-balance depreciation for Year 1? $_____

9. What was the total depreciation using the sum-of-the-years' digits method? $_____

10. What was the total depreciation using the declining-balance method? $_____

UNIT 8 SPREADSHEET APPLICATION 3: Automobile Financing

The following automobile financing spreadsheet includes formulas to compute the cash price of the automobile, the total down payment, the unpaid balance, and the monthly payment on the loan.

```
         A          B          C          D        E           F        G
1                          AUTOMOBILE FINANCING
2
3     Date:        10/20/--                     Length of Loan         Rate
4     Borrower:    DEANNA K. ALLRED             in Months:      36    10.90%
5
6
7     Price of Car        13,762.00
8     State Tax              293.78
9     County Tax             26.54
10    Business Tax           10.66
11    *Cash Price         14,092.98
12    Cash Down            4,000.00
13    Net Trade            1,680.00
14    *Total Down          5,680.00
15    Official Fees           8.75
16    Other                  68.75
17
18    *Unpaid Balance      8,490.48
19
20    DEANNA K. ALLRED          36 monthly payments of $289.03
```

Answer the following questions based on the financing spreadsheet shown above:

1. What was the length of the loan? _____

2. What was the financing rate for the loan? _____

3. What was the unpaid balance to be financed? $_____

4 What were the monthly loan payments? $_____

5. How much cash down did Deanna pay? $_____

6. How much was the county tax on the automobile? $_____

7. How much were the official fees on the automobile? $_____

8. How much was the cash price of the car? $_____

9. How much was the net trade value? $_____

10. How much was the price of the car before taxes? $_____

UNIT 8   SPREADSHEET APPLICATION 4: Weekly Payroll

The following weekly payroll spreadsheet for an on-the-job training program includes formulas for computing weekly pay, total hours worked, total hourly wages, and total weekly pay.

	A	B	C	D	E	F
1	CRENSHAW HIGH SCHOOL - DISTRIBUTIVE EDUCATION ON-THE-JOB TRAINING (OJT)					
2						
3		WEEKLY STUDENT PAYROLL				
4	**					
5	Student	Student		Hours	Hourly	Weekly
6	Name	Number	Employer	Worked	Wage	Pay
7						
8	Aguiree, Sandra	1438261	The Loft	22	3.75	$82.50
9	Allen, Coretta	1573420	McDonald's	20	3.80	$76.00
10	Bell, Jeff	4328615	Wendy's	30	3.75	$112.50
11	Carney, Monica	1420832	Wendy's	30	3.90	$117.00
12	Fitzgerald, Denise	1439680	Champions	20	4.00	$80.00
13	Lorch, Teppi	1083215	Red Lobster	24	3.75	$90.00
14	Mitchell, Andre	1392617	McDonald's	24	3.60	$86.40
15	Nanney, Doug	2882136	Seessels's	30	3.80	$114.00
16	Pardo, Jacob	4306915	Foot Locker	24	4.25	$102.00
17	Quillin, Joseph	3552100	Ticket Hub	20	4.10	$82.00
18	Ramsey, Brad	2361875	Library	20	3.90	$78.00
19						
20	TOTALS			264	42.60	$1,020.40

Answer the following questions based on the payroll spreadsheet above:

1. Who was Andre Mitchell's employer?   _____

2. How much did Andre Mitchell make per hour? $_____

3. How many hours did Andre Mitchell work each week?   _____

4. What was Andre Mitchell's weekly pay? $_____

5. What was Denise Fitzgerald's student number?   _____

6. Who worked the most hours for the week?   _____

7. Who made the most money for the week?   _____

8. What was the total earned by all students for the week? $_____

9. How many total hours were worked by all students for the week?   _____

10. Who worked at the Foot Locker?   _____

UNIT 8 SPREADSHEET APPLICATION 5: Personal Income and Expense Summary

The following personal income and expense budget spreadsheet shows income and expenses for the first quarter of the year. Included in the spreadsheet are formulas to calculate quarterly totals, total income, total expenses, and the surplus or deficit for each month and the entire quarter.

	A	B	C	D	E	F
1	F I R S T		PERSONAL	INCOME AND	EXPENSE	SUMMARY
2	Q U A R T E R			Jonathan K.	Hampton	
3	--------------	----------------	---------	---------	---------	----------
4			Jan	Feb	Mar	Totals
5	INCOME					
6		Parental Support	$200.00	$200.00	$200.00	$600.00
7		Interest Earned	$48.00	$48.00	$48.00	$144.00
8		Part-time Wages	$480.00	$480.00	$480.00	$1,440.00
9						
10		Total Income	$728.00	$728.00	$728.00	$2,184.00
11						
12	EXPENSES					
13		Food	$22.00	$22.00	$22.00	$66.00
14		Clothing	$25.00	$25.00	$25.00	$75.00
15		Recreation	$20.00	$20.00	$20.00	$60.00
16		Car Loan Payment	$257.25	$257.25	$257.25	$771.75
17		Car Insurance	$60.00	$60.00	$60.00	$180.00
18						
19		Total Expenses	$384.25	$384.25	$384.25	$1,152.75
20	SURPLUS OR DEFICIT		$343.75	$343.75	$343.75	$1,031.25

Answer the following questions based on the personal budget spreadsheet above:

1. What was the largest source of income for the quarter?   _____

2. What was the largest expense item for the quarter?   _____

3. What was the quarterly income from interest earned? $_____

4. What was the quarterly income from parental support? $_____

5. What was the total income for the quarter? $_____

6. What was the monthly car insurance expense? $_____

7. What were the total expenses for the quarter? $_____

8. What were the total expenses for the month of February? $_____

9. What was the monthly car loan payment? $_____

10. What was the quarterly surplus? $_____

UNIT 8   SPREADSHEET APPLICATION 6: Bank Statement

The following customer bank statement spreadsheet shows account activity for a 1-month period. Formulas are included in the spreadsheet to calculate the new investment balance and the interest earned on account.

```
        A       B           C           D           E           F           G
1   Date:  12/31/--    FIRST NATIONAL BANK              C U S T O M E R
2                      P.O. Box 8927                    S T A T E M E N T
3                      Gulfport, MS
4   -----------------------------------------------------------------------
5   Carl Jamison or                     Account Number:     32-907326
6   Allison Jamison                     Social Security:    526-07-4830
7   1387 Great Oaks
8   Gulfport, MS
9                                       Balance of
10              SUMMARY                 Your Funds
11
12  Previous balance, 11/28/--          $46,832.96
13      4 deposits totaling              $8,546.08
14     42 withdrawals totaling           $5,360.50
15  New investment balance, 12/31/--    $50,018.54
16
17
18  Average daily interest rate     5.362
19  Interest earned on account                  $270.20
```

Answer the following questions based on the banking spreadsheet above:

1. What was the customer account number?   _____

2. What was the average daily interest rate?   _____

3. How much interest was earned on the account for the month? $_____

4. What was the account balance at the end of November? $_____

5. What was Carl's Social Security number?   _____

6. What was the total deposited for the month? $_____

7. What was the total withdrawn for the month? $_____

8. What was the account balance at the end of December? $_____

9. How much more was deposited than withdrawn during the month? $_____

10. This customer statement shows account activity for what month?   _____

Employment Test Problems

Businesses and governmental agencies include business mathematics as a part of the employment test for many jobs. These tests may vary with the type of business and/or region of the country. The problems presented in this unit are typical of problems that are included in many employment tests. The content in this text should provide good preparation for employment tests.

UNIT

9

EMPLOYMENT TEST 1

1. Add: $14.95, $9.02, $7.69, $30.

$ _____

2. What is the quotient when 44,283 is divided by 87?

_____

3. What is 19 3/8 − 5 2/3?

_____

4. How many quarters are there in $856.50?

_____

5. How much is 16 more than 7 3/4?

_____

6. Write 85% as a fraction in lowest terms.

_____

7. $15 is what percent of $600?

_____

8. A man earns $500 during the week. On Friday, he earned $120. What percent of his weekly salary was earned on Friday?

_____

9. Three candidates ran for office in a class election. Candidate 1 received 1/3 of the votes, and Candidate 2 received 1/4 of the votes. What part of the votes did Candidate 3 receive?

_____

10. Two men work as sales clerks. Man 1 sells twice as much as Man 2. What portion of the sales is made by Man 2?

_____

11. Mr. Smith owns 1/7 of the outstanding shares of stock in a corporation. If he sells 1/7 of his shares, what fraction of the stock does he still own?

   _____

12. There are 60 students in the school who own a car. If this represents 15 percent of the total students, how many students attend the school?

   _____

13. A county has an assessed property valuation of $3,600,000. The rate for school taxes is 90¢ per $100 valuation. If all but 3% of the taxes are collected, how much was collected?

   $ _____

14. Susan Smock owns 2/3 of the interest in a partnership. She sells half of her interest for $97,500. What is the value of the entire company?

   $ _____

15. John Thomas buys 15 candy bars for 50¢ each. Doris Hall buys a dozen bars for $4.80. Tim Preston buys 3 bars for $1.20. What is the average price per candy bar?

   $ _____

16. How much longer (in minutes) does it take an automobile to travel 1 mile at 15 miles per hour than at 30 miles per hour?

   _____

17. Two trains are headed toward each other on the same tracks. One train travels 45 miles per hour, while the other train travels 35 miles per hour. If they begin 360 miles apart, how many hours will pass before they meet?

   _____

18. Nancy Freeman is 3 times as old as her son Ralph and half as old as her father. The grandfather is how many times as old as Ralph?

   _____

19. The charge for a telephone call is $3.80 for the first 2 minutes, plus $1.35 for each additional minute. How much will a call lasting 18 minutes cost?

   $ _____

20. Three skilled workers can paint a building in 20 days, or 5 unskilled workers can paint the building in 30 days. If all work together, how many days will it take to paint the building?

   _____

414

EMPLOYMENT TEST 2

These problems are typical of the wide variety of problems that may appear on employment tests containing a business math section.

1. The Barron Department Store had a 20% increase in sales amounting to an increase of $1,800,000 this year. What was the sales amount for last year?

   $ _____

2. How much longer (in yards) is a 100-meter race than a 100-yard race if 1 meter equals 1.09 yards?

   _____

3. John earned $50, Bill earned $80, and Sue earned $20. What percent of the total earnings did Sue earn?

   _____

4. Twenty gallons of gasoline are added to a tank, moving the gauge from 1/8 to 3/4 full. How many gallons of gasoline does the tank hold when full?

   _____

5. What number must be added to 24, 28, and 21 to obtain an average of 25?

   _____

6. Two trucks leave the station at the same time. One truck averages 46 miles per hour, while the other truck averages 49 miles per hour. How many hours will it take the trucks to be 78 miles apart if they are traveling in the same direction?

   _____

7. On a data processing test, 92 percent of the students passed the test, but 16 students failed the test. How many students passed the test?

   _____

8. A product cost the company $88. If the markup is 25% of cost, what is the selling price?

   $ _____

9. A man owes $8,000 on a note. If he earns $2,800 with deductions of 23 percent, how much will he owe on the note if he applies his net pay to the loan balance?

   $ _____

10. One pole is 6 yards, 4 feet, and 9 inches long. A second pole is 9 yards, 5 feet, and 8 inches long. How long are the two poles combined?

    _____

11. Sales taxes of 6.5% are added to purchases of $18. What is the total amount due?

$ _____

12. Boyce, Dockery, and Elwell invest $8,000, $5,000, and $7,000 respectively into a partnership. If profits are distributed according to the proportion of the original investment, how much will Elwell receive if profits are $3,300?

$ _____

13. A car sells for $10,250. If markup is 25%, based on cost, what is the original cost of the car?

$ _____

14. If 55 pounds of fertilizer cost $22, what will 33 additional pounds cost?

$ _____

15. Babette reads ¼ of her book in 3 hours and 15 minutes. How long will it take her to read the entire book at this rate?

_____

16. The Brown Appliance Manufacturing Company has 8 departments. Each department has 10 to 16 bureaus. Each bureau has between 40 and 60 workers, with 10% of the workers being typists. What is the minimum number of typists in a department?

_____

17. Six people can code 800 documents in 45 minutes. How many documents can 9 people code in 7 1/2 hours?

_____

18. The Cook family spends their annual budget as follows: 1/10 for clothing, 1/4 for housing, and 1/3 for food. After these expenses, $7,600 remains. How much is the total annual income?

$ _____

19. In a class of 45 pupils, 24 are boys. If 4 more boys are admitted, what part of the class will be boys?

_____

20. At Ridgeway High School, 4/5 of the graduating class plans to go to college. If 3/4 of those planning to go to college go to a local college, what part of the graduating class plans to go to a local college?

_____

416

ANSWERS TO SELF-TESTS

Unit 1 Self-Test

1. $556.34
2. $111.00
3. $8,785.59
4. $840.74
5. $760,000.00
6. 385 miles
7. $57.88
8. 12.9 minutes

9. (a) $116.74
   (b) $134.55
   (c) $ 60.13
   (d) $179.82
   Total $491.24
10. $784.14
11. $487.41
12. $2,367.75

Unit 2 Self-Test

1. (a) Five tenths
   (b) Eight hundredths
   (c) Thirteen thousandths
   (d) Eighteen ten-thousandths
   (e) Seven hundred-thousandths
   (f) Four and two hundredths
   (g) Five and seventy-one ten-thousandths
   (h) Seventeen and one hundred twenty-three thousandths

2. (a) 3/10
   (b) 1/4
   (c) 2 3/4
   (d) 5 4/5
   (e) .7
   (f) .8
   (g) .5
   (h) .625

3. (a) 23.5
   (b) 41.23
   (c) 44.351
   (d) 9.2498
   (e) 825.028
   (f) 311.261

4. (a) 570
   (b) 3,000
   (c) 560
   (d) 65.5
   (e) 2.52
   (f) 10.8
   (g) 8.238

5. (a) 9.34
   (b) 79.018
   (c) 19.793
   (d) 22.9348
   (e) 565.431
   (f) 208.879

6. $175.26

7. (a) 4.2
   (b) 31.435
   (c) 109.62
   (d) 475.9375
   (e) 3.09
   (f) 0.0034

8. (a) 5.03
   (b) 65.7
   (c) $40.30
   (d) $3.50
   (e) 0.17067
   (f) 17.1739
   (g) 51.96
   (h) 36.56
   (i) 3,256
   (j) 13.28

Unit 3 Self-Test

1. (a) $108.00
   (b) 9.624
   (c) $52.80
   (d) $153.00
   (e) $54.00
   (f) $170.12
2. $2,203.20
3. $2,249.53
4. $240.00
5. $1,250.00
6. $2,500.00
7. 25%
8. 40%
9. 25%

10. 25%
11. (a) $13.00
    (b) $3.00
    (c) $50.00
    (d) $6.00
12. $1,500.00
13. 208
14. $1
15. $9.75
16. (a) $46.50
    (b) $13.50
17. (a) $44.50
    (b) $44.10

18. (a) $7,560.00
    (b) $1,100.00
    (c) $8,660.00
    (d) $279.35
    (e) $2.79
19. 396.26
20. 49.66
21. 8.3267
22. 1024.0211
23. 353.1
24. 0.2269
25. (a) $3,600.00
    (b) $516.67
    (c) 15.57%

Unit 4 Self-Test

1. (a) $8.52
   (b) $417.34
2. (a) $1,152.00
   (b) $1,176.00
   (c) $1,200.00
3. (a) $652.80
   (b) $666.40
   (c) $680.00
4. (a) April 7
   (b) April 15
   (c) April 30

5. $1,500.00
   $75.00
   $1,425.00
   $285.00
   $1,140.00
   $114.00
   $1,026.00
6. $2,400.00
7. (a) $140.00
   (b) $3.60
   (c) $376.40

8. (a) $216.00
   (b) $936.00
9. (a) $15.95
   (b) 44%
10. (a) $4.80
    (b) 30%
11. (a) $13.92
    (b) 43.5%
12. (a) $30.00
    (b) 25%

13. $29.68
14. (a) 40%
    (b) 66 2/3%
15. (a) $5.10
    (b) $1.70
16. $57.60
17. $350.00
18. $363.00
19. $437.50
20. $202.00

Unit 5 Self-Test

1. (a) $384.00
   (b) $72.00
   (c) $456.00
2. $260.00
3. $340.00
4. $30.42
5. $2,812.50
6. $6,758.50
7. $20,076
8. $434.10
9. $67,250.00
10. $8,813.75

11. $9,828.00
12. (a) $54.00
    (b) $52.00
    (c) $52.90
13. (a) $236,000.00
    (b) $208,000.00
    (c) 6.5
14. (a) $9,600.00
    (b) $19,200.00
15. (a) $14,240.00
    (b) $10,680.00

16. (a) $7,680.00
    (b) $4,608.00
17. (a) $3,100.00
    (b) $4,960.00
18. (a) $40,000.00
    (b) 1.5 to 1
    (c) 3 to 1
    (d) 0.5 to 1
19. (a) 25%
    (b) $65,125.00
20. $831.28

418

Unit 6 Self-Test

1. $35.28
2. $29.17
3. $410.00
4. $11.98
5. August 14
6. 82 days
7. 36 days
8. 77 days
9. (a) $27.00
   (b) $1,173.00
10. (a) $8.00
    (b) $792.00
11. (a) 90 days
    (b) $27.90
    (c) $1,832.10
12. (a) $624.32
    (b) $5,624.32
13. (a) $410.00
    (b) $4,410.00
14. (a) $247.30
    (b) $3,247.30
15. (a) $9,776.00
    (b) $10,167.04
    (c) $10,573.72
16. $6,123.95
17. $4,038.29
18. $20,645.86
19. $24,255.74
20. $1,377.60
21. $680.00

Unit 7 Self-Test

1. (a) $315.29
   (b) $310.00
   (c) $310.00
2. (a) 151.1
   (b) 150.5
3. (a) 86.85
   (b) 88
   (c) 87-93
4. (Mark line graph in text)
5. (Mark line graph in text)
6. (a) $23,000.00
   (b) $27,600.00
   (c) $4,600.00
7. $2,340.00
8. $210.00
9. 30.43%
10. $10,000.00
11. (a) 15 days
    (b) $30.00
12. $4,180.00
13. 7.61%
14. (a) $7,120.00
    (b) $55.00
    (c) 10.75

COLLEGE BUSINESS MATHEMATICS
ACHIEVEMENT CHART

Assignment Number	Assignment Title	Date Completed	Score
1.1	Addition		
1.2	Addition		
2.1	Subtraction		
2.2	Multiplication		
2.3	Division		
2.4	Division		
3.1	Sales Slips		
3.2	Sales Invoices		
4.1	Bank Statement Reconciliation		
4.2	Bank Statement Reconciliation		
5.1	Wage Computation Spreadsheet		
5.2	Balance Computation Spreadsheet		
5.3	Units Sold Spreadsheet		
5.4	Monthly Absentee Report Spreadsheet		
6.1	Decimals		
7.1	Decimals: Addition		
7.2	Decimals: Subtraction		
8.1	Decimals: Multiplication		
8.2	Decimals: Division		
9.1	Basic Computations Using the Electronic Calculator		
9.2	Business Applications Using the Electronic Calculator		
10.1	Percentage Amount Applications		
10.2	Percentage Amount Applications		
11.1	Base Applications		
11.2	Rate/Base/Amount Applications		
12.1	Finance Charges		
12.2	Consumer Credit		
13.1	Discount Applications		
14.1	Computing Cash Discount		
14.2	Computing Cash Discount		
15.1	Trade Discount Applications		
15.2	Computing Trade Discounts: Equivalent Rates		
15.3	Computing Trade Discounts: Complete Invoice		
16.1	Markup Applications		
16.2	Markup Based on Selling Price Applications		
16.3	Markup Applications		
17.1	Markdown and Sale Price Applications		

17.2	Markdown and Markdown Rate Applications		
18.1	Commission on Sales		
18.2	Commission on Consignments		
19.1	Computing Payroll: Straight Salary and Hourly Wages		
19.2	Computing Payroll: Piece-Rate and Worksheet		
19.3	Computing Payroll: Payroll Register		
20.1	Computing Income Tax Due		
20.2	Computing Payroll Withholdings		
21.1	Tax Rate and Assessed Valuation		
21.2	Property Tax Computations		
22.1	Computing Cost of Merchandise Inventory		
22.2	Computing Cost of Goods Sold and Merchandise Turnover		
23.1	Computing Depreciation: Straight-Line Method		
23.2	Computing Depreciation: Accelerated Cost-Recovery System		
24.1	Financial Statement Analysis: Balance Sheet		
24.2	Financial Statement Analysis: Income Statement		
25.1	Computing Simple Interest		
25.2	Computing Interest and Due Date		
26.1	Computing Discounts on Non-Interest-Bearing Notes		
26.2	Computing Discounts on Interest-Bearing Notes		
27.1	Computing Compound Interest: Formula Method		
27.2	Computing Compound Interest: Table Method		
28.1	Computing Present Value		
28.2	Computing Present Value of Annuities		
28.3	Computing Annuity Investments and Sinking Fund Deposits		
29.1	Computations for Life Insurance		
29.2	Computations for Property Insurance		
30.1	Ungrouped Data Analysis: Basic Statistics		
30.2	Grouped Data Analysis: Basic Statistics		

INDEX

NOTES

NOTES

NOTES

1— 3.96

NORMANDALE

COMMUNITY COLLEGE

9700 France Avenue South

Bloomington, Minnesota 55431

DEMCO